Leadership of Inclusive and Sustainable Cultural Organisations

Leadership of Inclusive and Sustainable Cultural Organisations: A Practical Guide is the first book to provide guidance on how to lead cultural organisations that are inclusive, diverse and sustainable, and responsive to the public, their communities, their own staff and to popular movements.

The book's seven parts cover the qualities and skills a leader needs, and practical advice on how to develop an organisation that is sustainable, inclusive and diverse. It covers the role of the governing body, how to create an organisation that is constantly learning and adapting, how to deal with political, public and financial pressures, and what external sources of support they can call on. Each chapter is devoted to a specific issue that might be encountered on the leadership journey and is extensively cross-referenced to other relevant chapters.

Including a list of helpful suggestions of useful and practical publications for further reading, *Leadership of Inclusive and Sustainable Cultural Organisations* is a unique guide to cultural leadership. This book is an essential resource for all cultural practitioners with a leadership role within an organisation or aspiring to such a role. It will also be instructive to students of cultural heritage management.

Piotr Bienkowski has over 40 years of experience across the cultural sector, working in Europe and the Middle East. He was Professor of Archaeology and Museology at the University of Manchester, Director of Manchester Museum, and has developed inclusive practice with museums, galleries, science centres, the performing arts and community trusts. He now advises a wide range of cultural organisations as a consultant, working with them to embed inclusion and participation, and on organisational change and leadership at all levels.

Hilary McGowan works throughout the cultural sector. She helps organisations to improve their leadership and governance so they can thrive in the future. Her distinguished track record includes a background as an arts, museums and heritage director, and as a coach. Hilary established her own business 30 years ago and has worked with 250 different clients. As a Trustee of Bletchley Park, she played a leading role in its transformation; she is now a Trustee of the Egypt Exploration Society.

They are the co-authors of *Managing Change in Museums and Galleries: A Practical Guide* (Routledge 2021).

Routledge Guides to Practice in Museums, Galleries and Heritage

This series provides essential practical guides for those working in museums, galleries and a variety of other heritage professions around the globe.

Including authored and edited volumes, the series will help to enhance practitioners' and students' professional knowledge and will also encourage sharing of best practices between different countries, as well as between different types and sizes of organisations.

Titles published in the series include:

Marketing Strategy for Museums
A Practical Guide
Christina Lister

Fundraising Management in a Changing Museum World
Kate Brueggemann and Donna McGinnis

Practitioner Perspectives on Intangible Cultural Heritage
Joanne Orr

An Introductory Guide to Qualitative Research in Art Museums
Edited by Ann Rowson Love and Deborah Randolph

Institutional Change for Museums
A Practical Guide to Creating Polyvocal Spaces
Edited by Marianna Pegno and Kantara Souffrant

Ethics of Contemporary Collecting
Edited by Jen Kavanagh, Ellie Miles and Rosamund Lily West with Susanna Cordner

Cultivating Futures Thinking in Museums
Edited by Dr Kristin Alford

Leadership of Inclusive and Sustainable Cultural Organisations
A Practical Guide
Piotr Bienkowski and Hilary McGowan

For more information about this series, please visit: https://www.routledge.com/Routledge-Guides-to-Practice-in-Museums-Galleries-and-Heritage/book-series/RGPMGH

Leadership of Inclusive and Sustainable Cultural Organisations

A Practical Guide

Piotr Bienkowski and Hilary McGowan

Routledge
Taylor & Francis Group
LONDON AND NEW YORK

Designed cover image: abdudesigns / Getty Images

First published 2025
by Routledge
4 Park Square, Milton Park, Abingdon, Oxon OX14 4RN

and by Routledge
605 Third Avenue, New York, NY 10158

Routledge is an imprint of the Taylor & Francis Group, an informa business

British Library Cataloguing-in-Publication Data
A catalogue record for this book is available from the British Library

ISBN: 978-1-032-54243-0 (hbk)
ISBN: 978-1-032-50752-1 (pbk)
ISBN: 978-1-003-41588-6 (ebk)

DOI: 10.4324/9781003415886

Typeset in Times New Roman
by SPi Technologies India Pvt Ltd (Straive)

Contents

Illustrations

Figures

Tables

Acknowledgements

Heartfelt thanks to our wonderful advisory group (see Introduction), whose insightful comments and suggestions on diversity, equity, inclusion and the language and terms that we use hugely improved the book and made it, in itself, more inclusive:

Amparo Leyman Pino (Yellow Cow Consulting)
Fiona Slater (Science Museum)
Mark Miller (Tate)
Nuala Morse (University of Leicester)
Thanh Sinden (Hoa Lotus)

Needless to say, the final content and any mistakes, omissions or infelicities are entirely the authors' responsibility.

We would also like to thank the anonymous reviewers of the original proposal. This form of peer review is vital to ensure that our field remains relevant, up-to-date and vibrant, and their comments helped us tighten up aspects of the book at an early stage.

Of course, thanks to Heidi Lowther, our commissioning editor at Routledge, who also saw us through our previous book, and as always was extremely supportive and responsive; and to her colleague Manas Roy for his advice.

Piotr Bienkowski would like to thank:

In particular, Amparo Leyman Pino, not only for doing double-duty as author of the Foreword and member of the advisory group but for her constant inspiration, guidance and unswerving mission for inclusion and social justice in cultural organisations. Ampis: thank you.

Shaaron Leverment (Chief Executive of the Association for Science and Discovery Centres) for originally sowing the seed of this book in my mind. Shaaron, I bet you don't even remember!—but I'm very grateful for your faith in me.

Catherine Gillespie (Orchestra Manager, Scottish National Jazz Orchestra) and Jennifer Martin (formerly Chief Executive, The Cumnock Tryst) for discussing various aspects of practice with me and suggesting references.

My friends, colleagues and clients over the years (and these diverse categories intersect and overlap!) who have all contributed to my practice and to what is in this book.

Hilary McGowan would also like to thank:

Pippa Hill, Head of New Work and Justine Themen, Leadership Associate, at the Royal Shakespeare Company for kick-starting my thinking.

Hannah Khalil and Juliet Gilkes Romero, playwrights, for friendship, hugs and laughter.

Reyahn King for opening my eyes about her own experience.

Directing Change colleagues for always giving me another viewpoint.

Numerous actors of colour who have shared their experiences, including Amber James and Giles Terera for their friendship.

My cultural sector friends, colleagues and clients over the years who have all contributed to my business and to what is in this book.

My husband Grant for his unfailing support in difficult times.

But most of all to my co-author, Piotr, without whom this book would not exist: thank you more than I can ever say.

Foreword

The last decade of my career has been focused on two topics: leadership and inclusion. I am a proud alum of the Noyce Leadership Institute, and until the present day, I am continuing my peer-learning journey to improve my leadership skills. Funnily enough, I have been participating for the last five years in a peer-learning group focused on anti-racism, white fragility, trauma and lately on emergent strategy.

Since a very early age, I have been exposed to opportunities to work with communities at-promise:[1] orphans, people living in poverty in small towns far from big cities, Indigenous groups, runaway children, and, when I moved to the United States, immigrants—being an immigrant myself. I am from Mexico City, which is highly stratified, complex and with lots of contrasts. Growing up in my neighbourhood, I learned that my neighbours and I, regardless of our background, socio-economic status or location, were members of the same community. Being a member of the church choir in my teenage years allowed me to experience true inclusion: everyone was welcomed to be part of the choir, even those of us who didn't have a privileged voice or musical talent.

All these experiences have prepared me to understand, learn and put into practice the strategic initiatives I have co-led with institutions to support their efforts in becoming places for inclusion, belonging and therefore diverse. While some of our colleagues in the field have provided relevant research on inclusion and how it works, I have benefitted from their findings and put these principles into practice.

We can ask ourselves: how can we be leaders and provoke change? The most effective way to create change in organisations—from my humble perspective and based on the projects I have conducted in institutions in the United States, Switzerland, Ireland and Denmark—is by recognising, untapping and using the individual's place of power and influence. Each person in the organisation, regardless of their role and level, has the opportunity and the ability to provoke and drive change. This doesn't mean that they need to do more work or different work; instead, they can do it through their everyday work in a different way, what I call an equity lens.

In this book, the authors explain that leadership is a role rather than a characteristic linked to a position of power within the organisation. This resonates with the idea of using individual power and influence to provoke shifts and changes. The authors also state that organisations need to have champions of inclusion at every level; therefore, leveraging each person's leadership, power and influence becomes a strategy for successful change.

The author and activist adrienne maree brown compares fractals—complex geometric patterns that are similar across different scales—with the way change should and could successfully happen in society, from the micro to the macro universe.[2] She explains how nature repeats itself and 'what we practice at a small scale can reverberate to the largest scale'.

Nature itself is teaching us to embrace our own power and influence, believing that we are able, competent and capable to make a difference.

It is important to note that I have used the words 'leverage' and 'embrace' when I refer to power and influence, instead of referring to this act as 'empowering' people to use their power and influence—their leadership—to provoke change. The word 'empowering' implies that the person does not have power, and therefore, another person with power will give or share their abundance of power so they can do something. I find this a little bit disturbing and condescending. I believe that every person has power; maybe they do not know they have it, so we can help to untap it by giving them a task where they can practice it. It is there.

Recognising the assets of people, communities and organisations is a great starting place. It would be easier to do the work thinking of the things people are able to do, as opposed to thinking that they are under-achieving, at-risk or under-served (ahem, who is not serving these communities?). This is an invitation to discover and assume that people, communities and institutions have assets, wealth and too much to learn from them.

In my practice helping organisations to become more inclusive, I start the work with an assessment. Every institution I have worked with is already inclusive in one way or another, and has many assets to scaffold from to become even more inclusive. As an immigrant from the Latin American diaspora, I can also assure you that my Latin American fellows have a lot of assets that they can bring to the table and work together to create spaces for inclusion and belonging, and diverse points of view, walks of life and learning. This is again like the fractals: it can be applied for many diasporas, groups and communities, and it repeats itself for every human being and culture on the planet.

The fact that more and more colleagues are fine-tuning their practice to add this equity lens gives me hope that we will get to a point where we do not need to teach it anymore, as it is a common practice, a given, it is understood, and put into practice. I have high hopes.

Amparo Leyman Pino, M. Ed.
Principal and Founder, Yellow Cow Consulting LLC.

Notes

1 'At-promise' is an asset-perspective term that is more positive and implies potential, than the more common 'at-risk', which is more negative and stigmatising. See B.B. Swadener and S. Lubbock (eds.), *Children and Families "At Promise"* (SUNY Press 1995).

2 a.m. brown, *Emergent Strategy* (AK Press 2017), p. 54.

Introduction

What kind of leaders do the cultural organisations of the future need?

There has been a transformation in recent years in what is expected of cultural organisations, and increasing public, political and financial pressures on them. Diverse communities are demanding to be included in decision-making and that cultural organisations respond to their agendas and engage marginalised audiences; local and national politicians expect them to fit into their ideological frameworks in return for funding and support; and, financially, for at least 15 years, the cultural sector has been on the front line for cuts and demands for ever more value for money and new business models.[1]

These are the factors that make leadership of cultural organisations distinct from leadership in general. More than ever, there is a need for informed, confident and reflective cultural leadership that embraces diversity and understands how to build a values-based organisation.

This book is about how to lead cultural organisations that are sustainable, inclusive, diverse and responsive to their public, communities and staff, and to popular movements and hot topics. The authors' starting point was to consider what sort of cultural organisations we need in the future, in an increasingly fractured and polarised world, and then to imagine what the ideal leader of such an organisation would look like. Admittedly, our idea of the ideal cultural organisation and leader might not be shared by everyone, but we know from our own professional work that, for many people across the globe, what they look for in a cultural organisation is one that actively practices and champions diversity and inclusion, works closely with its communities in a participatory way, responding to community agendas and sharing authority and decision-making both on projects and wider strategy, and is sustainable financially, socially and environmentally.

So this is a leadership book that is not just about the leader as an individual (and is definitely not about the sole, heroic leader). In our experience, many cultural leaders act in an over-confident manner but lack awareness of their own weaknesses, are unwilling to delegate and are wary of criticism (for outdated leadership models, see below).[2] Furthermore, diversity and inclusion are too often pursued as somehow separate, divorced from the need to make an organisation sustainable in all ways.

We define leadership as working with an organisation, its stakeholders and communities to help it become sustainable, inclusive and diverse, and building an organisation that is able to learn and grow and to find a mature way of being effective in the medium and longer term, even given the myriad pressures it faces. Our two favourite quotations about leadership succinctly summarise our own approach:

DOI: 10.4324/9781003415886-1

> Leaders are at the heart of a network, not at the top of a pyramid.[3]
> An effective leader is a connector, a convener, a communicator and a listener.[4]

This understanding of leadership is a constant thread weaving its way through the entire book, like the words and patterns embedded throughout a stick of rock.

When we first submitted our proposal for this book to Routledge (in 2022), one of the anonymous reviewers commented that its concern with diversity and inclusion was 'very much of its time (two or three years' back it would have been called timely)'. There may be some truth in that statement—although in our defence, two or three years' back we were busy writing another book which we also felt was timely and dealt with an important topic.[5] Nevertheless, even in the relatively short period between the reviewer's comments and now, there is evidence of a backlash in some countries and regions against diversity, inclusion and 'identity politics', a rise in anti-semitism, Islamophobia, social prejudice and abuse faced by social minorities such as disabled people, refugees and migrants, and increasing rather than decreasing intolerance of different sexual and gender orientations. There is overt political criticism of equity, diversity and inclusion initiatives.[6] Sometimes these negative reactions are fuelled by international events such as invasions, wars, violence and protests, subsequently enhanced and distorted by the echo-chamber of social media. It is actually becoming harder for cultural organisations to navigate these stormy seas—for example, in their social inclusion or decolonisation work—without being criticised, sometimes by their own funders and stakeholders (often portrayed as 'culture wars'). This book is a practical guide, not a political manual—we would argue that our values of diversity and inclusion are moral and ethical rather than political (discuss…)[7]—but we believe its practical approach remains timely, and necessary.

The book draws on the authors' direct experiences of leading cultural organisations themselves, advising and mentoring leaders, and developing directors/CEOs, managers and governing bodies at more than 250 cultural organisations of all types and sizes, across the United Kingdom and Europe.

We are acutely aware that both authors are white and middle-aged, and as individuals have not experienced discrimination or exclusion. Despite our wide experience of leadership across the cultural sector, some readers may question whether we have the lived experience and moral authority to write about diversity and inclusion and why they are vitally needed. Indeed, we spent considerable time exploring the idea of an additional author, but such a solution would only bring in one additional perspective, and there are many factors to consider in deciding whether there is a good 'fit' with a co-author, not least of which are shared commitment to schedules and deadlines. Our solution has been to work with a small but diverse group of cultural practitioners from across the international cultural sector to sense-check what we write and the language and examples we use, and to ensure that our writing is itself inclusive and sensitive. These people not only have different life experiences from us but also have wide knowledge of their particular area of the cultural sector today, providing us with a global perspective and insight. Their input has been particularly focused on elements of the book that deal directly with diversity and inclusion, to include leadership perspectives in the non-English-speaking world and the need for leadership to tailor responses to various cultural contexts, and to ensure that language and examples are not (unconsciously) exclusive and insensitive. The members of this invaluable 'advisory group' are named in the Acknowledgements.

Definitions

Throughout the book, and indeed in its title, we make frequent use of certain terms that it is useful to define unambiguously, so that readers are clear exactly what we mean by them. All these terms have been discussed extensively in the cultural sector, and organisations and practitioners will have their own understandings and definitions of them. Our own definitions that follow are not some sort of distillation of all of those nor do they claim to be definitive: they are simply what we, as authors, understand by these terms and how we use them in the book.

Diversity—variation in personal, physical and social characteristics, not all of which is visible, for example, gender, race and ethnicity, religion, socio-economic background, sexual orientation, age, national origin or education, and how these differences intersect and combine.

Inclusion—the processes that embed diversity within an organisation, so that people of all types feel welcome, accepted, respected, valued and that they belong (we tend to think of diversity as *what* you want to achieve, and inclusion as *how* you achieve it).

Sustainability—we identify three types of sustainability, all three of which are vital for cultural organisations: financial, social (building long-lasting relationships with communities) and environmental (reducing impact by lowering emissions and reducing waste, but increasingly important is adapting buildings to a changing climate).

Equality—ensuring that everyone has access to the same resources and opportunities.

Equity—recognising that each person has different circumstances and requirements because of their own diversities and how they intersect, and ensuring that everyone has access to the resources and opportunities necessary to ensure an equal outcome.

Community—a group of individuals who share a common attribute or affinity, for example, shared locality, interest or work.

Learning—this is not about formal education programmes, but how an organisation improves and changes, including changing its culture, and the mechanisms it has in place for learning from what went well or not so well and what it might do differently.

Leadership vs. management

It is helpful to distinguish between leadership and management which, though linked, are distinctly different.

> Leadership shapes the future; management delivers it.[8]

Table 0.1 lists the main differences between them. While both are important in an organisation, it can be useful to consider if the balance between them is appropriate in a

Table 0.1 Leadership vs. management

Leaders	*Managers*
Focus on the future	Focus on the present situation
Secure resources	Organise current resources
Focus on the bigger picture	Focus on detail
Present a compelling—and shared—vision of the future	Think of ways of stretching resources further

Source: Adapted from Y. Gabriel, *Organizations in Depth*, Sage 1999, p. 139

particular case—depending on the needs of the organisation and its external environment—and how much the two roles are carried out by the same person.

Outdated leadership models

Why cover outdated leadership models? Because we believe that they are still present in parts of the cultural sector, and many cultural leaders and leadership courses continue to practise and promote them:

- 'heroic' (solitary).
- 'Alexander the Great' (don't know when to stop).
- 'hair shirt' (taking the flak and carrying the weight of the world).
- dictatorial (do what I say, not as I do).

What all these have in common is that the leaders who embody these models know of no other way than to do it themselves, and truly believe that how they behave is the best way of leading an organisation. They believe that for others to share in their leadership is not how a leader should behave and have an inability or unwillingness to see the alternatives.

This is not a style of leadership that inspires staff to help you build an inclusive and sustainable organisation. They are all solitary leadership models which do not leave a legacy of a stronger and more sustainable organisation, as their emphasis is entirely on the leader themselves. Most leadership training in the early years of this century focused on developing the individual, not on their organisation. Good leaders take the long view and build organisations for the longer term.

The **solitary, heroic** leader is a very traditional figure, like Horatio holding the bridge against the invading Etruscans, while his Roman colleagues crossed to safety: he (and it is usually male) standing alone and believing it to be the only way of protecting his people.[9] Those who find delegation difficult, who do not enjoy managing, inspiring and motivating others are heroic leaders. They are often selfish, and dislike sharing the limelight, wanting to take all credit for themselves, but determined to do it as they believe it is the right way of leading.

The **Alexander the Great** style of leader doesn't know when to stop but carries on regardless of the circumstances in which their organisation finds itself. This book recommends horizon scanning and developing political antennae to prepare the organisation for the future (see Chapter 12). The Alexander the Great leader would not consider this to be important as they live in the moment, ploughing on with determination and, often, initial success.

The **hair shirt** leader carries the weight of the world on their shoulders and makes sure you know it. They take all the flak and criticism on themselves in the mistaken belief that this is their role. Sharing responsibilities never occurs to them.

The **dictatorial** leader believes their staff should *do what I say, not as I do*. It is quicker and easier for them just to tell people what to do and order them to do it quickly, than to begin to understand how to lead and motivate them. They believe that this is the job they have been appointed to and that this is the best way of delivering it.

All these models will have organisations with high turnover, and high levels of sickness and absenteeism, which are an indicator of a lack of whole-hearted commitment from the staff as a result of flawed leadership.

In contrast, the newer leadership models are more relevant for contemporary needs and support the development of an inclusive and sustainable cultural organisation:

- transformational
- capacity building

and

- distributed.

Transformational leadership was first defined by American leadership expert James MacGregor Burns.[10] A transformational leader seeks to engage the hearts, minds and values of their staff through leading with their own high standards of integrity and empathy (see Chapter 10). They constantly remind the staff about their mission, why they're there and what impact they are striving to make; staff respond by being personally loyal to the leader, highly committed and proud of their work. Their levels of turnover, sickness and absenteeism are very low.

Capacity-building leadership primarily concentrates on building skills and ability for the future. The most effective way of helping an organisation is to help it to build its future capacity. An organisation must develop the skills and knowledge it needs for its own future as an inclusive and sustainable business, even when the current inspirational leader has moved on. This type of leader is focused on the future, beyond their own tenure, putting in place a culture which should continue to operate along the same principles (see Chapter 36).

Distributed leadership (see Chapter 32) means empowering individuals across an organisation to take ownership of leadership responsibilities and share decision-making. It is a deliberate move away from a traditional, hierarchical, top-down model of leadership, aiming at developing leadership throughout the organisation. In this model, authority does not reside in one key individual but emphasises a teamwork approach to overall strategy and goals. Consequently, the organisational culture is overtly one of democracy where the talents and capabilities of others, besides the director/CEO, are recognised and where they can flourish.

The structure of this book and how to use it

The objective of this book is to identify the various problems and challenges of cultural leadership and give practical advice on how to deal with each one. It is aimed at all cultural practitioners with a leadership role, whether aspiring, emerging, early career or established leaders—directors/CEOs, managers, members of governing bodies and members of staff at different levels in an organisation. This is not necessarily limited just to roles for paid staff. Many cultural organisations depend on volunteers who can have significant leadership or management responsibilities, some smaller ones being entirely volunteer-run. Indeed, even in certain larger cultural organisations, the majority of front-of-house staff are volunteers, sometimes with just a single duty manager as paid staff. Furthermore, in the sector as a whole, volunteers are increasingly involved in decision-making, and therefore much of this book is as relevant to them as to paid staff.

The guidance applies to all types of cultural and heritage organisations whatever their size, both publicly funded and not-for-profit—museums, galleries, arts centres, archives, libraries, science and discovery centres, theatres, music and dance companies, and community and arts trusts. Although both authors are UK-based, we have deliberately taken into account varying international environments, contexts and case studies, particularly with the help of the advisory group (see above), so that the book is applicable globally.

The book is divided into seven parts:

Part 1: Developing the individual as a leader
Part 2: The tool box: the skills you need
Part 3: Leading a sustainable organisation
Part 4: Diversity and inclusion
Part 5: Governance for an inclusive and sustainable organisation
Part 6: Leading a learning organisation
Part 7: Advocacy and external networks

The book comprises 68 short, focused chapters on all the different aspects of inclusive leadership, divided between these seven parts. Each chapter is devoted to a specific topic that you might encounter on your leadership journey, for example, 'How to have difficult conversations and deal with uncomfortable issues', or 'Identifying and dealing with racism and bias'. Of course, these topics are often interlinked, and so each theme-based chapter is cross-referenced to other relevant chapters. At the end, there are lists of Resources to Help (a list of practically focused web-based resources on cultural leadership) and an annotated list of Useful Publications—these are, deliberately, not an exhaustive list of literature on leadership, but strictly books that practitioners might find useful when dealing with the practical aspects of leadership.

Inevitably, there is overlap with some topics we covered in our previous book, *Managing Change in Museums and Galleries*, although, of course, there are major differences: the present book is about leadership, not specifically about managing change, and it covers a wider range of cultural organisations, not just museums. In all cases, our approach to these topics has been revised, reworked and updated.

Accounts of case studies have been kept to a minimum. The purpose of this book is to offer concise and practical guidance, not detailed case studies, which in any case can occasionally date quickly, or are perceived (rightly or wrongly) as not relevant to a particular cultural organisation or type of organisation. For that reason, our preferred approach has been to use quotations from practitioners, where relevant, which reveal their responses and insights regarding particular approaches to leadership. In other work, we have found that readers respond positively to these sorts of short quotations rather than lengthy and perhaps less immediately relevant case studies. Similarly, the references we cite are to case studies that the reader can follow up, to works that treat aspects of a topic in more detail, or to publications that have influenced our own thinking and writing. Our approach to references is not comprehensive: this is not an academic or theoretical book where the requirement is to cite all previous work on a particular topic, but a practical guide, so cited references are limited to aspects that we believe will be practically useful to readers.

We envisage that the typical practitioner–user, in search of practical and concise guidance, will start by consulting a particular chapter whose topic they are encountering on their leadership journey, and will then find cross-references to other related chapters—thus using the book in the manner of a trouble-shooting guide, rather than something necessarily to be read systematically from cover to cover.

Notes

1 In some countries, too, changing demographics, with increasing cultural and ethnic diversity, are putting pressure on cultural organisations to diversify their audiences. For the United States, see B. Farrell and M. Medvedeva, *Demographic Transformation and the Future of Museums* (AAM Press 2010).

2 Or worse: for a study that reveals endemic unacceptable behaviour by leaders in the cultural sector, see M. Nisbett, B. Walmsley and E. McDowell, 'Bullying bosses, broken boards and a crisis of accountability', *Arts Professional* (23 February 2023).

3 R. Hewison, J. Holden and S. Jones, *All Together: A creative approach to organisational change* (Demos 2010), p. 121.

4 Gloria Rubio-Cortes (President, National Civic League), quoted in M. Broussine and R.F. Callahan, 'Public leadership,' in T. Bovaird and E. Loeffler (eds), *Public Management and Governance* (third edition, Routledge 2016), p. 282.

5 P. Bienkowski and H. McGowan, *Managing Change in Museums and Galleries* (Routledge 2021).

6 For example, in recent years, several US states have banned diversity, equity and inclusion programmes in public colleges and universities.

7 On the contested concept of values, their impact on European politics and contemporary attitudes to different social groups, see R. Polak and P. Rohs (eds), *Values-Politics-Religion: The European Values Study* (Springer 2023).

8 M. Broussine and R.F. Callahan, 'Public leadership,' in T. Bovaird and E. Loeffler (eds), *Public Management and Governance* (third edition, Routledge 2016), p. 280.

9 T.B. Macaulay, *Lays of Ancient Rome*, 'Horatius at the bridge', 1842.

10 J.M. Burns, *Leadership* (Grove Press 1978).

Part 1

Developing the individual as a leader

This part is about the qualities necessary in a successful leader and how to develop them. It not only covers self-belief and self-confidence but also stresses the importance of self-reflection, recognising blind spots and compensating for your own weaknesses, having a flexible approach, welcoming different perspectives and learning how to respond to criticism, whether it is justified or not. Managing your own well-being will strengthen your mindset, as well as provide you with the stamina to be a good leader over the long term and inspire your staff. It is also important for a leader to personally model the inclusive values and behaviours they are developing in their organisation. Personal peer networks help to support a leader throughout their career and are a vital source of help and advice in a crisis.

DOI: 10.4324/9781003415886-2

1 Self-belief and self-confidence

Research shows that the biggest barrier slowing progression and development as a leader in the cultural sector is a lack of confidence in one's own abilities.[1] It is not uncommon for potential or aspiring leaders to have a negative perception of their abilities and how they come across to other people, and to compare themselves unfavourably to others. This is often termed 'imposter syndrome', an inner voice telling you that your success is undeserved and fraudulent.

There are tried and tested methods for bolstering one's self-confidence:[2]

- Make a list of your achievements, things you are proud of, and challenges you have overcome.
- Acknowledge your personal strengths and talents, including things you do outside work, that make you the person you are.
- Set realistic goals for yourself (not necessarily the same as your organisational goals).
- Don't wallow in negative thoughts, but regularly practise self-reflection (see Chapter 4), looking at what you do well, or not so well, and what you might do differently.
- Take inspiration from leaders you admire—not necessarily in the cultural sector—and think about what it is that they do well that you might emulate (see Chapter 2 on role models).
- Consider having a mentor, an experienced leader who can give you guidance, advice and support (see Chapter 64).

Don't over-compensate: confidence should not mean arrogance

Too much self-belief and confidence often create poor leaders—such as the heroic leader, unable to do wrong, imagining that everything depends on them, and that acknowledging mistakes is a sign of weakness (see the section on outdated leadership models in the Introduction). On the contrary, acknowledging you can be wrong, and being a good listener, are signs of strength, genuine self-confidence and effective leadership.

There needs to be a balance: self-belief and self-confidence cannot come at any cost. It is important to:

- Recognise your weaknesses and blind spots (see Chapter 5).
- Acknowledge you are not always right.[3]
- Be open to challenges and other perspectives, especially cultural approaches and life experiences different from your own (see Chapter 7).
- Be able to take criticism and use it constructively (see Chapter 9).

DOI: 10.4324/9781003415886-3

- Acknowledge that others in your team are better at some things than you are and may even have a higher professional, public or academic profile—you should build on that and support and nurture them, rather than feel threatened, remembering that effective leadership is shared, and does not depend on an individual at the top of a pyramid (see Chapters 25 and 32).

Balancing all these aspects is not the work of a moment, but an ongoing task throughout one's whole professional life. The key to finding the balance—as well as coping with frequent knocks to your self-confidence—is reflection and building one's emotional intelligence (see Chapters 4 and 13). Take the time, regularly and systematically, to look back honestly on your day/month/year, contemplating your behaviour and its consequences, your decisions, good and bad, and how you relate to others.

Notes

1 For example, *Scoping the Leadership Development Needs of the Cultural Sector in England* (TBR 2013), pp. 26–7.

2 For example, G. Bryce, *Unmask the Confident Leader Within* (Rethink Press 2023), and any number of 'self-help' books, but all based on the same principles.

3 For not being afraid to acknowledge problems or 'failure', see P. Bienkowski and H. McGowan, *Managing Change in Museums and Galleries* (Routledge 2021), pp. 98–9; and L. Jancovich and D. Stevenson, 'Failure seems to be the hardest word to say', *International Journal of Cultural Policy* 27/7 (2021), pp. 967–81.

2 Role models or finding your own style?

What sort of leader do you aspire to be? You may already have a clear idea of your values and leadership style, but those will undoubtedly have been influenced—both positively and negatively—by (good and bad) leaders you have worked under in your earlier career, those you have observed in other organisations or sectors, teachers who may have inspired you, and even fictional leaders (the authors know several cultural leaders whose role models are starship captains from the *Star Trek* franchise).

It is often from such experiences and observation that we begin to sift the leadership qualities that we value, and, sometimes unconsciously, aspire to emulate at least some of the behaviours and traits of those role models. The qualities we look for in a leadership role model might typically include passion, commitment, communication style, listening, trust, empathy, teamworking and being value-driven, socially engaged, inclusive, supportive, motivating, innovative or risk-taking.[1]

On the plus side, a role model can:

- Inspire you to reach your goals.
- Show you what is possible.
- Help you see the impact of different leadership approaches, so that you can develop your own distinctive style.
- Keep you motivated during hard times.
- Motivate staff and model organisational behaviours.
- Ideally, develop into a mentor who gives advice, support and guidance on your professional and leadership development (see Chapter 64).

Having positive leadership role models is perhaps particularly important for social groups who have been historically marginalised and not often, at least until relatively recently and even then patchily, represented in the leadership of cultural organisations, such as women, people of colour, disabled people and younger leaders.[2] It feels energising to see people like you, from similar backgrounds, in positions of leadership—conversely, the lack of such role models can make progression seem a hard, lonely road, with no-one to light your way or support you.

But there are also disadvantages in having a role model:

- A role model may not have the same background, situation or resources as you, and may have experienced different struggles, so it may be difficult to understand and replicate what lies behind their distinctive approach to leadership.

DOI: 10.4324/9781003415886-4

- It may put unnecessary (and, occasionally, unachievable) expectations and pressure on yourself (we can't all be starship captains).
- It can be limiting in terms of your perspective, growth and development as a leader.
- It may feel a little like failure if you do not live up to your image of them.

Role models can be useful as inspiration for what sort of leader you want to be (and what sort you *don't* want to be) and can help fill you with confidence and motivation that you can achieve your goals. But it is important to look beyond a role model to determine your own values, behaviour and leadership style: what leadership qualities are most important to you, and how do you express them?

See also:

8. The power of a personal network
64. Strategic peer networks and mentoring

Notes

1 For the characteristics of a leader as role model, see J.T. Scarnati, 'Leaders as role models: 12 rules', *Career Development International* 7/3 (2002), pp. 181–9.

2 See, for example, D. Ladkin, 'Creating an aesthetic of inclusivity: a new solution to the "problem" of women leaders', and J. Williams, 'Black leadership and the white gaze', both in S. Kay and K. Venner (eds.), *A Cultural Leadership Reader* (Cultural Leadership Programme/Creative Choices 2010). To address the lack of cultural leaders—and hence role models—from marginalised groups, the latter (p. 42) proposes that organisations roll out a positive action/guest programmer/guest curator/in-residence programme.

3 Learning on the job vs. being trained

If you have spent time on a leadership training course, the good news is that it was probably not time wasted. The bad news is that the most important things can only be learned through hands-on experience. Most leadership learning and development comes from on-the-job experience, and not from formal courses. In fact, research in different countries and sectors has spawned the 70-20-10 rule for leadership development:[1]

- 70 per cent of learning comes from on-the-job experiences and challenges.
- 20 per cent of learning comes from other people (such as managers, colleagues, mentors and coaches—see Chapter 64).
- Only 10 per cent of the learning comes from leadership courses and formal training.

How to make the most of on-the-job learning

Developing as a leader through hands-on-experience cannot be a passive process. You need to be in the right frame of mind and be prepared to learn from both successes and mistakes. The most valuable leadership development comes with a dose of discomfort—so push yourself, expect to get some things wrong, and learn from those mistakes. Be strategic: seek out experiences, assignments and projects (both in and outside work contexts) that push you out of your comfort zone and challenge your abilities. These might include facing unfamiliar and wider responsibilities, leveraging and managing change, influencing across organisational boundaries or working with diverse groups of people. Your advocacy and people skills will mainly improve through practice, rather than from attending a course.

To make the most of the learning, self-reflection is vital (see Chapter 4): make sure you get feedback and reflect on how you can improve. Across all countries and sectors, the most important leadership lessons learned from hands-on experience have been shown to be: direct line management, self-awareness and effective problem solving and decision-making.

Leadership courses as amplifiers

Nevertheless, leadership courses can have a supporting, clarifying or amplifying effect, boosting the remaining 10 per cent of your learning. Across the world, different cultural leadership courses usually offer something along the lines of the following:[2]

- Learning about yourself and your leadership style.
- The skills and strategies of leadership.
- Tips for successful influencing and motivation.

DOI: 10.4324/9781003415886-5

- Guest speakers on their leadership journeys.
- Often a secondment in an organisation (and sector) different from your own.
- Mentor or coach support.
- A research project, sometimes collaborative.
- A chance to step back from daily responsibilities and consider your leadership style, skills and any gaps in your experience.

Alumni of leadership courses often single out self-belief and a lifelong supportive network as the most important outcomes of that experience (see Chapters 1 and 8).

Notes

1 M.M. McCall, Jr., M.M. Lombardo and A.M. Morrison, *The Lessons of Experience: How Successful Executives Develop on the Job* (CCL Press 1988); see also the excellent guidance and resources from the Center for Creative Leadership on ccl.org, on which this chapter draws.

2 Such as Clore Leadership and Oxford Cultural Leaders in the United Kingdom, or leadership programmes run by Americans for the Arts. These can be residential or online or a mix.

4 Self-reflection

Leaders derive their long-term effectiveness from their ability to learn and to develop the organisation's capacity to learn. By far the most effective way to learn, grow and develop as a leader is through the regular practice of self-reflection; on the flip side, lack of regular reflection almost certainly means that you won't learn and develop as a leader.

Self-reflection is the moment of stepping back to think about your skills, strengths, weaknesses, actions, decisions, behaviour and how you influence others—essentially, to reflect on yourself as a leader. If you see yourself as a heroic leader (see Introduction), you may think that admitting the need to self-reflect and learn undermines your public image of certainty and security. But the ability to reflect and learn is vital in the context of change and uncertainty—a situation cultural organisations find themselves in most of the time. Leadership and learning go together.[1]

Reflection and reflexivity

This chapter defines self-reflection as combining two skills that are often treated as separate and distinct but are both essential for leaders: reflection and reflexivity. It is helpful to think of *reflective* practice as looking *inwards* and *reflexive* practice as looking *outwards*. Reflection (inwards) is thinking about what you have learned personally, from what went well or not so well, and how you can apply it to become more self-aware and confident in your practice. Reflexivity (outwards) is learning in relation to others: thinking critically about how your assumptions, values and actions impact the broader context in which you work, your relation to other individuals, and what your role is.

The practice of self-reflection by leaders must look both inwards and outwards. Thinking more critically about your assumptions and actions also helps to develop more collaborative and responsive ways of managing organisations.

The benefits of self-reflection for cultural leaders

Self-reflection is a way of addressing three broad questions:[2]

- Who am I, and what kind of person and leader do I want to be?
- How do I relate to others and to the world around me?
- How does my leadership impact others, and what should I change or do more of?

Honest self-reflection can be unsettling at first, as it often reveals that current assumptions (e.g., about yourself, your role and impact) can be questioned, so don't be surprised to feel outside your comfort zone. The benefits of regular self-reflection include:

DOI: 10.4324/9781003415886-6

- Testing our assumptions.
- Increased self-awareness and confidence.
- Increased understanding about our practice.
- Exploring what has gone well, and not so well, and what you might do differently.
- Awareness of our behaviour, impact and influence (including how they might vary between different individuals and groups).
- Flexibility to change and adapt—continuous questioning whether current ways of leading need changing according to new circumstances.
- Navigating conditions of ambiguity and uncertainty—including identifying and accepting things you can't control.
- Better relations with colleagues and stakeholders.

How to build in regular self-reflection

When discussing with leaders and managers how to schedule regular self-reflection, the response the authors often get is that they can find little time during working days to think and reflect, because work time is dominated by the need for action (or, more usually, by endless series of meetings). The trick is to block off regular, protected time in your diary for reflection: it may only be 10 minutes a day or week, which is not too much to ask for such an important learning mechanism. The authors have experienced some resistance from many who should be practising reflection, doubting that it would be possible or worth the effort. However, fairly soon you will find that it becomes an integral part of how you work and find the time more readily as a result. Former US President Barack Obama reports that he found clarity as a leader through the regular habit of self-reflection and journaling, starting as a young Chicago community organiser and continuing through his presidency.[3] If he managed to find the time in his busy and stressful life—dealing with 'the heavy and the weary weight of all this unintelligible world'[4]—then there is really no excuse for leaders of cultural organisations.

Here are some tips for how to make self-reflection work and fit in to a busy schedule:[5]

- In your diary, block off 10 (or 30) minutes a day (or week) to protect time for reflection. At first, it may seem difficult to find time every day, so make time at least once a week.
- Choose a way to record your reflections—this helps to filter and embed them. There are different formats: a reflective journal, dictating into a recorder, filming a video on your smartphone or a reflection app. Experiment with times and formats until you find something that works for you, and stick with it.
- For each reflective session, choose one prompt or theme and see where your thoughts take you. You might reflect on a specific meeting, a difficult conversation, a key decision or action, an awkward moment, a problematic work relationship, or generally the week in review, both looking back and looking ahead.
- These are the sorts of questions you might ask yourself: what went well; what could have gone better; what did you put off and why; what might you do differently; can you delegate it or forget it entirely; what could you do more of; how do you feel your team sees you as a leader; what type of leader do they require? Above all, what did you learn? The leading management thinker Peter Drucker recommended writing down what you expected to happen whenever you take a key decision or action—comparing the results with your expectations shows you where your strengths are, what you are failing to do, and what *not* to do.[6]

- Describe your emotions—be honest (these are private reflections!). Recording your emotions will help you recognise, work through and make sense of them.
- Reflect with others, for example, with a mentor or coach, or in action learning sets with peers (see Chapters 8 and 64).
- Finally, think about—and record—how you will act on your learning: what are your strengths and weaknesses, what areas do you need to work on and what will you do differently? You might commit to taking a specific action before your next reflection session.

See also:

5. Recognising your weaknesses and blind spots
7. Flexibility: welcoming challenge and different perspectives
13. The emotionally intelligent leader: listening, empathy, sensitivity, care and compassion
58. Organisational reflective practice
60. Don't avoid uncomfortable issues

Notes

1 M. Broussine and R.F. Callahan, 'Public leadership,' in T. Bovaird and E. Loeffler (eds), *Public Management and Governance* (third edition, Routledge 2016), pp. 285–7.
2 A.L. Cunliffe, 'On becoming a critically reflexive practitioner', *Journal of Management Education* 28/4 (2004), pp. 407–26.
3 See M. Scherer, '2012 Person of the Year: Barack Obama, the President', *Time* (19 December 2012).
4 From William Wordsworth, *Lines Composed a Few Miles Above Tintern Abbey*.
5 See P. Neale, 'Seven tips for designing a leadership self-reflection practice', *Forbes* (22 December 2021), at forbes.com.
6 P.F. Drucker, 'Managing oneself', *Harvard Business Review* 77/2 (1999), pp. 64–75.

5 Recognising your weaknesses and blind spots

Everyone has weaknesses, areas in which we know we are less competent or comfortable (typical ones for cultural leaders are finance, business planning, fundraising and advocacy). Often, we are aware of these and can take steps to mitigate them through training and coaching.

Blind spots, however, are areas where we are unaware of our weaknesses. It is being blind to what we most need to improve, unaware of our ineffectiveness in certain areas and how we are perceived, and unaware of what we have a tendency to miss. This leads to poor interpretation of situations, bad decisions, and staff, stakeholders and strategic partners not feeling listened to and understood. Sometimes, others in a team might compensate for the leader's weaknesses so that they do not immediately develop into problems; but eventually they will show up and bite you. An effective leader acknowledges that they probably have blind spots they are unaware of and takes steps to identify and address them before they become problems.[1]

Typical leadership blind spots

Research shows that 30 per cent of leaders have at least one 'fatal flaw', that is, weaknesses so extreme that they can have a dramatic negative effect on a leader's performance and impact, seriously hampering their contribution to the organisation. Usually, these flaws are the result of inaction or omission, for example, lack of strategic thinking or an inability to build strong relationships and trust.[2]

Typical blind spots for cultural leaders can be divided into three types (Table 5.1). The first relates to the leader's level of self-confidence and its impact; the second is about the leader's relation to others, inside and outside the organisation; and the third is about how one approaches or understands the work of a leader.

Actions you can take to become aware of blind spots

The actions to fix blind spots are mostly about soliciting—and being open to—regular feedback, and becoming more aware of your knee-jerk emotional reactions. Once you are aware of those blind spots, then you can take steps to change your behaviour.

- Encourage your team to give you feedback and challenge your assumptions (see Chapter 7). For this to work, you will need to be approachable and to cultivate an atmosphere of trust and openness (Chapter 19), so that your colleagues feel it is safe to raise concerns without fear of recrimination.

DOI: 10.4324/9781003415886-7

Table 5.1 The three types of leadership blind spots

1. Self-confidence and its impact	*2. Relation to others*	*3. Understanding the leader's work*
Lack of self-confidence and 'imposter syndrome' (see Chapter 1)	Poor interpersonal relationships and inability to build mutual trust (see Chapter 19)	Reluctance to delegate (see Chapter 21)
False over-confidence in one's abilities and arrogance (sometimes leading to bullying of staff)	Insensitivity and lack of empathy and emotional intelligence (see Chapter 13)	Micromanagement—focusing on the minutiae of operations rather than thinking strategically (see Chapter 11)
Going it alone, and being unwilling or afraid to ask for help or advice (see Chapters 8, 64 and 67)	Not truly listening and not valuing diverse perspectives (see Chapter 7)	Resistance to change and clinging to the status quo (see Chapter 27)
Not admitting when one is wrong	Assuming that others think the way you do and have the same values	Underestimating how much work certain tasks take for staff
Valuing being right over everything else	Isolation from colleagues—and being the last to know something	Blaming others or circumstances when things go wrong (see Chapter 9 on dealing with criticism, Chapter 23 on uncertainty and risk and Chapter 35 on crisis management)
	Avoiding difficult conversations (see Chapter 24) Not showing appreciation (see Chapter 33)	Believing the rules don't apply to you (see Chapter 10 on modelling behaviour)

- Undertake regular formal feedback, for example, through a 360-degree assessment.[3] This will help you to discover your strengths, weaknesses and blind spots.
- Work on developing self-awareness and emotional intelligence through regular self-reflection and analyse situations in hindsight to explore what went well or not so well (see Chapters 4 and 13).
- Listen: it is not enough just to ask for feedback. You must listen to what people around you are saying (and what they are *not* saying—that is, what are they not telling you and why?), and also see what their body language is telling you. When others suggest or hint at a potential blind spot, encourage them to explain what they mean.
- Surround yourself with diverse thinkers and those who are better than you at certain things. Learn from them but also give them opportunities to do what they are good at (see Chapter 32 for distributed leadership).
- Identify possible triggers—your blind spots may have specific triggers that set off particular behaviour patterns, for example, when you are especially busy or stressed, or when private life impinges on work life. Use self-reflection to identify and address these and to change your instinctive reactions and behaviour.
- Examine what you avoid and keep on putting off, and why.
- Don't get defensive when your viewpoint is challenged (see Chapter 9 on dealing with criticism).

- Enlist help, for example, from a coach or mentor (see Chapter 64). These can help a leader see themselves more accurately and can assist with devising an action plan based on a 360-degree assessment.

Notes

1 R.B. Shaw, *Leadership Blindspots: How Successful Leaders Identify and Overcome the Weaknesses That Matter* (Jossey-Bass 2014).

2 J. Zenger and J. Folkman, 'Most leaders know their strengths – but are oblivious to their weaknesses', *Harvard Business Review* (21 February 2018).

3 In a 360-degree evaluation, the person being reviewed receives feedback from people with whom they work regularly. There are usually four elements to this: self-appraisal, superior's appraisal (this may be the chair of the governing body), and subordinates' and peer appraisal, giving a fully rounded picture of how you are perceived. It is nearly always instructive to compare one's self-appraisal with those others.

6 Managing your own well-being

Prioritising and managing one's own well-being is essential in order to sustain effective leadership and balanced judgement over many years. It is not unusual for leaders to suffer poor physical and mental health that affects their judgement, as the weight of personal responsibility and long hours takes its toll on one's emotional well-being—particularly the stress of responsibility for things that go wrong and the impacts on members of staff and their families (e.g., in decisions related to restructures, redundancies and cuts—see Chapter 34).

It has been argued that leaders in the cultural sector are particularly prone to this sort of stress of feeling responsibility for others, as people-related aspects are seen as vital to the role (and to the role of culture), so they often put the needs of the organisation and their team before their own needs—or do not recognise that their physical and mental well-being (and their judgement) have been affected:

> When things have got very unstable, in my earlier years I struggled really badly with the stress of that and feeling I was totally responsible for some things that go down the plughole.[1]

Bad habits

Sometimes, leaders can be their own worst enemies, by following bad habits and routines that lead to tiredness and stress and eventually build up to affect their physical and mental health and judgement. For some leaders, in the authors' experience, it seems to be a point of pride and a mark of their status and importance to be visibly worn out and stressed as a result of overwork—not realising that a tired and stressed leader does not come across as competent and in control. Unfortunately, many of these bad habits also create pressure for your team to follow your (bad) example: if they see you working in a certain way, they may feel you expect them to do the same.

Typical bad habits to be aware of are:

- Working long hours—starting early, finishing late, being the last to leave.
- Taking on too much, and an inability to say 'no' to projects (see Chapter 29).
- Being accessible at all times of day and night and at weekends.
- Not taking breaks, but working through coffee/tea/lunch breaks.
- Checking and sending work emails during out-of-work hours (e.g., in the evenings, at night and on holiday)—this is a bad habit that has a particularly negative impact on colleagues.

DOI: 10.4324/9781003415886-8

- Insisting on remaining in touch while on holiday.
- Not trusting senior colleagues to manage the organisation and make decisions in one's absence.
- Not carving out time for self-reflection (see Chapter 4).

A plan for managing your well-being

To make your well-being a priority, it is good practice to consider your work style and any bad habits and put in place new habits or rituals that will create a better work-life balance and make you more effective and resilient as a leader. Below are some practical suggestions of the sorts of actions you can take, based on research into well-being at work, but each person will have their own preferences for what works for them:[2]

Set well-being goals, for example:

- Exercise at least three times a week (e.g., a 30-minute walk at lunchtime).
- Go to bed at a particular time, preferably early.
- Read or listen to one book a week.
- Set aside regular time for listening to music.
- Attend one fitness class a week (e.g., yoga, Pilates, spin class, circuit training, dance).
- Go on a date or outing once a week.
- Take 10–15-minute micro-breaks every few hours throughout the day to self-reflect, have a short walk, stretch, meditate, practise breathing exercises, listen to music, do a puzzle, or watch a funny video.
- Create a routine that helps you to decompress and destress in the evening or after work—switch off your phone, go for a walk or run, listen to music, read a book, or cook.
- Try to develop these into a routine that becomes second-nature.

Set boundaries with your team

- Do not let work spill over into non-work time, for example, evenings, weekends and holidays.
- Be online no later than 6 p.m. on a working day (or equivalent for organisations that do not operate on a standard working day). Do not send and check emails after that.
- Do not send emails to your team while you or they are on holiday, and make sure they know that you don't expect them to check emails until they return to work.

Block off time in the diary

- For personal and social commitments.
- For self-reflection.
- Even for writing/preparing presentations, to prevent the stress of being unprepared.
- If it's not in the diary, the time won't be protected, and you'll end up in a meeting instead.

Stay connected to prevent isolation

- Make time to connect with your team, for instance, through an open-door policy, regular walkabouts (MBWA or Management By Walking About is a well-established management tool), or joining them for breaks. You should anticipate that they will behave differently in your presence, so give them space to relax on their own, but show that you are interested and human.

- Ask your team meaningful questions and be interested in what they have to say. Learn everyone's names. Share your own personal experiences with them, remembering one of the key principles of this book, that leaders are at the heart of a network, not at the top of a pyramid (see Introduction).
- If working remotely, use video-conferencing tools to see your team face-to-face and encourage them to do the same. Hold virtual informal coffee chats and lunches online. Experiment with what works for you and your team to help keep a sense of connection.
- Take part in peer discussions. There are lots of communities of practice and peer support groups online, where you can share experiences and problems (see Chapter 64).

See also:

8. The power of a personal network
13. The emotionally intelligent leader: listening, empathy, sensitivity, care and compassion
33. Staff morale and well-being

Notes

1 Quoted in *Museum Leaders' Report: Challenges and responses for leading with purpose* (University of Oxford: Saïd Business School 2018), p. 20.

2 The following draws on *Managing Your Well-being as a Leader*, on the online learning platform LinkedIn Learning, and C. Cooper and I. Hesketh, *Wellbeing at Work: How to Design, Implement and Evaluate An Effective Strategy* (Kogan Page 2019).

7 Flexibility

Welcoming challenge and different perspectives

One of the most difficult lessons for some leaders to learn is the importance of welcoming disagreement and challenge. This is understandable: leaders are usually appointed (and paid) to make decisions and defend them to the governing body, stakeholders and the wider public. When you are in a leadership position, you (and others) might interpret your role as developing a vision for others to follow and having all the answers. It can be uncomfortable when others challenge or improve upon your ideas or opinions, but it is vital to acknowledge that other perspectives help you make better decisions and understand the diversity of your audience.

Flexible leaders are able to modify their approaches in response to uncertain, unpredictable or changing circumstances—nowadays the normal environment of most cultural organisations across the globe—and in response to challenges from staff, who may have different perspectives. Leading a diverse and inclusive organisation means acknowledging and welcoming those different perspectives and valuing that they have something to offer. The leader is not in it alone, at the top of a pyramid, but is part of a network.

Leaders should not feel threatened if they do not generate all ideas and solutions. Challenge brings fresh perspectives on the process of managing an organisation—there are always different ways of doing things (see also Chapters 4, 58 and 67, on reflective practice and external voices). Sadly, the authors know many leaders of cultural organisations whose response to challenge is to dismiss disagreement as unimportant, leaving staff feeling undervalued, uninspired and demotivated, or, worse, to remove or sideline those who disagree with them. An environment where people are afraid to speak up and ask challenging questions will always be hampered and unable to achieve its potential.

In many cultural organisations, the role of a leader is to foster, facilitate and support the creativity of the staff and enable them to flourish in what they do best. What is arguably distinctive about cultural organisations—especially museums, galleries, science and discovery centres, libraries, archives or performing arts—is that many staff are specialists in the key areas of the organisation's work, whereas the director/CEO may not be. In such cases, staff will often be able to articulate different options better than the leader, whose role then is to facilitate a discussion about the best way forward, and obtain and marshal the necessary resources.

Good leaders make a point of surrounding themselves with individuals who feel comfortable providing criticism and alternative perspectives. They proactively seek individuals for their leadership team who will challenge and question their decisions, ideas and initiatives. It is good practice to consciously recruit a team with a diversity of perspectives, backgrounds and lived experiences (see Chapters 39: Equitable recruitment and 41: Building a

DOI: 10.4324/9781003415886-9

diverse leadership team). Without in-built challenge, there is the risk of conformity and poor-quality decision-making leading to groupthink, herd mentality and an inability to think outside the box.

Staff should be empowered to share perspectives and make constructive challenges without fear of consequence, and this is an integral part of being an inclusive organisation. A nurse will have a different opinion about the strengths and weaknesses of a health service from a consultant surgeon, and the same is true of cultural organisations. The opinions of members of staff will be coloured by their background, education, skills, job, their colleagues and whether they have regular and frequent contact with members of the public/users or with the governing body. If you work with the public all day every day, your view of the needs of the organisation could be radically different from someone who works behind the scenes. A director will never see the same reaction from users as someone who is on the admissions desk—yet to be made aware of those user reactions is vital in terms of policy and decision-making.

It should also be acknowledged that people have different ways of communicating. If you are a logical, 'bullet-point' type of person, don't get frustrated when someone challenges you in a more discursive, roundabout way. Some individuals may not have the confidence to challenge openly, and as a leader you can support them with communications training, so that they feel confident expressing their views.

Any leader should be able to articulate their vision in order to build support from members, shareholders, the public or staff, but also be open to new ideas from whatever quarter and welcome the expertise and insights of others:

> Leadership is sometimes about stepping out in front of the crowd offering a vision to follow. More often it's about carving out and holding open a space for the ideas and expertise of others to grow and take shape. This is the challenge—leadership is about making a space for the leadership of others to come through.[1]

Embracing this diversity of opinions and perspectives and incorporating them into the decision-making process can only make the organisation stronger, more creative and more inclusive.

See also:

5. Recognising your weaknesses and blind spots
9. How to respond to criticism
13. The emotionally intelligent leader: listening, empathy, sensitivity, care and compassion
28. Balancing conflicting priorities
37. Why valuing and respecting difference makes your organisation better

Note

1 Liz Kidd, Wiltshire County Council, quoted in M. Broussine and R.F. Callahan, 'Public leadership', in T. Bovaird and E. Loeffler (eds.), *Public Management and Governance* (third edition, Routledge 2016), p. 286.

8 The power of a personal network

An effective leader is not an isolated individual who thinks they know it all and who requires no external advice or support. On the contrary, the best leaders are usually those who have built up personal networks that provide support, feedback, insight into new developments and opportunities to exchange ideas.

Much has been written about the importance of networking for effective leadership. In organisational studies, networking is often divided into three types: operational (or internal), personal and strategic.[1] In this book, these are addressed in separate chapters, as their context and purpose are different. This chapter covers personal networks, which are largely about enhancing personal and professional development. Chapter 59 is on internal (or operational) networks, which are about knowledge sharing and learning within organisations. Chapter 64 is about strategic peer networks that focus on the future of the organisation and creating new opportunities. These networks are not mutually exclusive and will almost certainly overlap, but it is useful to acknowledge their different aims and objectives, and recognise that each requires a different type of effort and time allocation and the development of different types of relationships.

Developing a personal network…even if you hate networking

No matter what stage of your career you are in—whether an aspiring leader or an established one—you need a web of personal contacts to give support, advice, help, exchange ideas and challenges and, of course, provide references and testimonials when necessary. Ideally, these will be people with a range of skills and experiences, working at different levels in various types of organisations.

Quite a lot of people in cultural organisations—including established leaders—hate networking, for various reasons: they are naturally shy, or they see it as taking time away from their creative work, or they regard it as insincere, manipulative, relying on favours, who rather than what you know, or someone else's goodwill. But you don't need to be an extrovert to be a good networker—it is a skill to be learned and practised, not a talent you either have or haven't got. In fact, constant networking helps build confidence by meeting new people, getting out of your comfort zone and building social skills, essential attributes of an effective leader. Nowadays, with the prevalence of social media, it is very easy to build up a network of personal contacts—people with whom you can exchange information and ideas and ask for advice; in fact, you don't even have to meet someone face to face.

The important first step is to find common ground and shared interests, even if your contact is in a different type of organisation or sector, or is at a very different level in terms

DOI: 10.4324/9781003415886-10

of seniority. Even if you are just starting out, you probably already have a network, although you might not think of it as such:

- Start with people you talk to and perhaps socialise with in your own organisation.
- Professional/membership organisations often organise networking events, either in-person or virtual, which encourage you to meet new people, often through ice-breaking exercises akin to speed dating.
- Attend conferences and events and make the effort to talk to new people, as well as catch up with old friends and previous contacts.
- Actively participate in virtual networks and workshops, by giving presentations, asking questions and making comments—develop your own distinctive voice.
- Create a profile on professional social networks, such as LinkedIn, which will automatically suggest potential contacts for you. Don't be shy about asking to connect with someone: explain why you want to connect and what your shared interests are. Most people on such online networks are very used to receiving connection requests from complete strangers and accepting them if they see the relevance.
- Follow, share and comment on various social media platforms: people will respond and ask to link up with you.

Effective networking takes time and requires constant nurturing (weekly if not daily)—but it is time well spent, as getting support and advice from your contacts may one day save you even more time, help you avoid mistakes and might create unexpected ways of getting things done or new openings for your career.

There can be some practical problems with networking:[2] entry barriers (such as membership fees for professional organisations or conferences), competition rather than cooperation between network members, network management and sustainability (networks can appear and suddenly disappear) and lack of immediate pay-off. It is not always clear who, among your contacts, is relevant or when they may be useful to you (or you to them: remember that networking is a reciprocal arrangement). The two authors of this book first met on a museum's diploma course in 1984 and, although they never worked together, they kept in touch. Thirty-five years later, chatting at a conference, they realised that they were both contemplating writing the same book and that co-authoring would make it better.[3]

The lesson is that you never know when you might reap benefits from someone in your network during your leadership journey, so keep up a wide range of personal contacts. It has been said that networking is like investment: it takes time, but yields benefits for years.[4]

See also:

59. How to harness internal networks
64. Peer networks and mentoring

Notes

1 H. Ibarra and M.L. Hunter, 'How leaders create and use networks', *Harvard Business Review* (January 2007).
2 L. Varbanova, *Strategic Management in the Arts* (Routledge 2013), p. 130.
3 The result was P. Bienkowski and H. McGowan, *Managing Change in Museums and Galleries* (Routledge 2021), and the current book is the second output of this longstanding personal networking relationship.
4 Original quote attributed to D. Helbig, *Lemonade Stand Selling: Accelerate Your Small Business Growth* (Sales Gravy Press 2010).

9 How to respond to criticism

Accept that receiving criticism is an inevitable (and necessary) part of a leader's job. As a leader, you are a legitimate target: not everyone will agree with you, and sometimes you will get things wrong. As the person with whom the buck stops, you will take a disproportionate amount of flak and blame. Some of it might be deserved, some might seem unfair. At its best, though, constructive criticism is to be welcomed, as it helps you to become aware of blind spots, alternative perspectives, facts you may have missed and solutions you may not have thought of (see Chapters 5 and 7). It is an opportunity to learn.

Response to criticism should always be measured and thoughtful: it does a leader's authority and reputation no good to become emotional, angry or defensive. It is useful to think of your response in three steps: stepping back and considering the context of the criticism; not responding emotionally or negatively; and providing a positive, evidence-based response linked to actions.[1]

Step 1: Context

- Step back to assess and understand the context of the criticism: take time to think, and don't feel forced into an immediate response, which may be knee-jerk and emotional.
- Try to understand the critic's perspective: who is the criticism from and why—is it about someone else's agenda, do they want to undermine you or to do things differently? (the latter is not always a bad thing).
- Try not to take it personally, but examine the criticism objectively: was it constructive, or hostile and judgemental, perhaps a personal attack or a lashing out in frustration?
- Do you have any objective data—such as an evaluation—connected with the topic of the criticism, which might be evidence of things going well or not so well?
- Consider if the criticism is justified (see Chapter 4 on self-reflection).
- Is the criticism connected to your behaviour? (see Chapter 10).

Step 2: What not to do

- Don't ignore criticism or dismiss it out of hand: it can be useful. Even if a particular criticism is invalid, if you ignore it, then people will tend to be less open with you in the future.
- Don't be defensive and stay calm.
- Don't be aggressive in response.
- As a leader, don't try to pass the blame on to someone else in your team—it is your job to take personal responsibility.

DOI: 10.4324/9781003415886-11

- Don't become thick-skinned, unfeeling and immune to criticism: look after your emotional well-being (see Chapter 6).
- Don't allow dwelling on criticism to divert you from your overall plan (unless, of course, you think the criticism is justified and you need to change tack, in which case, this becomes a wider strategic discussion with your team).

Step 3: Positive responses

- Be prepared to acknowledge your mistakes (for the importance of learning from mistakes, see Chapters 1 and 3).
- Set the record straight with facts, not emotions—especially if the criticism is based on inaccurate information or 'fake news'.
- Be transparent—do not obfuscate or avoid the issue.
- Be clear about any action you can take. When you do take action, report back.
- What can you learn from the experience? There will always be something you can take away, perhaps do differently in the future, or not make certain assumptions. Inexperienced leaders often say things out of turn, to the wrong people, using inadvisable words that can be misinterpreted—wisdom comes from the harsh experience of being criticised.

Increasingly prevalent is online criticism of cultural organisations and their leaders and staff on social media. Especially when it is anonymous, this can be challenging, harmful to the organisation and stressful for individuals. It can spread quickly and lead to negative perceptions and feedback. Post a measured response to the original post, using the guidelines above—stick to facts and actions. If individual members of your team are affected or targeted, be proactive in defending them (even if you think they are at fault—such issues should be dealt with internally and in confidence, not in a public forum) and ensure they have support (see Chapter 33).

See also:

13. The emotionally intelligent leader: listening, empathy, sensitivity, care and compassion
24. How to have difficult conversations and deal with uncomfortable issues
60. Don't avoid uncomfortable issues

Note

1 This section partly draws on and adapts R. Carucci, 'How leaders should handle public criticism', *Harvard Business Review* (12 December 2022).

10 Modelling values and behaviour

A leader's behaviour has an impact on everyone around them, inside and outside the organisation, and it has been demonstrated that staff behaviour is strongly shaped by leaders' behaviour.[1] Leaders therefore have a responsibility to set the tone for their organisation and to model values and behaviours for the staff they lead and manage. If the leader does not act out positive values and behaviours, why should anyone else? A leader's behaviour is also key to the external perception of the organisation—as an ambassador for the organisation, they must be willing to account for their personal actions. This does not apply only to CEOs, chairs and senior leadership teams: all leaders and managers throughout a cultural organisation, at every level, have a responsibility to act as role models for their staff and audiences (for role models, see Chapter 2).

Leaders are constantly being observed and evaluated, internally and externally, based on their behaviour, conduct, actions and what they say or don't say. Research shows that negative behaviours and role models can have a deleterious domino effect throughout an organisation: toxic behaviour, such as verbal abuse, can be modelled down the line by managers, becoming an ingrained part of the culture of how people work and are treated.[2]

It is therefore important for an aspiring leader to have a clear set of positive values that they will stand up for and act upon. Typical personal values voiced by leaders are honesty, integrity, transparency, collaboration and risk-taking. Usually—but not always—these align with organisational values, which are the common principles guiding the behaviours of everyone in the organisation, collectively and individually, whatever the circumstances. Most cultural organisations nowadays have clearly articulated public statements of their values, such as professionalism, trust, integrity, excellence, diversity and inclusion, creativity, dialogue and debate.[3] Formulating and agreeing organisational values requires a participatory approach and is an opportunity for everyone—including the leader—to reflect on their personal values, what they are prepared to commit to collectively, and how the personal and organisational align.[4] When personal and organisational values are incompatible, it can create problems of motivation and self-worth.[5]

Modelling behaviour that reflects positive values—and becoming a role model within an organisation—does not depend on eloquent statements of principle, but on consistency in words and actions and on simple daily acts:

> It wasn't the grand gesture that had the most lasting impact. Instead it was the power of spending time with someone, of working side-by-side with colleagues...of being highly visible during times of uncertainty...[6]

DOI: 10.4324/9781003415886-12

There are fairly straightforward ways by which leaders can set an example, build trust, commitment and motivation among staff, and be a role model:

- Be respectful, empathetic and interested in staff in all roles and at all levels, and listen to what they have to say (see Chapter 13). Don't isolate yourself.
- Be honest and transparent in sharing information: if you don't know something, or need to keep it confidential, say so.
- Don't be afraid to admit to mistakes (see Chapters 1 and 3), rather than hiding them or blaming others.
- Be prepared to praise others: don't take all the credit yourself just because you are the leader. Publicly acknowledging the contributions of others builds a lot of good will.
- Always acknowledge that you are constantly learning and similarly encourage the development of all staff in your organisation so they reach their full potential.
- Be an active champion for inclusion and diversity and an ally to those with fewer advantages, not passive and reactive (see Chapter 42).
- If you need support, get it (see Chapter 6). Don't go it alone or assume that it sends the wrong message by showing your vulnerability. On the contrary, your staff will take confidence from your lead and be more prepared to ask for help if they need it, rather than getting into difficulties, making mistakes, becoming stressed and burning out.
- Regular self-reflection is important (see Chapter 4), to become aware of what is important to you, how you show it and what values and behaviours you think you are currently exhibiting.

See also:

4. Self-reflection
5. Recognising your weaknesses and blind spots
19. Building trust

Notes

1 S. Gächter and E. Renner, 'Leaders as role models and "belief managers" in social dilemmas', *Journal of Economic Behavior and Organization* 154 (2018), pp. 321–34.
2 M.-H. Tu et al., 'Breaking the cycle: the effects of role model performance and ideal leadership self-concepts on abusive supervision spillover', *Journal of Applied Psychology* 103/7 (2018), pp. 689–702.
3 L. Varbanova, *Strategic Management in the Arts* (Routledge 2013), p. 63.
4 For how the process of creating consensus on shared organisational values can work in practice, see P. Bienkowski and H. McGowan, *Managing Change in Museums and Galleries* (Routledge 2021), pp. 67–9.
5 N. Morse and M. McCann, *Becoming a Change-maker in Museums: Experiences, Opportunities and Challenges* (University of Leicester 2019), p. 16.
6 J.M. Kouzes and B.Z. Posner, *The Five Practices of Exemplary Leadership* (second edition, Pfeiffer 2011).

Part 2

The tool box

The skills you need

This part describes a selection of skills which are all essential for a cultural leader.

As a leader, you must be able to think strategically and understand implications at this higher level, but not get bogged down in operational details. The key qualities of a successful leader are outlined: these include emotional intelligence, political antennae and horizon scanning for the longer-term sustainability of the organisation.

Business planning, being aware of where your organisation is financially, and understanding law and rights are important elements in the health of your organisation, as is the ability to fundraise and to act entrepreneurially, including awareness of the knotty and often controversial problem of commercialisation of cultural assets (including digital cultural assets). Uncertainty and risk are often daily fare, but leaders cannot dodge them, so must embrace them without fear.

There are tips on how to build trust in you by your staff/volunteer/trustee teams. Influencing upwards, delegating in every direction and being comfortable having difficult conversations are analysed as essential skills.

DOI: 10.4324/9781003415886-13

11 Strategic skills

Don't get bogged down

A leader (or joint leaders) should always focus on the bigger strategic picture and leading your team to success, supporting them to develop their own strategic skills. Do not get bogged down in minutiae and operational details.

There are three key things that can support you to ensure this can happen:

- Have operational staff with the right skills and responsibilities to keep the organisation running safely and successfully.
- Be clear in your own mind what **your** role is so you are not seen to be interfering.
- Ensure that your operational staff understand where the demarcation lines are drawn between you for the smooth running of the organisation and for your peace of mind.

Certain staff may attempt to divide and rule to get their own way/pet project implemented: steer round them with the surety of a harbour pilot. If you are clear about the organisation's journey and final destination, it makes it easier to decide which projects to pursue and which to say 'no' to (see Chapter 29).

Some people are natural, strategic thinkers; some are naturally operationally focused and delight in the day-to-day tasks of operating buildings, staging events/concerts and solving practical problems. Leaders should ensure that those who are fulfilled by operational routine are doing just that. The leader's role should be to trust operational staff to *just get on with it*, but also support them if a crisis arises and help them to learn from their experiences.

You should not only have clarity about your own role but ensure that the rest of the staff understand your role too. This way they shouldn't pester you with details when they should be dealing with a matter in its entirety.

Being strategic is taking a helicopter view over a longer period of time than just the next few months. Your organisation may be scheduling plays, events or exhibitions over a season or even beyond, so this means that your staff will be planning details of the content and supplies to be able to deliver. Your role as the leader is to build a sense of common purpose (see Chapter 26), develop a programme ideally in partnership with staff and communities (see Chapter 44), generate the resources (see Chapter 15) and ensure you develop your team to deliver this.

DOI: 10.4324/9781003415886-14

12 Political antennae and horizon scanning

It is crucial for leaders to be looking ahead at what's coming up and to be aware of potential political, economic, social and environmental changes that might affect their organisation. As detailed in Chapter 62, cultural organisations rarely work in a political vacuum and often need to address priorities developed by governments at different levels. Political priorities can change, and so it is vital to be aware of the way the wind is blowing and its potential impacts, rather than stick your head in the sand and pretend it doesn't matter.

But horizon scanning is more than just keeping your eyes and ears open. There are actions you should be prepared to take to prepare and adapt for what may be coming around the corner.

- Once you identify a potential trend, consider what it might lead to, whether you can find out more, how you can keep track of it, and its likely impact on your organisation.
- Use all available avenues to help inform your thinking and register for email updates from relevant organisations, such as market and trends analysis provided by external agencies.[1]
- Keep an open mind. Be prepared to question your assumptions and be open to different possibilities (see Chapter 7). Thinking about what the trend might lead to, what might you be able to do differently?
- Involve your stakeholders in discussion about trends and their possible impacts (see Chapter 65). Some of the trends may affect your future funding, so it is best to be prepared as early as possible.
- Discuss trends with your personal network (Chapter 8), many of whom are also likely to be affected by any changes. Are there actions you might be able to take together? (see also Chapter 66 on developing partnerships)
- Ensure your leadership team and your staff, in general, are as diverse as possible, so that your internal discussions bring in many different perspectives and life experiences to help make sense of future trends (see Chapters 41 and 43).
- Get out to see new developments or attend openings/press nights if you can. What others are doing and how the public are reacting is informative and relevant.

See also:

11. Strategic skills: don't get bogged down
23. Engaging with uncertainty and risk
35. Crisis management

Note

1 Such as, in the United Kingdom, Association of Leading Visitor Attractions (ALVA).

DOI: 10.4324/9781003415886-15

13 The emotionally intelligent leader

Listening, empathy, sensitivity, care and compassion

The concept of emotional intelligence has been central to understanding what makes leaders effective since the term was first coined in 1990,[1] and especially since the publication of Daniel Goleman's seminal *Emotional Intelligence* in 1995.[2] Mental Health America defines it succinctly as 'the ability to manage both your emotions and understand the emotions of people around you'. This means identifying how you are feeling, what those feelings mean, how those emotions have an impact on your behaviour and on other people and awareness of—and empathy for—the emotions behind the behaviour of others.

For leaders, emotional intelligence brings greater self-awareness and understanding of their strengths and weaknesses and allows them to view situations objectively, avoid making impulsive decisions and manage relationships effectively. It is arguably a particularly important skill for leaders of cultural organisations that aim to be diverse and inclusive, as it allows them to better understand the benefits of different cultural perspectives and lived experiences, and to be an active champion and ally. Indeed, understanding the need for diversity and inclusion, rather than seeing them as a threat, itself requires some level of emotional intelligence. On the other hand, *lack* of emotional intelligence can result in an inability to understand and value other perspectives, poor communication, poor interpersonal relationships and collaboration, misunderstandings and workplace conflict.

Emotional intelligence is sometimes measured as emotional quotient (EQ), analogous to intelligence quotient (IQ). Unlike IQ, however (75 per cent of which is generally believed to be accounted for by genetics), emotional intelligence is a skill to be learned and practised, not something you innately have or don't have.[3]

In the literature, there are slight variations in the listing of the key elements of emotional intelligence, but they overlap and in practice cover much the same competencies. This chapter uses the following four elements: self-awareness, self-management, social awareness and relationship management (Table 13.1).[4]

Self-awareness

This is the ability to understand your own emotions and how they affect your behaviour, and to be(come) aware of your strengths, weaknesses and assumptions. The most effective way to develop and maintain self-awareness is through the regular practice of self-reflection. Chapter 4 explains the benefits of self-reflection for leaders and has tips on how to schedule it regularly into your working life.

DOI: 10.4324/9781003415886-16

Table 13.1 Emotional Intelligence Quadrant

	Recognition/awareness		
	Self-awareness • Understanding own emotions and their impact • Accurate self-assessment • Self-confidence	**Social awareness** • Active listening • Awareness of body language and things unsaid • Empathy, care and compassion • Welcoming different perspectives • Sensitivity to different cultural norms and values	
Self	**Self-management** • Emotional self-control • Managing own well-being • Awareness of strengths, weaknesses and blind spots • Admitting mistakes	**Relationship management** • Building bonds and trust • Teamwork and collaboration • Inspiration and influence • Developing others • Rewarding success • Conflict management	Others
	Regulation/control		

Source: Adapted from D. Goleman, R. Boyatzis and A. McKee, *The New Leaders: Transforming the art of leadership into the science of results*, Time Warner 2002

Self-management

This is about the mechanisms you develop to actively manage your emotions and their impact on you and others. An essential component is managing your own physical and mental health (see Chapter 6). A leader should always come across as being present, rather than appearing tired and distracted. Be aware of bad habits and routines that lead to tiredness and stress; set boundaries with your team; and have a plan for managing your well-being.

Be aware of your weaknesses and blind spots (for typical leadership blind spots, see Table 5.1). Be open to regular feedback from different sources and take action to change your behaviour (see Chapter 5).

Be prepared to admit mistakes, seeing them as an opportunity to learn, and don't be defensive in the face of criticism (see Chapter 9 on how to respond to criticism).

Social awareness

This is about awareness of the emotions and behaviour of the people around you, and the dynamics of their interactions. Empathy means putting yourself in someone else's situation (which does not necessarily mean agreeing with them), while care and compassion are responding to the feelings of others and making decisions that take those feelings into consideration rather than ignoring them (see Chapter 33: Staff morale and well-being).

Social awareness includes being sensitive to, valuing and welcoming perspectives, cultural norms and values that are different from your own (see Chapters 7 and 37), recognising that such diversity makes your organisation stronger. Don't feel threatened by such difference or dismiss it, but actively seek and welcome challenge and questioning of your approach.

A good way to develop social awareness is through active listening. Practise listening carefully to what those around you say or don't say (especially to you—are there things they are deliberately not telling you, and why?), and what they convey by body language and

Table 13.2 Relationship management competencies, cross-referenced to chapters with detailed treatment and practical tips

Competency	*Cross-reference to chapter*
Building bonds and trust	19. Building trust
Teamwork and collaboration	21. Effective delegation
	22. Influencing upwards
	26. Finding common purpose
	32. Developing distributed leadership and sharing decision-making
Inspiration and influence	10. Modelling values and behaviour
Developing others	32. Developing distributed leadership and sharing decision-making
	41. Building a diverse leadership team
	42. Supporting champions of inclusion across the organisation
Rewarding success	33. Staff morale and well-being
Conflict management	24. How to have difficult conversations and deal with uncomfortable issues
	60. Don't avoid uncomfortable issues

gestures, which is often more revealing than words. Coaching-style questioning is useful to understand how people are feeling and why—open-ended questions that encourage articulation of thoughts, rather than imposing your own ideas or diagnosis (e.g., 'I know how you feel', followed by a personal anecdote, when in reality you cannot know or share their experience). Regular self-reflection (Chapter 4) is also key, as it includes looking outwards and thinking carefully about your relations with others.

Relationship management

Arguably, relationship management is one of the most vital skills for leaders, and it builds on all the other three elements of emotional intelligence: unless you are proficient at self-awareness, self-management and social awareness, it is unlikely that you will be effective at relationship management.

Not surprisingly, therefore, the six competencies listed under relationship management in Table 13.1 are vital to leading a diverse and inclusive cultural organisation, demonstrating how important emotional intelligence is to effective leadership. Consequently, each of these competencies is covered in detail, with practical tips, elsewhere in this book. Rather than repeat or summarise, the cross-references to the relevant chapters are listed in Table 13.2.

Notes

1 P. Salovey and J.D. Mayer, 'Emotional intelligence', *Imagination, Cognition and Personality* 9/3 (1990), pp. 185–211.
2 D. Goleman, *Emotional Intelligence: Why it can matter more than IQ* (Bantam 1995).
3 See C.D. Connors, *Emotional Intelligence for the Modern Leader: A guide to cultivating effective leadership and organizations* (Rockridge Press 2020), with practical tips and case studies on becoming an emotionally intelligent leader, but also how to create emotionally intelligent organisations.
4 In Table 13.1, the individual, bullet-pointed competencies of the four elements have been deliberately adapted and re-worded to fit the leadership needs of cultural organisations that aim to be diverse and inclusive.

14 Financial skills

Managing the money

In larger cultural organisations, a leader/CEO is usually able to rely on a dedicated financial specialist or team, but in smaller ones, it is often the leader who is mainly responsible for managing the finances. In some organisations, budgets are devolved, so managers can end up running the finances for discrete projects. It is also true that:

> Many cultural managers and artists are afraid of dealing with finances because mathematics, accounting or financial analysis is not their strength.[1]

While they don't need to be qualified accountants, leaders do require a basic understanding of managing finances: without a confident grasp of financial statements, it is impossible to run a cultural organisation, make responsible decisions and sign off and submit financial documentation to comply with statutory requirements and annual reporting. This chapter covers the four *minimum* financial documents that leaders need to be able to read, interpret and be comfortable with: budgets/financial plans, balance sheets, income statements (or profit and loss accounts) and cash flow statements. These form the basis for analysis of the organisation's performance and serve as a guide for the next period of financial planning.[2]

Budgets and financial plans

Both budgets and financial plans are forecasts of how much money is needed by the organisation to achieve its objectives for a certain period and from where it will be secured. A budget is generally understood to be a short-term, tactical forecast, usually for a year, which tracks estimated income and expenditure in order to make operational decisions. It estimates costs of programmes, projects, events and overheads, typically based on previous years' actual expenditure. A financial plan is more strategic and long-term, looking ahead to three to five years or more. It will usually be less detailed than an annual budget, but its general structure is similar.

Every budget or financial plan consists of two parts: income (from all sources) and expenditure, and must be approved by the organisation's governing body. There are four steps to preparing a budget or financial plan:

- Agree the goals and programmes of the organisation for the financial period.
- Estimate income for the financial period and where it will come from.

DOI: 10.4324/9781003415886-17

- Identify the expenditure for the same period, including operational costs such as salaries, investment, new equipment and financial costs such as interest payments.
- Calculate the budget surplus or deficit for the financial period: will you have sufficient income to cover your projected expenditure? If not, what are your options for bringing in more income, cutting costs or changing your activity plan, and who needs to be involved in those discussions?

Balance sheets

A balance sheet is a statement that shows the overall financial position of the organisation at a specific point in time. It is divided into two main parts: assets and liabilities.

- Assets are divided into two: fixed and current. Fixed (or tangible) assets are long-term, physical assets such as property and equipment. Current assets are short-term, used in day-to-day operations and typically used up in less than one year, such as stock, consumables, cash at the bank and in hand.
- Liabilities are financial obligations and debts, divided into two: long-term and current. Long-term liabilities are things like loans, repayable over a number of years. Current liabilities are accounts or tax payable, salaries or short-term debt, payable within one year.[3]

Income statements (profit and loss)

An income statement—also known as a profit and loss account—shows whether the organisation has made a profit or loss over a period of time, usually a year. It is different from a balance sheet. Where a balance sheet reports assets and liabilities, an income statement reports total revenue and total expenditure, and so how an organisation has performed during the period. It is an important document for tax purposes, as it has to follow relevant legislation related to what expenses can be claimed as valid (and, if appropriate, tax-deductible).

Cash flow statements

A cash flow statement shows money coming in and going out of the organisation and—crucially—what is currently available in cash or in a bank account. It is a dynamic document, showing money in, money out and money net, giving a current picture on any day, rather than at the end of an accounting period. It is an important financial document, because any organisation needs to know what money it has available at a specific point ('cash flow') in order to pay salaries and suppliers. An organisation may be in relatively good overall financial health but may temporarily be unable to pay staff salaries because of temporary unavailability of cash (a 'cash flow problem')—for example, if it is awaiting payment of a grant.

Practical tips

- If you are not confident with managing finances, get help so that you *can* be confident, for example, with targeted training or a mentor (see Chapter 64).
- If you are dyslexic and struggle with financial management and understanding data in figures, don't be embarrassed, but ask someone to go over financial documents with you.

- Ensure you have a financial specialist in your governing body and don't be shy about getting their help—that's what they are there for (see Chapters 48 and 49).
- A lot of people on your governing body will not be confident about understanding the management accounts they will regularly see, so you can help them without patronising them.
- Ensure your financial statements comply with statutory requirements, which vary from country to country, as well as the requirements of your organisation's governing document. Always have an independent auditor to check this.
- Be aware of what your funding agreements say about financial management and what data individual funders require.
- Understand the differences between restricted and unrestricted funds. Restricted funds are granted for particular purposes and can only be used for those purposes and not, for example, to solve a temporary cash flow problem. The authors have often encountered cultural organisations that 'dip into' restricted funds without authorisation, for example, to pay staff salaries on time. Such unauthorised use of restricted funds can get you into trouble and may lead to withdrawal and repayment of funds. At the very least, ask a funder if they will authorise temporary use of restricted funds for other purposes. Some enlightened funders will allow this but will generally require guarantees and more frequent financial reporting (monthly or quarterly). Cash flow problems are sometimes symptoms of wider financial difficulties, and funders may get together to recommend a comprehensive business review of your organisation, to cover income, expenditure, staffing and programming.
- Understand the nature of financial risks, for example, loss of income through reduction in visitor/user numbers, ability to pay back long-term loans, loss of funding from a key stakeholder or costs of flood clear-up or protection and other adaptation to climate change.[4]

Notes

1 L. Varbanova, *Strategic Management in the Arts* (Routledge 2013), p. 248.

2 See L. Varbanova, *Strategic Management in the Arts* (Routledge 2013), pp. 248–89 for the best detailed practical guidance to financial planning and budgeting, with descriptions of different accounting methods, tips on interpreting financial data and the differences in approach for business and not-for-profit cultural organisations.

3 Most cultural organisations are either publicly funded or charities/not-for-profit, but for those that have issued shares, a balance sheet also includes shareholder equity: this is the difference between assets and liabilities and shows what is left for any shareholders after all the debt has been paid.

4 See also D. Langley and S. Royce, *Managing Financial Difficulties: Part A: Guidance for Arts and Cultural Organisations* (Arts Council England, no date) that breaks down the levels and characteristics of financial difficulty from 'troubling indicators' to 'severe risk of insolvency' and gives practical tips, such as more accurate and frequent cash flow forecasts.

15 Fundraising skills

Following the money

The leader of a cultural organisation is a key person in fundraising, whether you have a large, dedicated fundraising team who do most of the work or are largely responsible for fundraising on your own. This chapter outlines the fundamental principles of a leader's role in and approach to fundraising, which are applicable to all types of cultural organisation, irrespective of size, nature, the amount you are seeking or the type of funder. It does not cover the details of how to develop an organisation's fundraising plan or strategy, or how to run a fundraising campaign, which are dealt with comprehensively by others, as well as in numerous online sources.[1]

The leader as advocate

One of the main roles of a leader of a cultural organisation is to be its 'front' and chief advocate. You must not only believe in your organisation and whatever projects you are fundraising for—you must demonstrate that passion openly. If you don't show that you believe in them, then why expect anyone else to? Don't just put your signature passively on the bottom of a grant application, but let your actions show that you actively champion it. Make yourself available to support your fundraisers in practical ways, whether they are staff or external consultants. Some leaders find it embarrassing, awkward or even intimidating to be constantly asking for money, but if you believe in your cause and its social impact, then remember that it's your job to bring in the resources to facilitate its work.

Be specific: why, what, how much, impact

Always be specific with your funding request: what you will do, why it is necessary, how much it will cost and what the impact will be. Stress its urgency and show that you have a plan in place to evaluate the impact (ideally not only in terms of audience/visitor numbers but in terms of the impact on people's lives). Never ask for funding full stop—for example, just for running costs to keep your organisation open or to offset a budget deficit. Some organisations still ask for funding for 'outputs' (i.e., particular programmes) without considering the 'outcomes' (the difference the programmes will make). A funding pitch should ideally consist of a statement of content and need:

- what exactly you will do (content/output).
- why (need).
- how much you require (precise amount, with justification).
- and what difference you will make with this funding (outcome).

DOI: 10.4324/9781003415886-18

Address priorities and interests of funders and donors

Why should funders or individual donors give to your organisation? In every case, you need to find a way to appeal to their interests and motivations.

Institutional funders invariably list their criteria and priorities for funding, so look carefully at their guidelines and ensure there is a match with what you want to do. Some funders are open to initial discussions about a potential grant application to see if there is a good fit; similarly, some will provide feedback if you are unsuccessful, although others don't have the capacity. Increasingly, there is a focus by many funders on social impact (this is especially true of local governments, whose priority is to support work that improves the lives of their communities), as well as what an organisation might learn from a particular piece of work and how that will help it to develop, rather than merely funding delivery of programmes and measuring success by numbers of visitors/audiences.

With commercial sponsorship, it is always a case of finding the mutual benefits: what can your organisation offer a company in return for their support? Sometimes it takes several conversations to find a solution (usually promotional, public relations or marketing). Don't expect a commercial company to know intuitively all the things your cultural organisation does: they will almost always be surprised by the range of your work that is hidden from public view.

With individual donors, and approaches such as crowdfunding, you have to appeal to the interests of a wide range of people: make your project sound worthwhile, exciting and impactful, something worth supporting that they would like to be a part of.

Demonstrate the broad base of your support

Show what other support you already have for your organisation or project, including financial, in kind, and community/stakeholder support. Consider fundraising in partnership with other organisations or community groups. The latter, especially, sends a strong message that your organisation is not alone but has a community role, impact and support.

Be realistic and don't overreach

Fundraising is time-intensive, so it is important not to overstretch your resources. Obviously, you need to be aware of the main sources of funding available for your type of cultural organisation.[2] But be realistic in what you are asking for: is the funding available, what are other organisations requesting and what sort of bids are successful? Fundraising from the private sector is particularly time-consuming—and the success rate can be low—so be strategic and choose wisely: focus on two to three main sources rather than diversifying too widely. It is not uncommon for a well-meaning but unrealistic trustee to suggest crowdfunding as the solution to all your funding problems; but, unless this is a deliberate part of your fundraising strategy, this sort of scattergun approach risks diverting you from your main targets, creating bottlenecks in fundraising teams, and not necessarily yielding good results. So think carefully about the most effective cost–benefit approach, which does not always mean maximum diversification of sources.[3]

Clarify responsibility for fundraising

Be clear who in your organisation is leading on fundraising, preparing or signing off grant application forms and liaising with funders and donors. Avoid overlap of responsibilities, as this can create confusion for funders and donors, who usually prefer to deal with one nominated person or team.

Ensure everyone can be an advocate

Although it should be clear who is leading on fundraising, it is also important to involve your wider team and trustees, so that they too can be advocates. Create a pitch for your organisation or the project that you are fundraising for, so that everyone can give a quick and effective summary to potential supporters. Involve people at all levels and make sure particularly that board members are on message.

Cultivate relationships with networks and donors

Use your networks to expand the donor pool. Keep them engaged and updated with newsletters, press releases, social media, thank you notes, personal messages from the leader and donor rewards such as private views, launches and behind-the-scenes/backstage tours. Ideally, establish a donor management system to track all interactions and follow-up.

See also:

17. Being entrepreneurial
26. Finding common purpose
29. Chasing funding and how to say ‘no’
64. Strategic peer networks and mentoring
65. How to involve stakeholders

Notes

1 Particularly useful are M. Wright, B. Walmsley and E. Simmons, *Fundraising in the Creative and Cultural Industries: Leading Effective Fundraising Strategies* (Routledge 2022); L. Varbanova, *Strategic Management in the Arts* (Routledge 2013), pp. 251–70; and, still valid though slightly outdated by the advent of social media and crowdfunding, K.B. Hopkins and C.S. Friedman, *Successful Fundraising for Arts and Cultural Organizations* (second edition, Oryx Press 1997).

2 These include subsidies from national, regional and local government, often for overall activity rather than just specific projects, sometimes awarded via an arms’-length organisation such as Arts Council England or Creative Scotland; and project grant and capital funding from lottery funding, foundations and trusts, endowments, corporate sponsorship, patrons, crowdfunding and individual donations. For a helpful snapshot of financial sources for cultural organisations, see L. Varbanova, *Strategic Management in the Arts* (Routledge 2013), p. 254, Table 10.1.

3 See M. Wright, ‘How to develop a fundraising strategy’, *Arts Professional* (18 December 2018).

16 Business planning

A business plan is a detailed, strategic overview of the future activities of an organisation over a period of time—usually between three and five years. It outlines an organisation's goals and how it plans to achieve and pay for them. It is a useful document because it demonstrates the viability of your planned activities, why you want to undertake them, the resources necessary and any potential risks or problems. Any cultural organisation seeking external funding needs to have a competent business plan in order to show that its plans are viable, but it is not in itself an application for funding.

Preparation of a business plan should always be a collaborative effort, not something written in isolation by a director/CEO or senior manager. It should involve your staff, governing body (who will need to sign it off) and stakeholders in discussion about overall aims, assigning discrete parts of the plan for research and drafting and providing feedback on early drafts. The business planning process is a key tool in achieving a sense of common purpose within the organisation (see Chapter 26). A business plan should be reviewed and updated annually, and organisations should have a mechanism and schedule in place to ensure that this happens—it can be a lengthy, iterative process, so make sure you set aside enough time for drafts and re-drafts.

Typical structure of a business plan for a cultural organisation[1]

- Executive summary: this distils the content of the whole plan to give a concise and structured overview, usually not more than a page or so long. It's the last part to be written; be aware that it is also the only part that some people will read, so make sure you label the sub-sections clearly for ease of reading.
- About your organisation: a brief background of your organisation, what it does, its legal status, funding, staffing and volunteers, governance and management structure (often presented in diagrammatic format), audience/visitor numbers, and its vision, mission and values.
- Strategic aims and objectives: aims are the key overall areas the organisation intends to focus on for the duration of the plan. These will be areas like participatory practice, diversity, income generation or touring. Keep the number of these within single figures, and explain why each is important and what you hope to achieve. Objectives are the measurable activities that you will undertake within each aim in order to achieve it. For example, if income generation is an aim, then the individual objectives might be increasing venue hires, functions and events.
- External environment: this describes the external factors that have influenced the nature of the plan and your key aims—usually factors your organisation has little or no

DOI: 10.4324/9781003415886-19

control over. For example, it might refer to the impact on your organisation of a pandemic, flooding, a war, rising prices or reductions in key funding that the new business plan has to take into account.

- (Market analysis: for business/for-profit cultural organisations, a market analysis is an integral part of a business plan. It describes your target market, how your organisation fits into its market, what the competition is and your pricing and marketing strategy).
- Resourcing: this section answers the question 'What do we need to develop or change in our people, tangible assets or systems in order to better deliver the business plan?' Typically, it will include elements such as staff training and development, restructuring, changes in governance, capital development plans or major changes to systems such as IT or box office.
- Finance: this summarises how much delivery of the plan will cost, and where the money will come from. Each element of the plan must be costed: provide evidence to support any assumptions, especially about earned income or audience numbers. Inclusion of graphs and charts is useful, but detailed figures and projections should be placed in an appendix. Usually, you will append a long-term financial plan (see Chapter 14: Financial skills: managing the money). Contingencies are an important part of the financial section of a business plan to allow for unexpected costs, rising prices or financial underperformance: they are generally calculated as a percentage of total costs.
- Risk assessment: this summarises the key risks or threats the organisation faces in delivering the plan, usually presented in tabular format. It describes potential risks (such as flooding or loss of funding), their probability from low to high, what effect each will have on the organisation and your plans for dealing with the risk.
- Monitoring and evaluation: this describes the mechanisms you have in place to check the progress of the activities in the business plan and take action to improve performance, including details of milestones (see Chapter 57 for more on evaluation).

Note

1 For detailed guidance on both process and content, see D. Langley and S. Royce, *Business Planning Guidance for Arts and Cultural Organisations* (Arts Council England, no date), which also usefully points out the difference between strong and weak business plans.

17 Being entrepreneurial

In the face of ever-scarcer resources, cultural organisations are increasingly being forced to become entrepreneurial in order to survive and thrive: to generate some or all of their own income, rather than relying solely, mainly or even partly on grant funding or donations.[1] While there is no agreed definition of 'entrepreneurship' (the word comes from the French *entreprendre*, 'to undertake, to adventure, to try'), for the purposes of this chapter we define cultural entrepreneurship as:

> Using cultural resources to create opportunities and take on financial risks in the hope of profit, in order to support activities in the cultural sector.

It is important to balance the need for generating income with all the other aspects of a cultural organisation's mission: so cultural entrepreneurship is not about profit for its own sake, but as a means to support the organisation's mission and activities.[2]

The heart of entrepreneurship is looking for and creating opportunities. For cultural organisations, there are three types of resources that they can potentially commercialise and turn into profit: creativity/expertise, tangible assets and intangible assets.

Creativity/expertise

This involves charging for the creativity and expertise that the organisation has in-house, through:

- Performances, events and exhibitions.
- Running workshops on particular topics.
- Hiring out expertise (e.g., specialist conservators or researchers).

Tangible assets

Most—though not all—cultural organisations have tangible assets such as property. These buildings or spaces can be used for retail, hired out or used in different ways. Museums and galleries have collections, which are also tangible assets, and these have the potential to generate income. Commercialisation of these assets includes:

- Venue hires (e.g., external conferences and meeting rooms).
- Functions (e.g., weddings).
- Partnerships: for example, the 20-storey M+ museum in Hong Kong leases some of its floors to local universities; and the Museum of Modern Art in New York paid for its

DOI: 10.4324/9781003415886-20

expansion and renovation by allowing a developer to add about 46 floors of condominiums to its six-storey museum, and it continues to receive a portion of the annual fees.

- Running a café: this is an obvious approach that many cultural organisations have tried, sometimes by outsourcing cafés to external companies. Be careful to do your market research thoroughly, though, as cafés can be an easy way to lose money. They require considerable resourcing in terms of staff, equipment and supplies, and the returns can be minimal. It is sometimes best to view cafés as ways of encouraging visitors to come and linger rather than making a profit.[3]
- Retail (which can also be outsourced): including creating and selling products based on the organisation's sphere of activity (e.g., artworks, replicas, souvenirs, books, posters or postcards).[4]
- Museums and galleries selling high-quality images of their collections for use in publications.
- Museums and galleries lending their collections to exhibitions in return for a fee.

Intangible assets

These can broadly be divided into two types, although they do overlap: digital cultural assets and knowledge/intellectual property (often abbreviated as IP):

- Digital cultural assets: these include digitised surrogates of corporeal material, such as photographs of objects and art;[5] original digital artwork, such as images, videos and music; recordings of performances; virtual museums and exhibitions; digital data or knowledge, such as catalogues, databases and spreadsheets. All of these can be sources of income, but in different ways:
  - Digital records that are not unique, such as museum catalogues, virtual exhibitions or recordings of performances, can be made available online for a fee.
  - Non-fungible tokens (NFTs) are unique digital assets, such as original or limited-edition artwork or music. NFTs have a unique digital identifier to certify ownership and authenticity and cannot be copied or substituted. Although there is a growing market in collectors of original digital art and music, it does require cultural organisations to find a reliable technical partner, and environmentally conscious organisations are wary of the huge environmental impact of the computing power necessary to produce NFTs.[6]
- Knowledge/intellectual property: this covers not only rights attached to digitisation of artworks but also new knowledge created by a cultural organisation, often through research (e.g., new conservation techniques or scientific analysis), which can be commercialised through partnerships with businesses.[7]

Risk

A key aspect of being entrepreneurial is accepting financial risk, with no guarantee that you will make a profit or even cover your initial outlay.

There are three types of financial risk associated with commercialisation in cultural organisations:

- Investment in the product/event.
- Investment in staffing—building a team with the required expertise.
- Investment in market research (often outsourced) and marketing.

The challenge is always: what level of investment is practical and acceptable? These are decisions that are usually made at governing body level, often following a feasibility study exploring the potential risks and rewards. It is vital that any feasibility study keeps its conclusions and recommendations realistic, achievable and evidence-based; overly optimistic feasibility studies on commercialisation opportunities can lead to considerable financial loss.

Staffing and expertise

Any serious attempt at commercialisation of cultural resources requires dedicated staffing: building strong commercial teams with expertise in understanding potential markets, market research, pricing, marketing and exploring business partnerships.

The leader and governing body must be open to opportunities and innovation and have a certain appetite for risk. They must also foster an organisational climate for innovation and creativity, to support their commercial teams—and other staff—to generate and build on new ideas.

See also:

23. Engaging with uncertainty and risk

Notes

1 Approaches to commercialisation in cultural organisations vary in different countries. In many, financial support from government, either direct or through agencies, is the largest source of income, often 50–70 per cent of total operating revenue. In the United States, Canada and the United Kingdom, it is usual for cultural organisations to generate about 25–30 per cent of their income from earned sources. For museums, see T. Silberberg and G. Lord, 'Balancing mission and money: critical issues in museum economics', in C. McCarthy (ed.), *Museum Practice* (Wiley Blackwell 2015), pp. 164–70. In the decade to 2018 in English arts organisations, earned income rose by 47 per cent while local government funding fell by 43 per cent: *Arts Index England 2007–2018* (National Campaign for the Arts 2020).

2 For the history and theory of entrepreneurship in the arts, see G. Hagoort, *Art Management: Entrepreneurial style* (Eburon 2003); L. Varbanova, *Strategic Management in the Arts* (Routledge 2013), pp. 14–23; and J. Woronkowicz, 'Arts, entrepreneurship, and innovation', *Journal of Cultural Economics* 45 (2021), pp. 519–26.

3 See C. Brown, *Successful Museum Cafes* (Association of Independent Museums 2020), whose opening heading is 'The road to riches or ruin?' He suggests that if a café is not taking six figures per annum, then you don't have much of a catering business.

4 See, for example, P. Holloway, *Successful Retailing for Smaller Museums* (Association of Independent Museums 2020), applicable to most cultural organisations.

5 Note that depending on the copyright law of a particular country, ownership of an object does not automatically mean ownership of copyright of an image of the object. So a museum may own an object, but may not own the copyright to its image, and so would not be able to sell that image.

6 See S. Reyburn, 'Museums are cashing in on NFTs', *New York Times* (25 March 2022). The British Museum sold three 'editions' of NFTs of works by Hokusai and Turner—unique (single copy), limited (1000 copies) and common (10,000 copies).

7 R.E. Pantalony, *Managing Intellectual Property for Museums* (WIPO 2013), which also covers opportunities for commercialisation of intellectual property.

18 Understanding law and rights

This book is not a primer for the legal knowledge that all leaders need to have at their fingertips. This chapter highlights three areas that all leaders, and emergent and aspiring leaders, need to be aware of, wherever they are on their career path:

- Don't try to be a lawyer unless you are one, as the law changes all the time.
- Employment law in particular is now very complex and even more complicated than you might expect.
- Get help rather than get into a mess: legal mistakes can be expensive and dangerous.

Don't try to be a lawyer

'A little knowledge is a dangerous thing', wrote the eighteenth-century poet Alexander Pope.[1] But a reasonable working knowledge of the current laws which affect you and your organisation is an essential tool for any leader. Much of it will be common sense and general knowledge, but there are significant areas of law which may wrong-foot you in certain circumstances. So don't second guess it.

Areas of the law which are likely to apply to a cultural organisation include:

- Employment, for both employees and employers.
- Limited company and charitable organisations.
- Taxes and insurance.
- Health and safety for employees and employers.
- Building fire and safety (if you own, occupy or operate from a building).
- Discrimination legislation, for example, protected characteristics such as age, disability, race and religion (see Chapter 37).
- Planning legislation, for example, listed buildings, scheduled ancient monuments and conservation areas.

Employment law

This is even more complicated than you might expect, and for very good reasons:

- Like charity law, it is a specialist area of expertise, so don't take advice from a generalist lawyer, as your employer/governing body would want reliable, specialist advice.
- If your organisation is unionised, work with them, not against them; you both want happy and secure employees and a successful organisation.

DOI: 10.4324/9781003415886-21

- The rights of staff can change with new legislation (and new governments). For example, in the United Kingdom, working rights changed after the UK's departure from the European Union.

Ask for help

- Legal mistakes can be expensive and dangerous, with reputational damage the very least of what is at stake.
- If you have a legal specialist serving on your governing body, even if they are not an expert in your problem, ask for their initial advice.
- They are likely to know someone who is ideal to help you, at least initially and possibly pro bono.

Note

1 Alexander Pope, 'A little learning' (1709).

19 Building trust

Trust enables people to work together more effectively. Trust must be earned, it cannot be bought or bottled, and it cannot be prized too highly.

If you are a leader developing a more inclusive and sustainable organisation, then you may be viewed with suspicion by those who are against some or all aspects of it or who are openly opponents of it (and there will be some). Asking your staff, whatever your role, to trust you is a pointless exercise, as naturally, unless you know someone extremely well and they are close friends, your audience will automatically be sceptical.

If you are the director/CEO, it is helpful to establish a strong, trusting relationship with your governing body (see also Chapters 22 and 53). Both sides should trust each other sufficiently to be open and honest about problems or potential crises and be able to discuss problem solving honestly. But, like trust between members of staff, this relationship will take time to build and will need energy to make it work. If you or they are new, then you need to prove that you are good at what you do and that you deliver what you promise. The top tips lower down this page apply as much to governing bodies as staff.

Some professionals in cultural organisations are inclined to be suspicious of leaders and managers who want to change things. As a first step, be visible in your buildings. If staff see you regularly 'on the shop floor', it helps them to start seeing you as a human being whom they can consider trusting, not someone who is holed up in an office and always in a meeting. The late Sir Michael Boyd, Artistic Director of the Royal Shakespeare Company, always left the building during the day via the public areas, so as many members of staff as possible could see him. This Management By Walking About technique greatly helps you to be seen as a human being who cares about their staff, who is approachable and who will listen. It will not dilute your authority as the leader if you appear human, quite the opposite!

Meanwhile, accept mistrust as the initial default setting from most or all of your staff, and you will be on the path towards building trust. To earn their trust, you must do six things:

- Never lose sight of the end goal of becoming an inclusive and sustainable organisation.
- Be honest about the future, however painful for you or them this might be.
- If events or new information cause you to change what you need to do, be open about this and explain your reasons; transparency helps to create a feeling of shared ownership.
- Actively listen to staff and ensure everyone has the chance for their voice to be heard, ask questions, get answers and voice concerns.

DOI: 10.4324/9781003415886-22

- Deliver what you promise: if you can't ensure it will happen, don't promise.
- Practise what you preach and don't have double standards; if you encourage people to work in teams, then collaborate yourself across teams and functions.

Trust takes time to build. You can't hurry it, but must give it space and time.

See also:

10. Modelling values and behaviour
22. Influencing upwards
53. Working with, and influencing, your governing body, and the relationship between chair and CEO

20 Understanding users' needs and agendas

Any cultural organisation that aims for sustainability needs to have the support of its users and to understand their interests and motivations in engaging with its offer. If it loses that support, then it loses its relevance. By 'users', we mean both in-person and virtual visitors/audiences (whether individuals, families, groups, adults or children), educational organisations, community groups, visiting scholars, artists or performers, and users of your ancillary resources (cafés, shops and meeting spaces). It is also important to understand the motivations and interests of non-users, and the reasons why they do not engage with your organisation. This information will help your organisation to make decisions about resources and programmes, make changes to your offer, build and diversify users and increase engagement with them.

There are two approaches to finding out users' needs and agendas: through third-party data and by involving users directly.

Third-party data

Companies and agencies in different countries provide data on demographics and cultural engagement of a particular area.[1] They can give information about the make-up of visitors and audiences, their attitudes towards culture, who is and isn't visiting, what they like to see and do, the frequency of their visits and what would make them visit more. The core data is gathered from census data, national and local government data, surveys, interviews and focus groups. Generally, this data is then analysed through audience segmentation. This is a way to look at a population by dividing it into groups whose members have similarities, grouping people by lifestyle, behaviour, attitudes and motivation. Since it is data-driven, this sort of information is ideal as a basis for an organisation to create an audience development plan. However, qualitatively such data can be fairly blunt, and to achieve real depth of insight requires the direct involvement of users.[2]

DOI: 10.4324/9781003415886-23

Involving users directly

Arm's-length mechanisms that cultural organisations can undertake themselves include surveys, feedback walls, observational research and mapping communities. But the best way to find out users' needs and agendas is to talk to them directly. Many, even regular, users may not understand the complexity of your organisation and what is possible, so begin with outlining options offering the range of what you could offer. Questions you then ask them will allow them to begin to develop their own ideas on what you should or could do. Then you can move onto: what can you do together, and what are the mutual benefits?

There are lots of mechanisms for direct involvement of users. Although, admittedly, they tend to be resource- and time-intensive, they are often also the first steps towards participatory practice and involving visitors, audiences and communities in longer-term strategy and decision-making. These mechanisms are covered in more detail in Chapters 43 and 44 in the context of developing diversity and inclusion but are summarised here:

- Collaborative workshops (e.g., creative cafés) to find out community needs and interests and potentially get them involved in jointly developing and managing programmes.
- Involving audiences and communities in strategy and decision-making, by including representatives on the governing body and advisory panels (e.g., youth boards or participatory forums).
- Building sustainable relationships with communities (for the common elements in this process, such as building trust and giving them agency in decision-making, see Table 44.1 in Chapter 44).
- Working with external third-sector agencies and networks in your neighbourhood to find out what their communities and clients are interested in—this way you will certainly reach non-visitors.
- Staff tours to find out what's going on in the community and to build relationships across a wider range of staff (see Chapter 65).

How far are you prepared to go?

The question inevitably arises of how far a cultural organisation is prepared to go to address users' needs and agendas, perhaps partly at the expense of pursuing its own creative journey (although these should never be mutually exclusive). The options are doing one-off projects or programmes, building long-term relationships, or welcoming ongoing community involvement in strategy and shared decision-making across the whole range of organisational activities. Depending on how far you are prepared to go, this can impact not just your public events and programmes, but potentially your long-term strategy, policies, budgets, communications and recruitment processes.

See also:

43. Diversifying staff and visitors/users
44. Building a participatory organisation
65. How to involve stakeholders

Notes

1 Such as The Audience Agency in the United Kingdom.
2 See E. Parsons, *Understanding Your Audiences* (Association of Independent Museums 2020), UK museum-focused, but in fact relevant to all types of cultural organisation.

21 Effective delegation

Delegation—the transfer of responsibility for specific tasks from one person to another—is a skill that needs to be learned and practised.[1] However, it is not unusual for leaders and managers to be unwilling to delegate, for several reasons:

- They think it will take longer to explain than doing it themselves.
- They need to feel indispensable by being the keeper of specific knowledge.
- They enjoy carrying out certain tasks and projects, so prefer not to re-assign them.
- They feel guilty about adding more work for employees.
- They lack confidence or trust in who they need to delegate to.
- They believe they are the only ones who can do the job right.

But reluctance to delegate can have negative consequences: it will overload your schedule, you may prioritise the wrong tasks and your team will miss out on valuable developmental opportunities. It is also important to acknowledge that others on your team will have expertise that is different from yours—in cultural organisations, many staff are experts in their field. Delegation is a way of showing confidence in staff and giving them space to show what they can do.

There are six principles of effective delegation:

- Choose what to delegate: not everything can be delegated (e.g., appraisal interviews or sensitive matters).
- Clarify the tasks and make sure they are manageable and achievable.
- Choose the right delegate: not everyone will be suited to every task, so play to people's strengths, their past experience, their development needs and their motivation to develop, and be aware of their workload and any other pressing deadlines.
- Communicate clearly what is to be done, why the tasks matter, the timeline and deadline, the outcome and how you will measure success.
- Ensure the delegate has the necessary training, resources and authority to carry out the tasks effectively.
- Ensure you have a process in place to monitor and support the delegate: judge how much support a particular delegate requires and find the right balance of monitoring and support. Always be ready to give praise and feedback.

DOI: 10.4324/9781003415886-24

See also:

22. Influencing upwards
32. Developing distributed leadership and sharing decision-making

Note

1 This chapter draws on the Harvard Business School blog by L. Landry, online.hbs.edu/blog/post/how-to-delegate-effectively.

22 Influencing upwards

As a leader in a cultural organisation—at whatever level, even as a director/CEO—you always have people above you that you have to get on board, such as chairs of governing bodies or more senior managers. Sometimes you need their agreement and support to pursue a course of action, and they may be unconvinced or even disinterested. Influencing upwards is a critical skill for all leaders, and it is essentially a form of communication with superiors above you in the organisational hierarchy.

There are several ways in which you can influence upwards, and these fall into two groups: tips for how to directly influence superiors, and, if these don't work, three 'if all else fails' approaches.[1]

Directly influencing superiors

- **Explain how your objectives support organisational goals and mission**, and therefore how your approach addresses the superior's priorities and helps them do *their* job better. As part of this, consider carefully what the superior's own personal goals and interests are—which may be subtly different from the organisation's goals—and where they might be feeling challenged. Make a concise business case for your approach, using evidence and statistics (including the experiences of other organisations) to back you up. Always lead with a summary of the key points.
- **Emphasise how the benefits outweigh the costs and risks**—senior leadership and governing bodies are often risk-averse (see Chapter 23). Present the benefits vs. costs/risks in a clear, logical and objective way, backed up by evidence, so it does not come across as your own subjective, unsupported opinion. Be prepared to argue that, in some cases, doing nothing is itself a greater risk.
- **Involve the superior**: acknowledge their experience and play to their ego by getting their input in discussion and problem solving. If unsure, ask them how and when they want to be involved, if at all. Ask them some leading questions to invite insight from their own experiences (though be ready to counter the depressingly familiar 'we tried this 20 years ago, it didn't work then, so it won't work now', with evidence demonstrating how the circumstances are different and the external environment has changed). In an ideal situation, such a collaborative effort will arrive at a better solution that avoids potential difficulties and enhances the likelihood of high-level support. With an unyielding superior, be brave and prepared to ask probing questions, such as why they seem uncomfortable with a particular idea, or what their alternative solution might be: this might spark them to re-think their views (or, vice versa, for you to re-think yours).

DOI: 10.4324/9781003415886-25

If all else fails…

- **Find an external champion**. In the authors' experience, sometimes middle-ranking leaders in cultural organisations become frustrated by lack of action, initiative, interest or support from more senior managers or directors. In those circumstances, if you have hit a brick wall, don't necessarily rely on the organisational hierarchy. Consider who is best placed to understand and support you and champion your approach, and who more senior leaders will listen to. Senior leadership is often more prepared to listen to influential external voices than those of its own staff (see also Chapter 67: External voices and critical friends). Think of potential champions on the governing body or among stakeholders (such as elected members in local government), Friends, patrons, funders or community partners: talk to them about your shared goals, develop a working relationship and see if they can use their influence with the senior leadership of the organisation to move things along. Think about how they like to be communicated with, how much time they have, how engaged they are and the level of their influence.
- **Work 'under the radar'**. Sometimes, leaders or governing bodies of cultural organisations are unwilling to publicly commit to a new strategy that they feel is risky or might alienate some sections of their audience. They are then reluctant to officially sanction a new approach by their staff. Typically, in cultural organisations, this risk-aversion can happen with participatory or inclusion projects, work with migrant communities, or decolonisation and restitution/repatriation programmes. In such cases, you are unlikely to get official support from superiors or a governing body. But, if you strongly believe something is the right thing to do and there is evidence of external need, it is possible to do such work, or at least its initial steps, 'under the radar', using broad budget headings to get it resourced; that is, not necessarily as part of a formal strategy, but quietly just getting on with it, without too much fanfare. Often, such 'under the radar' projects receive positive feedback and create a domino effect which, in time, affects the overall work of an organisation, so they are a proven and legitimate way of influencing long-term strategy. Some might feel such an approach is subversive, but we prefer to call it being creative (and being creative is what cultural organisations are all about). If in doubt, call such projects 'trials' that test out new approaches and gather evidence of their popularity and impact.
- **Take an 'unless otherwise directed' approach**. If your superior doesn't have time to get involved or respond, take the approach of indirectly asking for permission without actually asking for permission. You can do this by contacting them to say 'unless otherwise directed, I intend to do x…' They may respond, but if they do not, their silence implies consent.

See also:

53. Working with, and influencing, your governing body, and the relationship between chair and CEO

Note

1 This chapter draws on and adapts D. Robinson, '5 Ways to Influence Up in the Workplace', *Harvard Business Review* (28 March 2022).

23 Engaging with uncertainty and risk

In today's world, change is constant, whether planned or not—and in its wake comes uncertainty. Cultural organisations need to be able to adapt and be flexible, and for living with uncertainty and constantly changing circumstances with a manageable level of anxiety to become the norm. Unanticipated national or global events over which you have no control may have a chaotic and long-term impact on your organisation. Leaders must cope in these situations as best they can and it is often difficult, if not impossible, to plan ahead. Anticipating uncertainty or even chaos is therefore a valuable strength in a cultural leader. You will be able to deal with it more effectively and more swiftly if it is anticipated. If it comes around a blind corner to bite you unexpectedly, your response may be delayed and the results catastrophic.

It is a normal part of statutory requirements (at least for publicly funded organisations and charities) and standard business planning (see Chapter 16) to address key areas of risk, such as termination of external funding, fluctuations in investment, a drop in visitor/audience numbers or temporary closure due to unforeseen circumstances (e.g., flooding, fire or a pandemic). Although the risks a cultural organisation typically faces are both financial and non-financial, in most cases, the ultimate impact is financial and may lead to a need to cut costs—or even insolvency and closure (see Chapter 34 on dealing with cuts).

There are four basic strategies that can be applied to manage an identified risk[1]:

- transferring the financial consequences to third parties or sharing it, usually through insurance or outsourcing.
- avoiding the activity giving rise to the risk completely, for example, by not taking up a contract or stopping a particular activity or service.
- management or mitigation of risk.
- accepting or assessing it as a risk that cannot be avoided if the activity is to continue: for example, recognising that a particular activity carries a risk.

By identifying potential risks, an organisation can make informed decisions and take action and, hence, make the most of any opportunities and develop them with the confidence that any risks will be managed. Building up prudent financial reserves not only assuages anxiety over uncertainty but also encourages risk-taking (see Chapter 14). This frees you up for experimentation. 'Risk-taking' then becomes a way of trying things out, and learning what works, what doesn't and what you might need to do differently (for organisational learning and reflection, see Chapters 57 and 58).

DOI: 10.4324/9781003415886-26

Yet, the cultural sector is notoriously risk averse. Why risk trying something new and innovative, when it's often easier to do nothing, hope the worst-case scenario won't happen and that things can just stay the way they are? Of course, there are understandable reasons for this caution. Publicly funded institutions need to show that they are being careful and sensible with taxpayers' money, not throwing it away on crazy schemes that are not proven to work and that the media might build up into a scandal and create reputational damage (local authorities in the United Kingdom are especially sensitive on this matter). Independent organisations depend on paying visitors and philanthropy to survive, and sober commercial considerations often outweigh imaginative but potentially risky approaches which do not guarantee income and might alienate some supporters.

The risk of change is often seen by governing bodies, directors and staff as greater than the risk of doing nothing. At the Museum of Vancouver, sagging attendance, flat government funding, no support from sponsors or donors and little local awareness of the museum were all long-term symptoms of its increasing lack of relevance to the community, but some staff believed that the status quo could continue without consequence. There was 'a resignation that nothing could change because it was too risky'—because what was required were fundamental changes to programming, staff and structure.[2]

Negative institutional responses to risk can be subtle, rather than obvious. Sometimes, a response to an innovative and potentially risky approach is not a straight 'no' from leaders or managers, but redirection or a steer towards more acceptable or safer approaches, which are an unconscious symptom of their aversion to risk—often, an instinctive reaction to leaders' fear of making mistakes, making fools of themselves and appearing incompetent in the eyes of their peers and stakeholders.[3]

The Royal Shakespeare Company saw it as a duty to experiment and to conduct trials that opened up new, more effective and creative ways of working, because such small-scale innovations helped change things.[4] Inevitably, such experiments occasionally resulted in setbacks, failure and frustration, but they were also a valuable opportunity to learn from mistakes and embed the learning into further experimentation and change.

> If everything always worked perfectly, you're probably not taking as many risks as you might be.[5]

The *Our Museum* programme across the United Kingdom focused on embedding community participation through organisational change: funded by an independent foundation, it actively encouraged participating organisations to have the confidence to take risks and be more open to doing things differently—to try things out and to learn from what worked and what didn't.[6] Many of the organisations acknowledged that using the word 'pilot' allowed more risk taking, because any risk was perceived by staff, governing bodies and stakeholders to be short-term and could be contained. This approach of piloting alternative solutions was an effective way of trying something new without alarming these constituencies unduly.

But it is crucial to be clear *why* you are trying something new and potentially risky and to communicate this clearly to everyone—staff, stakeholders, funders and the media. Be proactive and anticipate what their reactions and reservations might be. Do not wait for adverse reactions after the fact, when you will be playing catch-up and reacting to negative media coverage. Take the lead and be in control of your own narrative: some cultural organisations are explicit in stating that an integral part of their mission is to experiment and take risks, sometimes with uncertain outcomes. Anticipate a worst-case scenario and explain up front what you want to achieve, that you expect some things not to go to plan and that you have a process in place to learn from any mistakes.

Funders are increasingly open to organisations admitting when things have not gone to plan and welcome evidence that they have learned from mistakes. Problems or 'failure' can be very useful—as long as the organisation learns from them—as they can signal that your approach needs revising (rather than abandoning). By providing clarity for your motivations and actions and showing that you understand the risk and that it is worthwhile, you will assuage most of the alarm from your stakeholders and audiences.

See also:

16. Business planning
17. Being entrepreneurial
68. How to respond to popular causes and campaigns and survive 'culture wars'

Notes

1 Adapted from the guidance document *Charities and Risk Management (CC26)* (Charity Commission for England and Wales 2010).
2 N. Noble, 'Museum of Vancouver – a transformation in progress', in R.R. Janes, *Museums and the Paradox of Change: A Case Study in Urgent Adaptation* (third edition, Routledge 2013), p. 226.
3 N. Morse and M. McCann, *Becoming a Change-Maker in Museums: Experiences, Opportunities and Challenges. Reflections on the Museums Association's Transformers Workforce Development Initiative* (University of Leicester 2019), pp. 13–14.
4 R. Hewison, J. Holden and S. Jones, *All Together: A Creative Approach to Organisational Change* (Demos 2010), pp. 49, 127.
5 Quoted in L. Jancovich and D. Stevenson, *Failures in Cultural Participation* (Palgrave Macmillan 2023), p. 43.
6 P. Bienkowski, *No Longer Us and Them: How to Change into a Participatory Museum and Gallery – Learning from the Our Museum Programme* (Paul Hamlyn Foundation 2016); *id.*, *Our Museum: What Happened Next? A Review and Further Learning Two Years on* (Paul Hamlyn Foundation 2018).

24 How to have difficult conversations and deal with uncomfortable issues

Twenty-first-century large-scale displays of emotion are now often expressed after the death of a celebrity icon, at the site of a murdered child or after a mass shooting. Mounds of flowers, messages and candles are used to express shared sympathy and horror at what has happened in a world now largely without a strong religious base. So in your drive to achieving an inclusive and sustainable organisation, emotions may run high as staff and, possibly your users, react to the inevitable changes which follow.

Being able to deal with strong emotions in other people, in addition to yourself, is a key skill in being a leader. If you, as the director/CEO, are aiming to ensure that your organisation is moving towards being inclusive and sustainable, then change is a necessary state and, with change, comes the emotional baggage of upheaval.

Robert Janes observed:

> Organizational change produces a cycle of emotions and reactions in people. Staff first felt shock and a sort of numbness, then denial. This moved into anger, and then negotiating and bargaining.[1]

Much like the emotional stages of bereavement, these stages are important to traverse in order to reach your destination of being an inclusive and sustainable organisation. You as the leader, however, must be able to cope with facing emotional staff and being forced to have difficult conversations as a result, not to mention dealing with your own emotions as you face distraught and angry staff.

As the director/CEO, if you have your own office, then ensure it is suitable for staff to enter if they are in a heightened emotional state. Make sure your immediate neighbours cannot hear your conversations or peer through a glazed pane in your door and see who is talking to you.

Have a vase of flowers in your office, preferably on a bookcase or a coffee table, to bring colour and freshness to what may be a dull corporate space. It will brighten up the room and soften it with the greenery of nature. Ensure that chairs can be easily rearranged round a coffee table or close together to create a more intimate, safe space for emotionally charged conversations. And always have a box of tissues readily to hand in your office.

If you are based in an open-plan office or can only use a glass-walled room for confidential meetings, it is more difficult to create the right environment. If you are able to, it is worthwhile designating a particular space during a time of major changes where any type of confidential conversation can take place, not only with individuals but with unions or smaller groups of staff. Many of these things are applicable to any leader's office, not only for times of major change.

DOI: 10.4324/9781003415886-27

As a leader, do not try to avoid or discourage emotional reactions; it is entirely natural to show them openly, even if it makes you personally feel uncomfortable. Coping with a member of staff in tears or visibly upset is not easy for anyone, but you must be prepared for this and know what to do. Don't be embarrassed, proffer the box of tissues, and all you need to say is 'take your time' or reassure them that they do not need to apologise; then don't speak until they do.

Your method of coping with heightened emotions will say more about how this makes *you* feel than how the staff member may feel. If you feel out of your depth, then you need to examine your reactions and work on your responses. Leaders should recognise that they themselves will go through a cycle of emotions during these periods of change—anger, frustration, hope and disappointment—that must not be vented on staff. You will personally have invested considerably in these changes towards inclusivity and sustainability, but your own disappointments must not be transferred to your staff. Be aware that emotions can take even you unawares and inhibit how a conversation turns out.

Sometimes staff members might be tasked with levels of responsibility in your drive to be more inclusive and sustainable which they feel are inappropriate to their professional role and for which they feel under-prepared, so trying to sustain their work takes an emotional toll. The converse can also be true: more junior staff looking to speed up the move to inclusion and sustainability might experience strain due to a feeling of lack of agency and support, and this has adverse effects on their morale and well-being.

As a leader, you must be able to conduct difficult conversations with staff without bottling out or being misleading. Four tips to help you to develop this ability are:

- Carefully consider the right time and place for the conversation—but don't put it off.
- Recognise that there may not be agreement, but start with an ideal outcome in mind: this will help you to stay focused and reduce your own anxiety.
- Keep your voice soft and low but enunciate clearly to ensure you can be heard.
- Take a deep breath so you don't run out in mid-sentence and state the problem—redundancy, disciplinary or job changes—simply and unambiguously.

Once this is openly acknowledged, more detailed conversations can follow. Do not get sidetracked by questions about other members of staff, but keep your focus on what you need this staff member to understand about their own situation and their future.

The responsibility to get these conversations right is yours, so preparing for them is key, as is being in the right frame of mind.[2]

See also:

13. The emotionally intelligent leader: listening, empathy, sensitivity, care and compassion
34. How to deal with restructures, redundancies, cuts and downsizing
60. Don't avoid uncomfortable issues

Notes

1 R.R. Janes, *Museums and the Paradox of Change: A Case Study in Urgent Adaptation* (third edition, Routledge 2013), p.71.

2 See S. Clark and M. Myers, *Managing Difficult Conversations At Work* (Management Books 2000 Ltd 2007).

Part 3

Leading a sustainable organisation

'Leaders are at the heart of a network, not at the top of a pyramid' is a key theme throughout this book, as leadership in an organisation does not automatically sit at the top of the structure. If an organisation is to be sustainable, it needs to take a long view and have a common purpose which all trustees, staff, volunteers and stakeholders share and in which they all believe. How to achieve this is described: this includes changing values, behaviours and the culture of an organisation—'the way we do things here'—which takes time and is best done step by step, working with allies and champions of change.

In order to be sustainable as an organisation, change will be required as your environment alters with time. Taking the workforce with you will be key to this, and there are tips for internal communications, developing distributed and shared leadership and decision-making, and being sensitive to morale and well-being. There are tips on the pros and cons of using external consultants, and how to deal with restructuring and redundancies which could support building capacity in an organisation.

DOI: 10.4324/9781003415886-28

25 Where does leadership sit in your organisation?

Strictly speaking, the chair of the board (or equivalent governing body) is the leader, and leadership of the whole organisation rests with them and the director/CEO in partnership.

But leadership is needed at all levels of an organisation, not just at the top. It is necessary for managing teams of staff or volunteers, for managing projects with people from different disciplines working on it and for ensuring standards in the public service of your building(s). A director/CEO can support the development of staff so they can lead in their areas and, in time, might move onto leading an organisation themselves (see Chapter 32 on distributed leadership).

Even if you are the director/CEO, you should not assume that you are automatically seen as the leader. Many cultural organisations have strong, charismatic leaders who are associated closely with the organisation and, in many cases, have made significant and lasting contributions to the identity and values of their organisation. But others have influential senior figures who are more emblematic than the actual CEO, be they a chair, a deputy chair, a senior manager, a principal or visiting conductor or an eccentric specialist.

For example, the historian and curator Lucy Worsley is a Curator of Historic Royal Palaces in the United Kingdom. As a regular and successful presenter of historical documentaries on television, she is closely associated with her organisation, but she is not the director or CEO, as she is a job-share curator. But many do mistake her for someone who has the top job because of her prominent public profile.

Does this matter? Depending upon your type of personality and your style of leadership, this may be a welcome distraction from being in the limelight yourself. If, on the other hand, you are hungry for exposure and feel this detracts from your own position, you should try to understand the nature of your leadership, as it should not exist simply to massage your ego, and it may be that you are insecure in yourself (see Chapter 1 on self-belief and self-confidence). The overall profile with stakeholders, funders and audiences is what matters for any cultural organisation; it should not be about one individual but the work you produce and the engagement with your audiences and communities. As individuals leave and new people are appointed, the spark of recognition about your organisation in the minds of the public is what is important, not the public profile of any one person, whatever their position or job title. So if you are the director/CEO of an organisation with one outstanding, popular and well-known person whom people recognise and believe is the organisation's leader, use them as a positive tool for the good of the whole organisation. They could become a champion for you as you lead the organisation to an inclusive and sustainable future.

DOI: 10.4324/9781003415886-29

For some years, many cultural organisations, especially in theatre and music, have split their leadership, making a distinction between 'artistic' and 'executive' posts, with the latter leading on finance, human resources, support services, and running sites and buildings. This means that the non-artistic services are much more effective as a professional is managing them, not someone who wishes to get back to what they really enjoy, for example, directing plays or curating exhibitions.

This trend to spread the load and responsibilities of leadership has grown recently with several cultural organisations turning senior roles into a co-leadership model, for example, the Director of Birmingham Museums Trust in 2020, the Co-Executive Directors at Explora Science Center and Children's Museum in Albuquerque, New Mexico in 2021 and the Royal Shakespeare Company's Artistic Director in 2023. The Royal Exchange Theatre in Manchester scrapped the post of Artistic Director, a role created over 45 years ago when the theatre was first built, to re-think the role. In 2024, they appointed a 'Creative Director' to work as part of a triumvirate with an Associate Director and a Dramaturg,[1] alongside the existing non-artistic Chief Executive.

This move by governing bodies of sharing a burden through co-leadership is a significant shift in understanding about leadership and the weight of responsibilities. It is an open acknowledgement that leadership benefits from different perspectives (see Chapter 7), but also that the well-being of leaders is of paramount importance (see Chapter 6). Equally, it is a response by individuals to protect their own mental health and avoid burnout from overwork. This trend is likely to continue and should be taken into account by all boards when considering changes to their leadership, programming or methods of working. The responsibilities of developing and leading an inclusive and sustainable organisation are considerable and all parties should acknowledge this.

See also:

33. Staff morale and well-being
41. Building a diverse leadership team

Note

1 Dramaturgs are specialists in the study of plays, musicals or operas. It is their job to provide the cast and crew with vital knowledge, research and interpretation about the theatrical work in question so that they can do their jobs more effectively; they should complement, and work closely with, a production director.

26 Finding common purpose

If you are developing a more inclusive and sustainable organisation, there will inevitably be changes in the way people work and behave, so it is crucial to explain and discuss the purpose and likely impact of any major changes. This is so that everyone understands the reasons for these changes, how they will affect them personally, what training and support they will receive, and are prepared for them.

Among the things to clarify are:

- Whether this move to be more inclusive and sustainable is a result of
  - political or community pressure
  - a new director/CEO or staff pressure
  - a funding stream that encourages inclusive practice and sustainability
- Whether the objective is to make the organisation more permeable to community voices and representation, through
  - change of governance
  - different approaches to recruitment, training and programming
  - shared decision-making, policies, values and behaviours
  - changes to staff roles and job descriptions
- How long the process is likely to take (two, three or five years?).

To maximise support and understanding of any future changes, these topics should be widely discussed beforehand throughout the whole organisation.

When the Association of Independent Museums carried out widespread market research with UK museums in 2015, they found the greatest risk to museums prospering was their lack of clarity of purpose. Asked why their museum existed and what it did, staff, volunteers, CEOs, trustees and other governing bodies all gave different answers. So establishing a clarity of purpose became the first Hallmark of Prospering Museums.[1]

Equally, getting everyone in the organisation to understand the reasons why these changes are needed and to support the desired outcomes is a significant step towards achieving them. As a leader you will know why these changes are needed, although, admittedly, in some organisations the push to be inclusive does not come from the leader but from other, committed staff. Wherever the motivation comes from, there must be a shared vision for a common purpose if the organisation is to succeed in being inclusive and sustainable.

This gives leaders the advantage of articulating the change process and to speak eloquently about the impact you are seeking. You must be able to answer such questions as 'what is inclusive practice?' and 'what does sustainability look like for us?' You will be

DOI: 10.4324/9781003415886-30

reiterating this often over the coming weeks, months and years. The authors have both seen major changes not being clearly explained, and subsequently many of those involved not being aware that change was either needed or expected.

Your starting point for identifying common purpose must be finding your 'Why?' so a first step may be to articulate why your organisation exists and what it exists to do.[2] Your change will be seeking to put you in a position to be as inclusive and sustainable as possible and therefore to fulfil your mission, whether this originates from your founders of long ago, from legislation, or from an inspirational leader such as a director/CEO or a trustee. Finding your 'Why?' should involve everyone in the organisation, and ideally external voices such as communities and strategic partners (see Chapters 66 and 67), as every aspect of your work should feed into the outcome. This can be done through discussions, workshops, focus groups or action learning sets. As a way of involving all staff/volunteers as well as community partners and stakeholders, it is a position of strength from which to launch your drive to be an inclusive and sustainable organisation.

Not only must the need for change be shared but the process and impact—what the change will mean for day-to-day work—must be understood too. Finding a common purpose is an effective means to win hearts and minds. This should ease the whole process and can help to identify both active supporters—who may become champions of your changes (see Chapter 42)—and blockers—who may seek to sabotage the process. For a cultural leader, being able to identify both as early as possible could be key to the success of your organisation becoming more inclusive and sustainable.

See also:

58. Organisational reflective practice
61. The importance of organisational memory

Notes

1 AIM Hallmarks www.aim-museums.co.uk/aim-hallmarks/.
2 See S. Sinek, *Find your Why?: A Practical Guide for Discovering Purpose for You and Your Team* (Penguin 2017).

27 Leading change

Organisational change has become an integral part of life for cultural organisations across the world, usually as a response to different external pressures, such as reduced funding, value for money or increasing diversity and participation. It is now a standard part of a person specification for a leader's role in a cultural organisation to be able to demonstrate experience of leading change.[1]

Change can start from anywhere in an organisation—top down, bottom up, from the middle or from the outside. But it cannot succeed or be sustained without the commitment and active championing of the leader and the governing body. Yet across all sectors—business, industry, health and culture—it is widely reported that 70 per cent of attempts at organisational change fail. Those that succeed do so only after about five years.[2]

There are common reasons why most change initiatives fail, and this chapter deliberately starts with these. If you know in advance what is most likely to go wrong, you can take steps to avoid or mitigate it:[3]

- There is rarely a shared understanding across a cultural organisation of what change involves.
- Change is often imposed from the top without consultation or even explanation, which can lead to resistance.
- People resist change often because of fear and how it will impact their jobs.
- Avoiding uncomfortable issues: unless unacknowledged problems within a cultural organisation are openly discussed and tackled, it is unable to learn, improve and change (see Chapter 60).
- Change can fail because the people involved have other priorities—often treating 'change' as a time-limited project that can be set aside for more interesting and urgent tasks, rather than something that runs through and impacts everything they do.

There is a logical, though sometimes iterative, sequence of actions involved in successful organisational change—before, during and after. You cannot just jump straight in: you need to understand what you are letting yourself in for, prepare for it, have a plan (even if that plan might have to alter), prepare staff for it, constantly monitor and learn from what is going well or not so well and be prepared to take action if you are off track.

Understanding what change is—and what you are changing

Any cultural organisation, including all its staff, volunteers and stakeholders, needs to understand up front what change may entail and be prepared for the (often painful

DOI: 10.4324/9781003415886-31

and lengthy) process. The purpose of your change programme should be to put your organisation into a better position to fulfil its mission, whether financially or in terms of staffing, structure, partnerships or ways of working. It is also an opportunity to radically shift, or at least rebalance, the priorities of the organisation. This sometimes, but not always, results in role changes, cutting hours or redundancies. For staff, 'change' is often perceived as shorthand for redundancies and can set up resistance, so it is best to be clear about what is involved right at the start, to ensure that staff understand and buy into the process.

Although the conventional wisdom is that organisational change takes three to five years, in fact, experience shows that it rarely stops or has a neatly defined end point. It takes time for several reasons: change is not necessarily linear or progressive and can lose momentum; one of the hardest things to change is the culture of an organisation ('the way we do things here'); and the financial, political and social environment continues to change around you, resulting in constant adaptation.

But 'change' often does not entail a single, transformative project. In cultural organisations, especially, frequently it is about small improvements and changes across different areas of work, which over time add up to a significant transformation. There are many advantages to breaking change down into a series of smaller projects: small changes are less threatening; they can allow you to experiment; and they create momentum through quick wins.[4]

Preparing for change

As well as fostering a shared understanding of the purpose and nature of the change programme, it is helpful to have a plan up front. Change management models help you to organise solutions, plan for potential problems and keep your team and stakeholders informed of progress. Most importantly, they clarify the connection between your current work activities and your long-term aims—what you want to achieve through the change. The plan may well change, but it gives you a sense of direction, with milestones that help monitor how far you have travelled, and what you might need to do differently.

There are many different ways of modelling change, and you should choose one that suits your circumstances and that you and your staff feel comfortable with.[5]

What makes a good change leader?

All leaders who are successful at change have a strong focus on the matter in hand and are not easily distracted or waylaid by other events or priorities. A leader of organisational change needs five key characteristics:

- Determination: to see the programme through, especially if you expect to face opposition.
- Flexibility: to adapt and take account of unexpected events and be open to alternative ideas and approaches (see Chapter 7).
- Political antennae (see Chapter 12).
- Empathy/sensitivity (see Chapter 13): be alert to the reactions of staff who may be worried about the impact of the change on their jobs.

- Belief: self-confidence is important for any leader (see Chapter 1), but in leading and championing change, it is vital to demonstrate belief in what you are doing. Leaders should actively champion the change, constantly reinforcing the message at every opportunity.

Involving staff and volunteers in change

Although commitment by leaders is essential for change to succeed, in practice they cannot do it on their own: they need the support of their staff, governing bodies and stakeholders. Change has to come from across the whole organisation—it is everyone's job—and leaders need to involve staff (and volunteers) in understanding and managing the change process. There are always actions anyone can take—whatever their role—to help shape and deal with change. Everyone has the capacity, and the responsibility, to be a change agent.

A good way of incorporating different voices into your change process is to use a diagonal slice of staff/volunteers in a change implementation group (although this depends on the size of the organisation). This is effective because a slice ensures all levels of staff/volunteers across different roles are included, and therefore all viewpoints should be represented. Ideally, this group will nurture champions of change, allies across the organisation who understand the need for change, buy into it, enthusiastically support it and disseminate it to other staff. As long as the leader is prepared to listen and adapt, these different perspectives should make the change process stronger and more sustainable, with less internal resistance.

Evaluating and learning from change

How does an organisation know that it is changing in a positive way and that the change is having the desired impact? The danger is that, over a long-term change programme, it can be easy to lose sight of the original aims—especially as staff change—and to just carry on doing what you planned regardless, even if the actions are not achieving those aims. Organisational change requires a robust and ongoing approach to evaluation, to track where real change is happening within the organisation, where it is not happening, where it might be happening too slowly, and if it is happening in the right way. Evaluation encourages you to look back and assess your practice, to see if you are heading in the right direction.

Evaluation is treated in detail in Chapter 57. Its primary function is not to appease funders, but for the organisation to learn from what went well, what could have gone better, what it might do differently and to help it develop even further. As part of this learning, change programmes particularly benefit from external voices and critical friends (see Chapter 67), who can bring fresh and independent perspectives and ensure that difficult and uncomfortable topics are addressed, without which the organisation cannot move on positively.

Notes

1 For a detailed treatment of all the aspects of leading and managing change, see P. Bienkowski and H. McGowan, *Managing Change in Museums and Galleries: A Practical Guide* (Routledge 2021), applicable to all types of cultural organisations.
2 Among the first to cite these figures was J.P. Kotter, *Leading Change* (Harvard Business Press 1996), pp. 12–13.

3 These reasons are covered in detail in P. Bienkowski and H. McGowan, *Managing Change in Museums and Galleries* (Routledge 2021), pp. 141–57; see also P. Bienkowski, 'Why change fails (and what YOU can do about it', *Journal of Education in Museums* 37 (2017), pp. 13–21.

4 For the advantages of continuous, experimental small changes, based on research at the Royal Shakespeare Company, see R. Hewison, J. Holden and S. Jones, *All Together: A Creative Approach to Organisational Change* (Demos 2010), p. 127.

5 For six change models commonly used in cultural organisations, see P. Bienkowski and H. McGowan, *Managing Change in Museums and Galleries* (Routledge 2021), pp. 35–8.

28 Balancing conflicting priorities

It is not uncommon, in cultural organisations, for different constituencies or stakeholders, both internal and external, to have different—sometimes incompatible—aims and objectives. For example, national or local governments, funders, community organisations, governing bodies and various groups of staff may all be pulling in different directions in terms of priorities. It can be difficult to strike a balance and ensure that people feel listened to and not alienated from the organisation.

In general, conflicting priorities tend to fall into one of two groups: conflict over different, possibly incompatible ends, and prioritising means (especially financial resources) over ends.

Reaching consensus over conflicting ends

A balancing problem occurs when different constituencies are aligned with different, seemingly incompatible goals. A fairly common example within cultural organisations is whether to prioritise visitor/audience numbers, make an impact on local communities or be a centre of academic or professional excellence and creativity. What is really at issue here is the process of agreeing on the goals of the organisation: who is involved in that process, what goals are prioritised and for whose benefit (and assessing whether some goals really are incompatible with others). The smaller and more restricted the group that decides goals, the more likelihood that there will be constituencies who feel that their interests and perspectives have not been taken into account. A strategy agreed in isolation by a governing body and a director will always be in danger of not attracting a broad consensus.

In many ways, the solution to these problems is very simple: increasing the diversity of voices involved in an open and honest process of setting goals increases the likelihood of reaching consensus. Even if some of those involved disagree with group recommendations, they may be more easily reconciled to the outcomes because there has been an opportunity for all to argue and justify their positions in good faith. Directors/CEOs and trustees sometimes counter that it is their job to make such strategic decisions, as that is what they were appointed to do. However, they still remain the ultimate decision-makers, as they are the ones who facilitate the process of goal-setting and sign off its recommendations.

Where a collaborative process of strategic goal-setting has been carried out successfully, it has involved the director/CEO and senior managers, trustees, staff, volunteers, communities and stakeholders—literally, everyone with an interest and stake in the organisation. Everyone's priorities go into the pot to be argued over and justified. Several examples of these sorts of collaborative mechanisms used successfully in cultural organisations can be found in Chapters 43, 44 and 65.

DOI: 10.4324/9781003415886-32

The tension between ends and means

Cultural organisations are increasingly concerned about long-term financial sustainability and income generation (see Chapters 15 and 17). What often then happens is that the generation of income becomes such an overwhelming priority that it becomes an end in itself. Staff members are given individual income-generation targets that they regard as a key part of their job, taking precedence over many other activities.

It is important to keep a sense of perspective and to remember that sustainability is not the organisation's reason for existing. Generating income may be a means of it surviving, but it is a means: it is not the purpose of the organisation. This is a typical 'what-how?' question: *what* is the organisation here to do, and *how* is it going to resource it? Activities such as generating income are a *how*, not a *what*, and elevating them to a *what* distorts the aims of the organisation. If the generation of income takes over as an overriding aim, then it is legitimate to ask whether the organisation is worth sustaining.

The best way of addressing any tension between *means* and *ends* is to confront it head-on and discuss it at board and senior leadership team level. Identify what are, ultimately, *ends* (e.g. impact on communities, or x number of visitors attending y number of events each year), and what are the *means* to achieve these (e.g. revenue generation, fundraising targets, commercial activities), and then tease out what might be tensions between them in practice. The discussion then focuses on which activities or programmes should be supported and how, and whether income from activities that generate more income should be used to support high priority activities that earn less well.

Different audiences or events generate different levels of income, and activities that are strategic imperatives need not be penalised for their lack of income-generating potential. Likewise, activities that generate higher income should not always be prioritised as a matter of course, if it means that other strategic imperatives cannot be carried out as a result. Means should not trump ends: generating income should never be treated as a priority on the same level as, for example, making an impact on your community. They are priorities *of a different kind*, with the former serving the latter. If you clearly distinguish between the two and ensure the whole team understands the distinction and the consequences, it will make decision-making more strategic.

See also:

65. How to involve stakeholders

29 Chasing funding and how to say 'no'

Particularly since the global financial crisis of 2008, cuts have been a way of life everywhere for the cultural sector. Public funding overall has been in decline ever since and it is now 'accepted', albeit somewhat reluctantly still in some organisations, that cultural organisations must raise their own cash to sustain even day-to-day activities.

Local authorities in the United Kingdom in particular have been targeted for savings by central governments who, since the 1990s, have sought to render them more and more harmless. The expenditure on culture has dropped by 16 per cent overall on museums alone since 2010.[1] Even within central government, reducing subsidies and close examination of all expenditures have become a way of life. In the United States, where philanthropy is more important as a source of funding, there has been a decline in charitable giving to the arts and culture sector in recent years.[2] So *doing more with less* has become a mantra for the cultural sector as it seeks grants, collaboration, external contracts and partnerships to stretch limited resources further.

As a direct consequence of this, most cultural organisations are chasing funding, with each new initiative, grants stream or funding criterion being considered for its relevance. Larger organisations are likely to have dedicated staff for fundraising and writing grant applications. This switchback of having additional income and doing additional work may disrupt the organisation, as periodically you will plunge downhill as funding comes to an end.

In 2024, the Wigmore Hall classical concert hall in London took the decision to launch their Director's Fund with a view to becoming completely financially independent (they were then 97 per cent self-sufficient). They considered the politically motivated hoops which Arts Council England funding would require them to jump through as not sufficiently important compared to the effort of complying. The artistic director acknowledged that, for organisations not in London (or in any other major capital city), it is more difficult to raise funds, so they are in a fortunate position. The specific criteria of grant-giving organisations, and the time-consuming and tedious task of adhering to their bureaucratic procedures, can be a distraction from your core business. Consequently, each situation must be evaluated on its own terms.

However, every application or fundraising initiative takes a considerable amount of time, energy and creativity, taking staff away from doing anything else. So why do it? How often does an organisation say 'no' to a potential opportunity? How should they be assessed? Is it from a fear of losing out, of being left behind, of not being in the cool gang, of being forgotten when the new trends are evaluated?

A key question to ask when considering a new funding stream is: what will we *not* do, or be able to carry on doing, if we do this? The extra workload—both of applying and of

DOI: 10.4324/9781003415886-33

being successful and having a new project to run—will have consequences and resource implications elsewhere in the organisation. A leader should assess if the price of applying for any particular funding stream is too high, rather than accepting a default setting of always trying. But if the organisation has staff capacity to spend time applying and/or has a good chance of achieving the funding, then the time and energy may be well spent. Otherwise, the decision should often be 'no'. The impact of declining funding means that you must not be afraid to say *no* to new ideas and opportunities if you cannot sustain activity at the higher level required, if your organisation and staffing levels are so much smaller.

See also:

14. Financial skills: managing the money
15. Fundraising skills: following the money
16. Business planning
28. Balancing conflicting priorities

Notes

1 *Research to Understand the Levels of Public Investment in Museums* (Arts Council England 2024).
2 *Giving USA: The Annual Report on Philanthropy*, at givingusa.org.

30 Leading a specialist workforce and the problem of silo-working

Most cultural organisations, unless they are tiny, have specialist staff and also some more generalist posts in areas such as front-of-house, security or administration/finance. As a leader, you need to value everyone, as no one type of role or personality could do the work of a whole organisation. However, leading such a disparate group of people means that everyone must play a part in creating a successful, inclusive and sustainable organisation.

As a leader, you must explicitly acknowledge, value and celebrate the expertise of specialist staff—they will definitely know more about their subject or craft than you do and will be able to offer different perspectives. Remember: it is their specialism that makes you the organisation you are. It is also important for staff across the organisation to be aware of the expertise that resides in the parts they do not work in: it is not unusual for staff in larger cultural organisations to be unaware of the knowledge, skills and experience that their colleagues have, even those in the support roles like finance, human resources and design, and it is always a revelation to them when they find out. Incorporating the disparate views of your staff will help to make the organisation more inclusive, so every opinion should be listened to and weighed in order to find sustainable solutions.

It is often specialist staff who are accused of silo working: this is departments, teams or groups in an organisation purposely not working together or sharing information and knowledge with other parts of the same organisation. This is an attitude found in many sectors and organisations of all sizes. Silos, like a patronising attitude to some of your less-specialised colleagues, can be a barrier to inclusion in cultural organisations today and this has been well documented.[1]

There are usually two causes of silo-working:

- One is a side-effect of bureaucratic structures and departmental divisions, often found in large organisations.
- The second is self-created when some specialist staff focus on their own subject areas to the exclusion of the wider work of the organisation.

Whatever the cause, silo-working is a danger to you changing your practice, especially if the staff resisting retreat further into their silos.

Specialist staff may feel their skills mark them out as more important to the organisation, and their manner to someone with skills which are more widely in demand may be seen as superior and snobbish, jealously guarding their special status; they often assume that things can only ever be done their way, and any other way is wrong. Specialisms should indeed be highly prized, but not to the exclusion of other skills elsewhere on the staff;

DOI: 10.4324/9781003415886-34

they're simply different. Good leaders should seek to create more democratic relationships between their staff and mutual understanding of the importance to the organisation of all skill sets.

In silos created through organisational structures, departmental divisions keep colleagues and departments apart in different ways: physically (occasionally locating some departments in completely different buildings), through the targets they are required to meet, or the specialist teams they work with, and through the hierarchy of management reporting systems. Ironically, some progressive organisations have flattened hierarchies to give people more responsibility and to improve performance, but in the process have created silos that have little contact with each other and different ways of doing things.

A post-COVID-19 pandemic challenge in trying to lead a sustainable organisation is remote working, 'working from home' or WFH. It is very difficult to build a cohesive organisation if several of your key workers—and they are often the more senior people—are not present on site(s) with the rest of the staff. It is undoubtedly an incentive for some people to work from home one or two days per week, especially if they have caring responsibilities or children who are ill. It is also often easier to concentrate, if you are working on a major policy document or grant application, not to be interrupted by colleagues or the bustle of daily cultural organisational life. However, doing it on a regular basis is more difficult to justify if you want to ensure your organisation is sustainable.

School absences jump by 20 per cent on Fridays, traditionally a WFH day, and unauthorised holidays were up 25 per cent on pre-COVID-19 levels in an analysis in 2024 of English school children being absent. These days give more opportunities for weekends away or departures for holidays before the weekend. In addition to the continuing impact of the pandemic lockdowns on school children, this demonstrates that the WFH impact is not only on the employer's business.[2]

Where your organisation runs building(s), WFH can exacerbate the divisions between front-of-house and back-of-house staff. The former are essential if your building is to open, so they are unable to work from home, while other staff, such as senior management, finance, fundraising/development, design or artistic professional staff do have the possibility of working from home. Consequently, the organisation needs a WFH policy, so the director/CEO and the board must consider the likely impact on staff relations before making a decision. Then the policy should be incorporated into specifications, job adverts and staff contracts to ensure that the policy of the organisation is clearly understood by new or prospective recruits (see Chapter 39). Being even-handed about this will assist in your drive for sustainability and not encourage silo-working.

There are two tried and tested ways to counter silos. The first is through creating and supporting internal networks which cut across departmental boundaries, encouraging and supporting collaborative working (see Chapter 59). These not only bring together the allies and champions of your changes but also help the silo-workers understand the important work that others in the organisation do and that they have their own specialist knowledge, skills and experience—*expertise*—which is just as valid as that of the silo-worker.

The second is a highly effective method of incorporating different voices to achieve your changes by using a diagonal slice of staff/volunteers (see Chapter 42). This will introduce silo-workers to the wider priorities of the organisation and encourage them to be involved in shaping the changes. Even if individual silo-workers do not take part, there will be a ripple effect across the organisation from colleagues with a wider perspective and a positive approach to your changes which, over time, will help break down the silos.

Notes

1 R. Hewison, J. Holden and S. Jones, *All Together: A Creative Approach to Organisational Change* (Demos 2010), pp. 123–4.
2 Gillian Keegan, UK Secretary of State for Education, *The Times* (10 May 2024).

31 Internal communications

Ask staff in any cultural organisation anywhere in the world how it could work better, and most will say 'better communication'. Effective internal communication is vital for sustainability and for keeping staff motivated and up to date. Rumour and murmuring gossip will fill any gaps and could destabilise your mission, so you need to avoid these at all costs.

Plan ahead, do not wing it. For effective communication in these circumstances, you need to make sure that your messages are clear, concise and accurate. This will avoid misunderstandings and ensure that your messages get through at every stage. Do not assume that a single all-staff email is sufficient—you need to use every conceivable method of communication to ensure the messages get through and are understood. Constantly reiterate the need for diversity and inclusion at every opportunity, so everyone understands that it is a priority.

> You simply cannot communicate too much.[1]

Many cultural organisations will have their busiest days of the week at the weekend and you may have many staff/volunteers who only work then, not during the week. If this is so, those who do not work full time Monday to Friday may not be able to attend briefings/staff discussions and can quickly feel 'out of it' and ignored. Consider introducing new staff meetings, discussion groups, emails, newsletters pinned onto staff notice boards and/or a WhatsApp group (or similar).

If you have elderly volunteers who don't 'do' technology, do not suggest they should learn just to suit you (see Chapter 46 on digital inclusivity). Ask one of your trusted lieutenants to print out copies of messages or newsletters for them and put them through their letterbox on the day they are issued. Ensure you write a note so they understand that this has come from you as the leader, what the contents are, what the status is and who else has a copy. If the volunteer is on duty on that day, give it to them directly, in an envelope. Ensure no-one feels left out.

Above all, ensure that your communications strategy is inclusive and flexible:

- Do not be economical with the truth but be truthful—do not withhold information unnecessarily.
- Use clear and concise language that can be understood by all (see Chapter 40 on inclusive language).

DOI: 10.4324/9781003415886-35

- Do not use jargon or acronyms.
- Ensure it is always correct and complete, so the reader will not be left hanging with several questions once they have read it.

Think carefully if there is to be a difference between the information given to staff and that provided externally (for external communications, see Chapter 63). In situations where staff might feel anxious about changes, it is difficult to keep matters confidential. Some staff may confide in a member of the Friends, for example, who may confront you. Beware of betraying confidential assessments or future plans in these circumstances. Never tell a stakeholder anything that is not readily available elsewhere.

You will also need to brief your governing body at every stage, as trustees especially will have contact with staff in the normal course of their duties. If they are lobbied about details, do not let them become caught in a 'he said, she said' discussion. Governing bodies, who should operate at a strategic level, need a statement on any sensitive topic that they can use if in a tight spot with staff, the press or a zealous member of the Friends.

Note

1 R.R. Janes, *Museums and the Paradox of Change: A Case Study in Urgent Adaptation* (third edition, Routledge 2013), p. 123.

32 Developing distributed leadership and sharing decision-making

Distributed leadership means empowering[1] individuals across an organisation to take ownership of leadership responsibilities and share decision-making authority. It is a deliberate move away from a traditional, hierarchical, top-down model of leadership, aiming at developing leadership throughout the organisation—thus placing the leader at the heart of a network and not at the top of a pyramid. In this model, authority does not reside in one key individual, but emphasises a teamwork approach to overall strategy and goals, and so it is based more on tasks than on one's position or title within the organisation.

The advantages of distributed leadership are that the talents and capabilities of others, besides the director/CEO, are recognised. They bring distinctive knowledge, skills, expertise, perspectives, ideas and ability to lead and motivate, thereby increasing initiative and creativity in problem solving without having to wait for approval from the top. A board of charity trustees or a political cabinet have collective responsibility. This spirit should carry through any organisation, whatever its structure, so there is effective, shared decision-making. As members of a senior, departmental or project management team, everyone will have their own areas of expertise and arena of responsibility, in effect distributed leadership (providing they are working to the organisation's plan and not creating their own private fiefdom).

Although this is about leveraging the power of others, it is still, of course, delegated authority: ultimate accountability to stakeholders and funders remains with the director/CEO. While the final decision on any matter may still rest with the director, this model of leadership shares responsibility. In times of crisis, or during a major project which takes all or most of the director/CEO's time, everyone else should share the burden of leading, each in their own area of skill. It makes for a more effective organisation which can then more readily respond to external forces or imposed changes and, in addition, helps the director/CEO or chair to be more effective in their job.

With this model of leadership, there should be several leaders at different levels of the organisation and in different skill areas. This is more than simply doing lots of delegating. The leadership element means that those individuals have actual authority, within agreed parameters, and are not simply carrying things out on behalf of someone more senior. In these less hierarchical organisational structures, the role of a traditional manager often changes, as they become coaches, mentors and advisers, who encourage rather than control and motivate rather than order. One thing to look out for is managers refusing to allow staff to assume greater responsibility, for example, by withholding information: delegation and sharing decisions in practice is a skill to be learned, like any other, and some staff may need help with this.[2]

DOI: 10.4324/9781003415886-36

There are three important aspects to bear in mind as you develop distributed leadership:

- Allocate leadership responsibilities and allow others to set agendas, processes and outcomes, as well as to lead meetings, especially about strategy. Everyone brings a different perspective and experience and will likely approach tasks in a different way from you. Be prepared to give others a certain level of autonomy within their field of responsibility; with that autonomy comes accountability for outcomes. If this is to be successful, it is essential that clearly established parameters of the shared responsibility for decision-making are understood by all. It does not mean people going away to do whatever they want to do. There will be limits to authority which must be spelled out before being put into practice.
- If, as a leader, you find this sort of 'letting go' challenging, you may need to learn to trust others more—if you don't, you will end up micro-managing, and the experiment will fail (see Chapter 19 on building trust).
- Ensure you communicate often and effectively—but without appearing to micro-manage (see Chapter 31). The best way is to agree up front with your distributed leaders how, and how often and in what circumstances, communication should happen.

See also:

5. Recognising your weaknesses and blind spots
7. Flexibility: welcoming challenge and different perspectives
21. Effective delegation
25. Where does leadership sit in your organisation?
41. Building a diverse leadership team
59. How to harness internal networks

Notes

1 See Amparo Leyman Pino's cautionary comments about the condescending implication of the word 'empowering', in the Foreword. For distributed leadership to work effectively, however, it needs to be a deliberate strategy supported by the governing body and director/CEO.

2 R.R. Janes, *Museums and the Paradox of Change: A Case Study in Urgent Adaptation* (third edition, Routledge 2013), pp. 48, 91.

33 Staff morale and well-being

Staff who are happy, healthy and positive are generally less tired and stressed, capable of producing more creative work, and better engaged with the overall mission of the organisation. Job satisfaction and a sense of common purpose (see Chapter 26) result in less likelihood of rapid staff turnover, which often slows projects down, with its consequent loss of skills and expertise and the subsequent recruitment process taking time away from other work. For a cultural organisation to sustain its values and mission, it is therefore vital to foster an environment in which staff feel safe, supported, valued and listened to. Staff well-being should be taken into account at all stages of planning, scheduling, budgeting, risk-assessment and decision-making. It is important to ensure that all activities are sufficiently resourced to deliver effectively without excessive demands and negative impacts on well-being. With the financial constraints faced by most cultural organisations, this ideal is not always possible: but in those cases, there is an even greater responsibility to provide support for staff whose well-being may have been adversely affected.

Here are 11 practical tips to foster and maintain staff morale and well-being.

Work–life balance

Promote a healthy work–life balance as an organisational value. Be prepared to discuss with your staff what that might look like in your particular circumstances. While many who work in cultural organisations are fiercely committed to the work, this does not necessarily mean that their social and family lives are not of equal or more value to them. Leaders should lead by example: don't make excessive demands; consider carefully how long a task should realistically take and what resources it requires; don't send emails out of hours and expect immediate replies; and don't expect staff to be available when they are not in work (for leaders' typical bad habits, and setting boundaries with your team, see Chapter 6).

Two-way feedback

Ensure feedback is two-way and be open to suggestions about improvements to the organisation or even about your own actions and behaviour as a leader (see Chapter 7 on welcoming different perspectives). Introduce mechanisms for staff comments—which can be anonymous—and report back how you have responded to them. Staff feeling they have been listened to is one of the major aspects in maintaining positive morale.

DOI: 10.4324/9781003415886-37

Acknowledge emotions

Be sensitive to, and acknowledge, the emotions of staff—and ensure managers understand the need to show empathy and receive appropriate training. Do not try to avoid or discourage emotional reactions by staff; it is entirely natural to show them openly, and it may also give you a valuable insight into their and/or their colleagues' perspectives and worries (see Chapter 13 on emotional intelligence and Chapter 24 on difficult conversations).

Stress and mental health

Be aware of staff stress and promote mental health awareness.

In January 2024, Mental Health UK published *The Burnout Report*.[1] Based on interviews with working adults throughout the United Kingdom, it identified that the lines between work and home life were becoming increasingly blurred, exacerbated by working from home and hybrid working. Nine out of 10 adults said that they had experienced high or extreme levels of stress over the past year. Many are working longer hours, and the societal changes caused by the pandemic are still present. As a result, stress has become the main reason for UK workers taking sick leave, overtaking skeletal problems such as back pain. It can surprise outsiders that workers in the cultural sector experience stress and mental health problems. As the sector is responsible for much of the public's enjoyment and entertainment, it seems easy for them to believe that we are all happy and fulfilled. But much cultural sector work takes place out of normal office hours, so it can be disruptive for family and social life if you are 'on duty' when everyone else is at leisure, and it is traditionally a sector that is poorly paid.

The Royal Shakespeare Company now allows actors to take time off for family birthdays, for example, which is one of the reasons why the company uses a full complement of understudies for their plays. They believe the consequent costs and additional work are worthwhile for both sides, in addition to the developmental benefit for younger actors.

Counselling and coaching should be available within larger organisations, or those with an external company providing human resources advice. Glenbow Museum organised formal stress management workshops for staff, delivered by a professional counsellor, as well as opportunities for individual counselling.[2] In more serious cases, occupational health assessments are the route to different types of therapy or psychiatric help.

Physical health

Provide resources, opportunities and freedom to focus on physical health, for example, healthy food, flexible working hours, working from home or hybrid working. Some cultural organisations, like Glenbow cited above, offer regular groups such as yoga and walking that help alleviate stress or have arrangements with local gyms or health clubs that give staff a discount.

Financial stress

Surveys show that 26 per cent of UK employees have financial worries that impact on their mental health, performance and relationships with work colleagues.[3] Cultural organisations are, in general, not that well paid, and financial worries are not uncommon. Employers can help by incorporating financial educational material into their regular internal communications, for example, about financial planning, debt management or state benefits, or making free resources available to employees. Another practical step is to invite a financial expert to give a talk on managing money. Human resources departments can rarely assist with individual financial worries, so you might signpost staff who need support to external organisations that have the expertise to help, for example, in the United Kingdom, Citizens Advice, or a number of charities that provide education, information, advice and guidance to help people manage their money well and increase their financial well-being.

The importance of conviviality

This is about creating a sense of togetherness and belonging by facilitating opportunities for colleagues to come together informally. This encourages conversations and communication between people from different areas of work and allows for light-hearted forms of interaction, humour and workplace friendships. Typically in cultural organisations this might involve quiz nights, real/virtual coffee breaks or seasonal parties, but it is important that these occurrences are inclusive. They can be counter-productive and even divisive if certain staff are unable to attend because of work commitments or because such events are seen as the preserve of a particular clique. The Royal Shakespeare Company created more opportunities for its staff to meet informally in a number of ways (see Chapter 59 on internal networks). The design of the premises was changed to ensure that people could meet by chance. Staff catering facilities were re-designed so that as many staff as possible could eat together (instead of eating sandwiches at their own desks). Lots of clubs sprang up: gardening, yoga and a choir. These helped break down hierarchical barriers and created links between different areas.[4]

Well-being during conflict

External conflicts can affect staff members emotionally and physically, especially if their families and friends are involved. In recent years, the Russian invasion of Ukraine and the Israel–Palestine conflict have impacted staff of cultural and other organisations. Do not allow harassment, discrimination or micro-aggressions by those who hold different views (see Chapter 38). Allow space for exploration of the issue in a safe and supportive environment. Reflect on your own views and ensure you do not have a biased approach (see Chapter 4 on self-reflection).

Training

Ensure that you and managers across the organisation have received training to understand that morale and well-being are a combination of mental, physical, social and environmental factors and that you all have the tools to support the well-being of others.

Measuring morale and well-being

Regularly measure staff morale and well-being, for example, through staff surveys (which must be anonymous). Ensure there are resources and mechanisms to take action to address any issues that arise and to consider suggestions for change made by staff.

Say 'thank you'

Good leaders, at whatever level in an organisation, should always acknowledge the achievements of their staff. Private and public thanks are often what any member of staff needs to feel proud, appreciated and motivated.

Notes

1 *The Burnout Report 2024*, www.mentalhealth-uk.org/burnout.
2 R.R. Janes, *Museums and the Paradox of Change: A Case Study in Urgent Adaptation* (third edition, Routledge 2013), p. 71.
3 *The Employer's Guide to Financial Wellbeing 2020-21* (Salary Finance 2020), p. 5. This is a very useful resource, updated annually, with lots of practical tips.
4 R. Hewison, J. Holden and S. Jones, *All Together: A Creative Approach to Organisational Change* (Demos 2010), pp. 71, 99.

34 How to deal with restructures, redundancies, cuts and downsizing

Leaders have to manage what are often painful processes. But limiting the negative impact on individuals of the changes and upheavals to the organisation as a whole is also vital, as the negativity of such events must not destabilise effective working.

The day-to-day life of the cultural organisation must continue during these processes, and everyone must accommodate the demands the day job makes on them. The financial challenges which lead to restructuring, redundancies and role adjustments will need to be incorporated into any other changes in ways of working, in addition to keeping the day job going alongside, with minimal impact on any public service. This can be a tall order for any leader, but the overall goal must drive activity.

The impact of restructures

Restructures, redundancies and staff changes can lead to a number of problems:

- Reduced staff capacity.
- Lack of continuity with current commitments and external partners.
- Lack of continuity with funding bodies.
- Gaps in organisational learning and memory (see Chapter 61).

Restructuring is often a way of life, as budgets and varying demands of funders put pressure on all revenue expenditure. Those who rely on public funding face regular challenges to do more with less, but also to deliver it with fewer people. Restructuring and the threat of redundancies are deeply unsettling for all staff, which in turn inhibits the organisation's ability to become more inclusive and sustainable. In addition to other types of change, many will feel destabilised and exhibit signs of stress and anxiety as a result.

Leaders should be honest about the impact of restructures and cuts on the organisation and ensure they clearly communicate both the implications, but also any revised objectives. This includes being upfront and honest with staff, breaking down any restructuring information into smaller pieces and setting reasonable expectations both for the whole organisation and for individual roles. To help your colleagues through the process, create peer support groups and connect staff with counselling.

Some staff may leave because any changes in ways of working do not suit their values. New projects and grants towards specific pieces of work may mean that different work priorities for some staff dictate that roles are changed or adjusted as a result. Overall financial changes are likely to be the driver for downsizing an organisation, and this may make any shift to be more inclusive even more challenging to implement. It can be difficult to

DOI: 10.4324/9781003415886-38

remain committed to a change journey amidst the constant disruption of key members of staff leaving or changing.

Redundancies, restructurings, cuts and downsizing often create a sense of loss—for colleagues who have left, for former departments and workplaces, or for old ways of working. It is important for leaders to acknowledge that such processes do not appear out of nowhere and that not everything that was done before was bad. Honouring and acknowledging the work of staff and members of the governing body that preceded changes of emphasis is crucial, and it can make a huge difference to those remaining staff who are still adjusting to the new ways.

Leaders should acknowledge the emotions involved and not assume that only those personally affected might have strong feelings. Leaders should always bear in mind their end goal in these circumstances, and not enter into debates or defence, whatever the emotion on display, and perhaps most crucial of all, do not take it personally. The emotion is stirred by many different feelings—worry, anger, sadness, loss, professional pride, irritation on behalf of someone else—so do not respond in kind. Keep a cool head but do not appear cold or unmoved by the outbursts of emotion. You can acknowledge it without needing to sympathise.[1]

Redundancies are sad, especially if the individuals are popular figures, but this does not mean they will automatically have a role in the new future; indeed, they may not be very proficient at their current job. Popularity and effectiveness do not necessarily go hand-in-hand. All staff may not recognise this, but a leader must not let emotion about individual personalities sway their judgement, so keep the end goal in mind.

See also:

24. How to have difficult conversations and deal with uncomfortable issues
33. Staff morale and well-being
35. Crisis management

Note

1 G. Anderson, 'Reflections on organizational transformation in the twenty-first century', in R.R. Janes (ed.), *Museums and the Paradox of Change: A Case Study in Urgent Adaptation* (third edition, Routledge 2013), p. 201.

35 Crisis management

Times of crisis require different styles of leadership from day-to-day organisational life, so additional qualities are needed. Especially in smaller organisations, professional staff are required to develop new leadership skills under intense pressure and often in the public eye. Irrespective of the nature of the crisis, there are key requirements to lead through recovery successfully:

- Be visible
- Be present
- Be focused
- Be honest
- Ask for help

Be visible: as the leader, and particularly if you are the director/CEO, then you must be visible in all of your sites, especially in the public areas, in addition to keeping in touch with your public-facing staff. MBWA—Management By Walking About—is a well-established management tool, but during a crisis, it is even more important, and you cannot be seen too often. If you are not open to the public, as happened during the COVID-19 pandemic, then be visible via video link for as many meetings or briefings as possible. All staff, whatever their job, find comfort in seeing and hearing their leaders in times of stress.

Be present: demonstrate that you're in this crisis too. This is the mental aspect of being visible—especially if you are listening to a member of staff during one of your MBWA walkabouts. Active listening is a challenge if you're stressed (see Chapter 13), but it is vital that staff do not get the impression that your mind is not on what they are saying.

Be focused: there is nothing more important than ensuring that your staff/volunteers and your users/customers/visitors are safe and your building(s) are as successful as possible. Pet projects or research trips, however long planned, must not take your focus. You must be seen to be concentrating on the matter in hand, even if you aren't and have operational managers who are responsible for the day-to-day.

Be honest: if you don't know the answer, then say so. If you are working through challenging times, no-one knows all of the answers, so if you are unsure, say so. Predicting what might happen when you do not have sufficient evidence or skills to do so is not recommended. Staff will admire you for your honesty more than if you guess and get it wrong.

Ask for help: any crisis is not the time for heroic leadership (see the Introduction for outdated leadership models). Asking for help is not a sign of weakness. Use your personal network, friends and contacts to keep yourself informed by every available means.

DOI: 10.4324/9781003415886-39

Use your governing body for support and for specific advice where they have expertise. They will want to be useful but make sure they do not get in the way of pragmatic action.

During the UK's Foot and Mouth outbreak in 2001, all rural museums and countryside sites kept in touch with one another and shared information and tips on what to do and what not to do. During the 2020/21 COVID pandemic, professional associations assisted by coordinating information gathering and disseminating to everyone. In the United Kingdom, the Association of Leading Visitor Attractions (ALVA) shared with everyone information normally only available to its members. The Association of Independent Museums and the Museums Association offered free coaching, mentoring and governance support to their members from senior leaders in the sector; while in the United States, the American Alliance of Museums, and museum associations at state level, compiled directories of resources, including leading in times of crisis. While this pandemic was global, if your own organisation has a crisis, your professional networks and associations can help support you. So use every available tool you can to ensure you are making well-informed decisions, based on evidence and not reinventing the wheel unnecessarily.

36 Capacity building

When to use consultants

Capacity building is a crucial skill for a leader to develop in their organisation.

For many, getting a new job, be it promotion or moving to another cultural organisation, is a significant step on your career journey. However, if it is a senior position, or the director/CEO, one of the questions you are likely to be asked as part of the recruitment process is *'what do you want this organisation to achieve on your watch?'* And even if it isn't asked of you, then for your own professional development, you should consider where you want to lead the organisation and where it should be when you come to leave. This may be an odd place to begin a new job but, as Stephen Covey wrote, 'begin with the end in mind'.[1] This helps to give you clarity of vision for your new responsibilities and to plan how you will get the organisation to where you believe it should be going.

As part of this corporate planning, you will be able to assess the areas where the organisation needs additional capacity in order to achieve its goals. This capacity may need to be in many different areas, for example:

- Members of staff in particular areas of work.
- Additional hours by existing staff, for example, if most of them work part time/seasonally.
- Additional revenue income to allow, for example, increased learning and participation work.
- Improved, or a wider variety of, skills in particular areas of work.
- Specialist skills to assist in short-term projects, for example, writing funding bids, project management, building-related skills and market research.
- Specialist human resources knowledge to support improved staffing.
- Governance or organisational development specialists to help you assess what skills you'll need and when.

For some of the above roles, employing staff, often on short-term contracts, will be the most effective method of acquiring the skills you need. But the cultural sector has many freelancers and consultants.

If your organisation needs specialist skills for a fixed period of time, for example, a lottery project or preparing a business plan, then using consultants is a good idea. You will be able to command a more experienced person with a higher range of skills than you would be able to afford to employ on a short-term contract. And when the need for them is over, you will not have the complications of redundancy. An experienced consultant will have a much broader range of relevant experience than any member of staff, so your organisation will have the best advice and expertise.

DOI: 10.4324/9781003415886-40

However, the drawback to using consultants and freelancers for specialist areas is that too often they themselves improve their skills and knowledge while working on your project, but does the host organisation benefit beyond the initial project? As a leader, you must ensure that your organisation learns about their particular area and that you retain knowledge about it within your organisation (see Chapter 61 on organisational memory and retention of knowledge).

The most effective consultants are capacity-building, who do not drop in and then out again, but work *with you*, helping you to gain understanding. One way of ensuring this happens is to attach a member of staff (or, if you're a small team, a trustee or project board member) to each consultant/freelancer so that the overall approach becomes your knowledge also.

Of course, the overall sector benefits from improved skills in its self-employed workforce, but you must ensure that all their knowledge does not disappear with them at the end.

Note

1 Begin with the End in Mind, Habit 2 from S.R. Covey, *7 Habits of Highly Effective People* (revised edition, Simon & Schuster 2020).

Part 4

Diversity and inclusion

A key thread running through this book is that valuing and respecting difference makes your organisation stronger. Being diverse and inclusive is not a 'politically correct' (or 'woke') thing to do, but a vital and necessary step to ensure that an organisation reflects its communities, bringing in different perspectives and lived experiences that enrich planning, decision-making and delivery of activities. This is achieved through understanding and learning how to recognise and value varying types of 'difference' and how they combine, associated biases and potential discrimination, including racial, ethnic, sexual, ability, class/socio-economic status, religious, gender and age, not all of which are visible or obvious.

Chapters look at equitable recruitment and the importance of using inclusive language both internally and externally—and being aware of the power of language to exclude. There are practical tips on diversifying staff and visitors, how to build an inclusive leadership team, nurture and support champions and allies of inclusion across all levels of the organisation, and on making your physical space accessible to all. There is a chapter on digital inclusivity, which has become increasingly important in recent years, including awareness of digital poverty and that a digital offer has the potential to exclude. There are also tips on how to become a participatory organisation, one that builds equitable and sustainable partnerships with communities, including Indigenous/First Nations peoples, involves them in decision-making and explores ways of relinquishing control of the narrative.

For definitions of key terms—diversity, inclusion, equality, equity and community—see the Introduction.

DOI: 10.4324/9781003415886-41

37 Why valuing and respecting difference makes your organisation better

Visible and invisible diversity

An equitable society is one that recognises people's different needs, situation and goals, and removes barriers—physical and social, such as discrimination, but also symbolic, such as baby-changing tables only in women's toilets—that limit what people can do and see, and where everyone has the same opportunities to flourish.[1] But people's different needs and situation vary enormously, and not all of that diversity is obvious because it is based on characteristics that cannot readily be seen. While the types of diversity in society are theoretically infinite, in a workplace context, diversity is usually broken down into the following categories:[2]

- Race and ethnicity.[3]
- Disability—physical or mental impairments that impact on the ability to perform day-to-day activities.[4]
- Age (often referring to unequal treatment of, and fewer opportunities for, older people, but there are also biases about being young or too young; see also Chapter 50: Board diversity and young trustees).[5]
- Socio-economic status (or social class[6]).
- Sex and sexual orientation.
- Gender identity.[7]
- Pregnancy, maternity, menopause and other gynaecological issues.
- Marriage and civil partnership.
- Religion and belief.
- National origin.

Across all societies, many groups—people of colour, women, LGBTIQA+ people,[8] disabled people and others—have historically not been treated equally but have faced discrimination and exclusion from certain jobs and positions, including participation in cultural activities.[9] What happens in practice is that most kinds of inequality amplify other types of inequality. This is what is meant by the term 'intersectionality': different forms of unequal treatment of diversity intersect, act together and influence one another, and so multiple factors creating disadvantage compound themselves to create even greater obstacles.[10] Intersectionality does, of course, also influence privilege, with advantages of gender, ethnicity, national origin and socio-economic status combining to create hyper-advantage.

This is why it is vital to understand all the different types of diversity and how they intersect: you cannot focus on just one. In the authors' work with many different cultural organisations on equity, equality, diversity, inclusion and belonging, we often hear acknowledgement

DOI: 10.4324/9781003415886-42

that they are good at one type of diversity but not others. Really, this is not good enough: unless you are taking action on all forms of diversity—ensuring that everyone has equal opportunities to be recruited, to progress, to be valued and treated with respect and to see themselves represented—your organisation is in danger of ignoring, or worse, compounding disadvantage for certain individuals and groups. It means acknowledging that some groups, statistically and historically, have been disadvantaged and that they compete with groups whose privileges give them an advantage. Equity is about finding solutions that address the unequal status quo and create different outcomes by increasing and retaining diversity.

The diversity problem in cultural organisations

Evidence shows that cultural organisations are not very good at diversity, with significant under-representation and entrenched inequality, especially around gender, race, disability and socio-economic background.[11] Individuals from higher socio-economic and educational backgrounds are over-represented in most creative occupations, particularly in leadership roles, while the most under-represented group of all are disabled people. It must be emphasised that the 'under-representation' is not a choice or characteristic of these groups or individuals, but a consequence of organisations limiting themselves by not reaching, representing and engaging the full demographics of their societies. The 'under-represented' are not represented as a consequence of the barrier of not being heard or included.

There are structural reasons for this, which reflect the intersecting and compounding of disadvantages:

- Those from lower socio-economic backgrounds often cannot access unpaid work experience or the right schools and universities that open up cultural networks—they are limited by their social and cultural, as well as financial, capital; they are often discouraged from pursuing careers in the cultural sector; and class-based exclusion at recruitment stage can be based on accents or lack of a specific set of shared cultural references and behaviours.[12]
- Disabled workers are often given restricted roles in cultural organisations, based on job descriptions that are ableist (for ableism, see Chapter 45); and they are significantly more likely to experience unfair treatment at work.[13]
- Racialised groups are often sidelined into special pathways and projects in cultural organisations, rather than mainstream work, for example, tasked with community engagement and audience development, championing under-served communities of which they are themselves a part.[14]

It must be acknowledged, too, that bringing in diverse staff and audiences is sometimes seen by existing staff of cultural organisations as a threat—to their jobs, to having their roles sidelined, or to their experience not being valued—rather than an opportunity to innovate and open up new aspects of heritage and culture. Being a new 'diverse' member of staff can also be isolating, with the extra load of often being the only one with visible difference, which creates an emotional burden. On the positive side, this puts pressure and expectations on the existing team members to work collaboratively and with trust; on the negative side, the 'diverse' recruit might be singled out and undermined, with no back-up (see Chapter 38 on racism and bias):

> What happens next is very typical for people of colour: I went from being pet to pest. Suddenly, I became a viable threat to more senior people in the organisation.[15]

How diversity makes your organisation better

There are five ways in which being diverse and inclusive makes your organisation more effective: the legal case, the business case, representation, the creative case and the social justice case.

Legally protected characteristics

In many countries, the diversity categories listed above—or variations thereof—are protected by law.[16] In addition, several European and South American countries include social origin as a protected characteristic, and there is considerable discussion in the United Kingdom as to whether social class should become a protected characteristic.

These laws legally protect people from discrimination in the workplace and wider society. In practice, you discriminate if you treat someone with a protected characteristic less favourably than you treat others.[17] Most of these legal statutes allow for positive action—such as targets—to encourage and train people from underrepresented groups, but do not allow for positive discrimination, such as quotas. This is an important distinction: treating someone more favourably because they have a protected characteristic is generally unlawful.

Business case

Although many cultural organisations still seem to struggle to make the business case for diversity, in fact, the argument was first articulated several decades ago.[18] The business case is essentially that diversity is critical to organisational performance and effectiveness, in four ways:

- Commitment to diversity ensures that, by not discriminating, you attract the best talent, irrespective of age, ethnicity, disability, etc.
- Diverse teams provide a better perspective and understanding of what the communities you serve want to see, hear or do.
- Diverse teams outperform homogeneous teams on problem-solving, with more creative dialogue, and deliver more innovative work.
- Diverse and inclusive organisations foster staff loyalty and engagement, resulting in lower staff turnover. The opposite is also true: lack of diversity and inclusiveness often leads to increased staff turnover and associated costs.

Representation matters

It is increasingly important for cultural organisations to demonstrate that they both serve their communities and audiences and are representative of them, and so to ensure that their workforce reflects the diversity of modern society and particularly of the community in which they are embedded. People want to see people like themselves working in your organisation, and a diversity of backgrounds fully represented—the alternative is a form of 'embodied exclusion' that perpetuates structural inequalities.[19] Building diverse teams attracts diverse audiences because people feel more comfortable that your organisation is a place for them. It is also inspiring for young people to see someone like them working in your organisation, raising awareness of a potential career path they may not have considered. Representation leads to belonging: your workforce, your offer and your audiences representing and being relevant to diverse contemporary society.

Creative case

There are three planks to this argument, partially articulated by Arts Council England as part of its funding framework:[20]

- Diversity is a condition for innovation: it enriches any art form by bringing in new people with fresh perspectives and influences to change, challenge and inspire creativity.
- It shifts perceptions of what diverse people can achieve—for example, disabled people—by removing barriers, actively growing opportunities for minoritised and marginalised people to unleash their potential, so that cultural organisations reflect the reality of social diversity. This also acknowledges the diversity of artists historically who have been marginalised through structural barriers and prejudice, such as women and ethnic minority writers, composers and artists.
- More broadly and ambitiously, diversity creates the conditions for imagining new and different structures, systems, organisations and arts that serve a diverse society.

Social justice and equity

This affirms that cultural organisations have a responsibility to take action on societal and organisational injustice and inequity. Genuine inclusion requires action not only in making external programming more diverse and inclusive but in recognising that social justice and equity begin inside the organisation. This can be done by addressing systemic exclusion, for example, in workforce practices that have constrained people of low income, racially minoritised groups or disabled people from accessing cultural employment opportunities.[21] It also requires building cultural capacity, so that existing staff understand the why and how of social justice, diversity and inclusion and are prepared for the shift, ready to welcome a more diverse workforce rather than see it as a threat.

See also:

7. Flexibility: welcoming challenge and different perspectives
20. Understanding users' needs and agendas
50. Board diversity and young trustees
68. How to respond to popular causes and campaigns and survive 'culture wars'

Notes

1 Definition based on *Fairness and Freedom: The Final Report of the Equalities Review* (The Equalities Review 2007), p. 126.
2 In 1990, Marilyn Loden and Judy Rosener developed the Diversity Wheel, a framework for the various dimensions of diversity within individuals and organisations. Arranged as four concentric layers of diversity—personality, internal, external and organisational—they encourage thinking about values, beliefs and identity and also consider a person's position or level in an organisation.
3 'Race' is usually more linked with physical characteristics, while 'ethnicity' relates to social and cultural expression and identification, but they are both fluid and complex constructs deeply connected to an individual's self-identity.
4 Including neurodivergence, although only some neurodiverse conditions are characterised as a disability under the laws of different countries.
5 L. Lang, 'Age discrimination in the art world', *Arts Professional* (6 June 2023); A. Benitez, 'The impact of the ageing population on museum audiences: challenges and opportunities for museums', *The International Journal of the Inclusive Museum* 5/1 (2012), pp. 1–9.

6 For social class in the United Kingdom, see D. Cameron, *How Diverse Are We, Really?* (Creative People and Places 2021), pp. 64–6; A. Biressi and H. Nunn, *Class and Contemporary British Culture* (Palgrave Macmillan 2013); S. Iervolino and D. Sergi, *Museums, Class and the Pandemic: An Investigation into the Lived Experiences of Working-Class Londoners* (Museum of London 2022), p. 55. But class is also important in Latin America: see, for example, E. Jessel, 'If I'm stratum 3, that's who I am: inside Bogotá's social stratification system', *The Guardian* (9 November 2017); and T. Stringer, 'Understanding social class in Mexico: an intersectional framework', *Middle Atlantic Review of Latin American Studies* 7/2 (2023), pp. 183–96.

7 Including gender identities that are not based on a binary framework of male/female, for example, transgender, transexual, non-binary and intersex. See *Trans-inclusive Culture: Guidance on Advancing Trans Inclusion for Museums, Galleries, Archives and Heritage Organisations* (RCMG, University of Leicester 2023).

8 LGBTIQA+ stands for 'lesbian, gay, bisexual, transgender, intersex, queer/questioning, asexual and other terms (such as non-binary and pansexual)'.

9 For example, Black Americans were excluded from visiting some cultural sites until the start of the Civil Rights movement: see P. DiMaggio and F. Ostrower, 'Participation in the arts by black and white Americans', *Social Forces* 68/3 (1990), pp. 753–78; or transgender opera singers insulted at auditions and urged to give up: C.N. Lester, 'Taking to the stage: life as a trans opera singer', Living Opera Series (12 June 2019), https://www.nationaloperastudio.org.uk/news/taking-to-the-stage-life-as-a-trans-opera-singer.

10 See P. Hill Collins and S. Bilge, *Intersectionality* (second edition, Polity Press 2020), especially pp. 1–36.

11 Obviously statistics vary across countries. For the United Kingdom, see *It's About Handing Over Power: The Impact of Ethnic Diversity Initiatives on Curatorial Roles in the UK Arts and Heritage Sector 1998–2021* (Art Fund 2022); M. Sharma, M. Riccardi and S. Islam, *If Nothing Changes, Nothing Changes: A Report Examining the Status of Anti-racism, Equity, Diversity and Inclusion in the Heritage Sector Across England* (Ahmed Iqbal Ullah Education Trust 2022); H. Carey, D. O'Brien and O. Gable, *Social Mobility in the Creative Economy: Rebuilding and levelling up?* (Creative Industries Policy and Evidence Centre 2021); N. Wreyford, D. O'Brien, and T. Dent, *Creative Majority: An APPG for Creative Diversity Report on 'What Works' to Support, Encourage and Improve Diversity, Equity and Inclusion in the Creative Sector* (report for the All Party Parliamentary Group for Creative Diversity 2021); D. O'Brien, O. Brook and M. Taylor, *Panic! Social Class, Taste and Inequalities in the Creative Industries* (Create London and Arts Emergency 2018). For the USA, see C. M. Topaz et al., 'Race- and gender-based under-representation of creative contributors: art, fashion, film, and music', *Humanities and Social Sciences Communications* 9, 221 (2022): https://doi.org/10.1057/s41599-022-01239-9; A. Olivares and J. Piatak, 'Exhibiting inclusion: an examination of race, ethnicity, and museum participation', *Voluntas: International Journal of Voluntary and Nonprofit Organizations* 33 (2022), pp. 121–33; P. Moore, R. Paquet and A. Wittman, *Transforming Inclusion in Museums: The Power of Collaborative Inquiry* (Rowman & Littlefield 2022), pp. 16–28; J. Hayes, 'Is the nonprofit sector doing enough for diversity?', *Profiles in Diversity Journal* (9 November 2012): https://diversityjournal.com/9897-is-the-nonprofit-sector-doing-enough-for-diversity/.

12 S. Koppman, 'Different like me: Why cultural omnivores get creative jobs', *Administrative Science Quarterly* 61/2 (2016), pp. 291–331; *Socio-Economic Diversity and Inclusion in the Arts: Toolkit for Employers* (Jerwood Arts 2019), p. 11.

13 K. Randle and K. Hardy, 'Macho, mobile and resilient? How workers with impairments are doubly disabled in project-based film and television work', *Work, Employment and Society*, 31/3 (2017), pp. 447–64.

14 S. Malik, C. Chapain and R. Comunian, 'Rethinking cultural diversity in the UK film sector: practices in community filmmaking', *Organization* 24/3 (2017), pp. 308–29; A. Saha, 'The politics of race in cultural distribution: addressing inequalities in British Asian theatre', *Cultural Sociology* 11/3 (2017), pp. 302–17; F. Linnehan and A. Konrad, 'Diluting diversity: implications for intergroup inequality in organizations', *Journal of Management Inquiry* 8 (1999), pp. 399–414.

15 Quoted in *It's About Handing Over Power: The Impact of Ethnic Diversity Initiatives on Curatorial Roles in the UK Arts and Heritage Sector 1998–2021* (Art Fund 2022), p. 29.

16 For example, UK Equality Act 2010; European Union Charter of Fundamental Rights; US Civil Rights Act 1964 and later federal laws on age and disability discrimination; Canadian Human Rights Act 1977; Australian Equality Act 2010. But the legal landscape is constantly evolving: for

example, in the United States, since 2015 there has been a huge increase in anti-LGBTIQA+ bills by individual states, which has shifted to target transgender and non-binary youth, rolling back existing legal protections; see *LGBTQ+ Americans Under Attack: A Report and Reflection on the 2023 State Legislative Session* (Human Rights Campaign, May 2023).

17 For example, in England, a former employee of Arts Council England felt forced to resign from the organisation due to hostile comments by colleagues over her gender critical beliefs, but won her harassment claim at an employment tribunal. It found that the organisation had not adequately protected her from harassment, although those gender-critical beliefs are protected under the Equality Act 2010; for summary of the case, see H. Siddique, 'Gender-critical woman wins harassment claim against Arts Council England', *The Guardian* (27 June 2023).

18 See the seminal paper by T.H. Cox and S. Blake, 'Managing cultural diversity: implications for organizational competitiveness', *Academy of Management Executive* 5/3 (1991), pp. 45–56; C. Herring and I. Henderson, *Diversity in Organizations: A Critical Examination* (Routledge 2015), chapter 3; also *Socio-economic Diversity and Inclusion Toolkit: Creative Industries* (Social Mobility Commission 2021), pp. 12–13, with quotes from cultural practitioners on the business case for diversity.

19 E. Dawson, *Equity, Exclusion and Everyday Science Learning: The Experiences of Minoritised Groups* (Routledge 2020).

20 *What is the Creative Case for Diversity?* (Arts Council England 2011); *Equality, Diversity and the Creative Case: A Data Report 2019–20* (Arts Council England 2020). Note, though, that the published data only provides a quantitative measure of the diversity of staff, leadership, boards, successful grant applicants and audiences, but does not attempt a qualitative evaluation of the aspiration for enriched creativity. In that sense, it does not effectively measure the 'creative' case.

21 This is particularly well articulated in *Facing Change: Insights from the American Alliance of Museums' Diversity, Equity, Accessibility, and Inclusion Working Group* (American Alliance of Museums 2018). For the tension between the business and social justice cases, see F. Tomlinson and C. Schwabenland, 'Reconciling competing discourses of diversity? The UK non-profit sector between social justice and the business case'. *Organization* 17/1 (2010), pp. 101–21.

38 Identifying and dealing with racism and bias

It is self-evident that a truly diverse and inclusive organisation aims to treat everyone equitably, no matter what their situation or background, and does not tolerate racism and inappropriate or unacceptable behaviour. The challenge is that values are not universal, and what is regarded as appropriate behaviour by some is not acceptable to others. You cannot assume that everyone shares the same standards, understanding and values when they join your organisation. If you want to achieve an inclusive working environment and a common understanding of what that means in practice, you have to work hard to create and maintain it—it won't happen by itself, nor will it be sustainable without constant care and attention. It means you have to invest time and resources into a process for agreeing shared values, diversity training, regularly updated policies, support systems and robust mechanisms for dealing with complaints.

Sadly, you should also anticipate some backlash against anti-racist and inclusion work (see Introduction, note 6). It remains the case that equity, equality and diversity are contested ideas and practices. There are some who are resistant to change, with vitriolic defences of the status quo and personal attacks on individuals and organisations that promote such work: increasingly common in the performing arts is online racial abuse following the casting of Black performers (see also Chapter 68: How to respond to popular causes and campaigns and survive 'culture wars').[1] This work can become confrontational, toxic and stressful for people. Anticipate this, provide support for staff and be clear about your organisation's continued commitment to diversity and anti-racism.

Understanding the roots of racism in organisations

Racism is often present in the workplace, even in cultural organisations that regard themselves as progressive, and it can badly affect those targeted.[2] Anyone in a leadership position in a cultural organisation, or aspiring to one, needs to be aware of the continuing impacts of racism and the terminology and debates around the topic. Although the history of racism is complex—many ancient cultures, such as Mesopotamia, Egypt, Greece and Rome, exhibited prejudice against people from other cultures and exaggerated their 'otherness'[3]—the roots of modern racism lie in European colonial exploitation, including enslaving African peoples and extracting resources from Latin America and Asia. The belief that white people are superior to those of other races—termed white supremacy—justified this exploitation, and enshrined cultural norms of whiteness as default in colonised and coloniser nations.[4]

It continues to have an insidious impact, in that, often, organisational policies, practices, biases and behaviours are based on colonial models and hierarchies and discriminate

DOI: 10.4324/9781003415886-43

against different racial groups—sometimes subtly—allowing privileges associated with 'whiteness' and disadvantages associated with 'colour'. In cultural organisations, this sometimes takes the form of protection of white 'norms', emphasising white culture, history and contributions, which becomes a blocker to making progress on racial equity. Leaders need to be able to look objectively and dispassionately at the practice of their organisations to see if there are forms of structural and institutional racism that should be tackled.[5]

Identifying racist and unacceptable behaviour

What does racist and inappropriate behaviour in the workplace look like? It includes bullying, harassment and victimisation. It involves actions, words or physical gestures that are unwanted by the recipient and are offensive or degrading, such as shouting, racist abuse, personal insults, sexual innuendos, spreading rumours or gossip, unwanted physical contact, but also persistent and unreasonable criticism and unreasonable demands and impossible targets by managers. It does not have to be face-to-face but can be through written, telephone or email communications or through social media. In most countries, racist and unacceptable behaviour contravenes equalities legislation.

Very common in the workplace are micro-aggressions, seemingly innocuous everyday statements, assumptions or acts that are insensitive, demeaning and subtly excluding, often related to someone's race, gender, sexuality, socio-economic background, accent or mental health.[6] Examples might be 'where are you really from?', implying that the person does not belong here; 'your name is so hard to pronounce', implying that the person does not fit in culturally or linguistically; or 'the way you've overcome your disability is so inspiring', conveying surprise that a disabled person accomplishes just as much as their non-disabled peers. Cumulatively they can have an impact on physical and mental health by creating a sense of not belonging, leading to depression, stress and trauma. If not checked, micro-aggressions can become part of an organisation's culture, so an inclusive organisation should have zero tolerance towards such exclusionary and discriminatory language and behaviour (see below under 'Practical tips for action').

Implicit (or unconscious) bias

We all have biases (even when we think we don't). People are often unaware that certain comments or behaviours may be causing distress or harm, and there may be no conscious intention to offend. But for an organisation to be truly inclusive, it must encourage self-reflection, exploration and understanding of individual implicit biases.

Implicit (or unconscious) biases are biases we are unaware of.[7] They are automatic judgements influenced by background, cultural environment, social stereotypes and prior personal experiences. They impact how we judge others' competencies, shape our expectations and even influence body language in certain situations. They can cause us to make decisions that are not objective, miss opportunities, limit potential and be actively prejudicial. Evidence shows that implicit bias impacts decisions around recruitment, salaries, promotion and progression, and programming, interpretation and representation in cultural organisations.[8]

The task is to recognise these biases and work to ensure that their impacts are mitigated. Dealing with implicit bias is a skill to be learned and practised. Implicit or unconscious bias training—either at an individual or organisational level—is about self-reflection and self-awareness to recognise these biases, consider whether an opinion is based on assumptions or facts and identify ways to manage bias (see also Chapter 58: Organisational reflective practice). Online tests and questionnaires are available that help identify your own implicit biases.[9] Having identified them, what you then do with them is what makes the difference.

Practical tips for action[10]

- Have a robust and confidential mechanism to tackle individual cases and respond to complaints:
  - For example, a nominated trustee—that is, ideally someone outside the organisation's departmental or line-management framework.
  - Ensure you acknowledge stress or trauma where it has occurred and provide support for affected staff.
  - Be seen to be taking prompt action.
  - Don't just move a person affected by racism or other unacceptable behaviour to another department, but ensure you deal with the perpetrator.
- Make it mandatory that all staff undertake diversity and anti racism training, ideally as part of the induction process; for front-of-house staff, this is essential to help them provide an inclusive and welcoming environment.
- Ensure that middle managers have regular diversity and anti-racism training, targeted to give them the skills to manage everyone appropriately and sensitively, irrespective of their background, including understanding how personal characteristics such as disability, faith, sexuality, ethnicity, etc. impact people's lives.
- Publish a diversity and anti-racism policy, ideally developed in collaboration with diverse external voices, revised regularly, that all staff must sign up to.
- Set up a diversity/anti-racism advisory group to monitor the organisation's progress, with a cross-section of staff at different levels, together with external voices.[11]
- Set up a network of diversity champions within your organisation (see Chapter 42: Supporting champions of inclusion across the organisation).
- Actively promote diversity, anti-racist and ethical practice, to create and maintain an inclusive environment, through:
  - Internal events, webinars and podcasts.
  - Physical and online forums for employees to share views and experiences.
- Avoid using exclusive or exclusionary language in all your communications, internally and externally (see Chapter 40: Using inclusive language).
- Consider what you might do about artworks that include racially sensitive words or outdated descriptions of minoritised groups. Options include editing, re-wording or re-contextualising titles, or adding addendums/complementary labels that explain or even apologise.[12] But be aware of accusations of censorship (see also Chapter 68): ideally set up a dialogue with all interested parties inside and outside the organisation to discuss and agree your organisation's response.

See also:

10. Modelling values and behaviour
33. Staff morale and well-being
39. Equitable recruitment

Notes

1 H. Liu et al., 'Anti-racism in the age of White supremacy and backlash', *Equality, Diversity and Inclusion* 40/2 (2021), pp. 105–13; J. Newman and R. Ashworth, 'Changing equalities: politics, policies and practice', in T. Bovaird and E. Loeffler (eds.). *Public Management and Governance* (third edition, 2016), pp. 348–60.

2 For alarming research on abusive leadership in the arts, which uncovered a spectrum of mistreatment: from racial, gender and age discrimination to sexual harassment, class prejudice and side-lining; and from fraud and financial mismanagement to bullying, victimisation and coercion, see M. Nisbett, B. Walmsley and E. McDowell, 'Bullying bosses, broken boards and a crisis of accountability', *Arts Professional* (23 February 2023).

3 See, for example, D.E. McCoskey (ed.), *A Cultural History of Race in Antiquity* (Bloomsbury Academic 2023); B, Isaac, *The Invention of Racism in Classical Antiquity* (Princeton University Press 2006); E. Wilson, 'The origins of foreigners', *The New Republic* (13 September 2012).

4 T.E. Givens, *The Roots of Racism: The Politics of White Supremacy in the US and Europe* (Bristol University Press 2022).

5 For the history and continuing impacts of colonialism, racism and white privilege on organisations today, and ways to disrupt inequality and create inclusive organisations, see S.M. Nkomo and A. Al Ariss, 'The historical origins of ethnic (white) privilege in US organisations', *Journal of Managerial Psychology* 29/4 (2014), pp. 389–404. For an updated version of the seminal (1999) paper on white supremacy and how it operates in organisations, see T. Okun, 'White supremacy culture: still here' (2021), at whitesupremacyculture.info.

6 T. Jana and M. Baran, *Subtle Acts of Exclusion: How to Understand, Identify, and Stop Microaggressions* (Berrett-Koehler 2020).

7 Although 'unconscious bias' is the better-known term, we prefer 'implicit bias', as this implies more self-awareness and responsibility that we all have in-built layers of beliefs and values that inform our judgements, decisions and behaviours.

8 For a literature review, see *Unconscious Bias and Higher Education* (Equality Challenge Unit 2013).

9 For example, the Harvard Implicit Association Test, https://implicit.harvard.edu/implicit/takeatest.html. Some universities have their own online implicit or unconscious bias courses, which you may be able to partner up with.

10 See also the Unlock Anti-racism Toolkit for the Arts: https://www.incartsunlock.co.uk/.

11 The Young Vic and Royal Court theatres in London collaborated for two years with a social enterprise to interrogate their internal structures and understand how they facilitated racism and inequality.

12 Be confident in contracting external knowledge and expertise for areas of work that do not have the required expertise in-house, but ensure there is a good brief that manages expectations and that the practice and knowledge are retained in the organisation's memory for future work (see Chapter 61).

39 Equitable recruitment

For an inclusive organisation, the aim of a fair and equitable recruitment process is to give everyone the same opportunity, irrespective of their background. For cultural organisations, given their relatively poor record for diversity (see Chapter 37), the particular challenge is to broaden the diversity of applicant pools, encourage under-represented candidates to apply (being aware that such candidates are not under-represented by choice, but by the organisation having failed to attract them) and ensure they are evaluating each candidate on the relevant skills for the job, rather than unnecessary qualifications. In some cases, this means treating people during the recruitment process differently, so that they can compete equally, for example, by removing or reducing disadvantages. A one-size-fits-all approach is not always equitable. By treating people in exactly the same way, there is a danger of actively creating barriers or constraints for some, such as those with disabilities or from lower socio-economic backgrounds, and preventing them from showing their true potential. Equitable treatment, not equal treatment, is the goal of an inclusive recruitment process.[1]

There are several stages in a recruitment process, and all need to be considered carefully to create equity.[2]

Person specification—qualifications or skills?

- Many cultural organisations, especially museums, galleries, and science and discovery centres, have expectations around qualifications such as university degrees and professional diplomas, even for entry-level (and low paid) jobs. Ask yourself whether these are absolutely necessary for the role or are based on biases or assumptions, for example, about graduates or previous experience.[3] You will attract more diverse applicants by focusing on skills and competencies, and by actively welcoming the possibility that candidates may be qualified in different—and sometimes unexpected—ways for a position, such as transferable skills from different sectors.
- Consider how this job might be done differently: be brave and set new expectations, and prepare to be surprised by what diverse candidates might bring to the role.
- Allow flexibility for the role where possible, especially around working hours and location. This will be more attractive to some groups, such as disabled people or those with caring responsibilities. Consider if the role must be located in your office or venue, or if remote working is an option (but be aware that, if it is remote, you will have to ensure that they have correct equipment, access to high-speed internet and appropriate working conditions—if not, do you have the resources to provide a budget to remedy this?).

DOI: 10.4324/9781003415886-44

- If you are aiming to build an inclusive organisation, include a statement about what you expect of an employee's approach, for example, that they 'demonstrate and evidence commitment to diversity and inclusion'.

Pre-application materials—accessible and encouraging

- Provide sufficient information about the practical elements of the role—working hours, workplace, access, etc.—so that people of all abilities, background and situation can assess if it is a good fit for them.
- Provide the information in accessible formats, for example Easy Read or even British Sign Language (or equivalent) versions of all written material.
- Rather than sending out background information in traditional written format, consider making a video showing the workplace and people involved.[4]
- Eliminate jargon and acronyms and check language for assumptions and hidden barriers, to see if it is off-putting to certain demographics (see Chapter 40: Using inclusive language). For example, it is now standard practice to use 's(he)' and 'his/her', which might appear to be inclusive but may be exclusionary to transgender, gender fluid and non-binary applicants. It is better to use second-person pronouns, 'you, your'. This is a more direct form of communication, avoids the risk of exclusion and invites applicants to consider themselves in the role.
- Refer explicitly to diversity and inclusion in the materials you send out, ideally by including a letter from the director/CEO about the benefits of diversity for the organisation.
- Explicitly encourage diverse applications.[5]

Advertising—broaden your reach

- Advertise beyond the usual sector websites, for example, on local jobs pages, through community organisations and through networks in touch with marginalised or under-represented groups.[6]
- Ask your community partners where their community members usually access job opportunities.
- Target local communities where you have not recruited in the past.

Application process—offer a range of communication options

Most cultural organisations, rather quaintly, still demand job applications in traditional written format, and it is usually assumed that the most fair and objective assessment is through an application form with set questions, these days often online. But people have a range of communication methods, and written formats, especially application forms, can disadvantage some. For example, research has shown that D/deaf, disabled and neurodivergent people find written applications a barrier, especially navigating complex online portals, and completing these forms can be very tiring particularly when applicants with limited energy are making multiple applications.[7]

Mobile phone and social media technology means that most people have easy access to and are comfortable using video or audio formats—which are also easy to upload to a recruitment portal—and, while total anonymisation of candidates during the assessment process is a valid consideration, it is worth considering if written applications should be the only option. Videos especially can get across more information about an applicant and what they offer than filling out a form.

The video application allowed me to show how I'm different, what I can offer, and the value I can offer to the sector. My life experience doesn't look good on paper, that's a fact. If it was a paper application I probably wouldn't be here today.[8]

It is more equitable, and encourages a more diverse range of applicants, to offer a range of application options, with word or time limits:

- Written application.
- Short video.
- Audio recording.

and

- Avoid application forms.

Assessment/interview—don't take the easy option

This is a crucial step, where bias can inadvertently creep in. A good rule of thumb is to avoid hiring someone because they are like you, or just because you feel they will be 'a better fit'. The American Alliance of Museums has suggested some useful prompts to ask during an assessment process, to ensure equity is considered in recruiting decisions:[9]

- What assumptions are we making about this applicant?
- What will we miss out on by not hiring this applicant?
- Are we open to hiring a candidate who can offer complementary skills?
- Are we open to hiring a candidate who can help shape our workplace culture, or do we just want a candidate who can fit into our existing culture?
- What are the perceived risks of hiring this applicant, and are they valid?
- Will we be truly living our values around equity, diversity, inclusion and racial equity by hiring this applicant? If so, how? If not, why not?
- Stop taking the easy way out by choosing candidates who we believe will need the least amount of training, because they have done the exact same job before or know the same people in our own networks.
- Choose to hire a candidate who is qualified in ways that are less familiar to us.

To ensure your assessment and interview process is as unbiased and equitable as possible, here are some actions to consider:

- Anonymised screening: omit candidates' names, addresses, ages, names of schools, graduation dates, gender and background to mitigate unintentional bias. Obviously, not all of this is possible if using video and audio applications.
- Clarify to all assessors that candidates from lower socio-economic backgrounds may not have had access to some elite experiences, such as extra-curricular activities, internships and studying abroad—keep in mind factors of diversity and intersectionality, so that you do not inadvertently create extra roadblocks for certain candidates.[10]
- Aim for diverse shortlists that reflect the demographics of your community.

- Who is on the interview panel? Invite diverse external voices to avoid bias and provide fresh perspectives.[11]
- Consider providing interview questions in advance.
- Prior to interview, ask short-listed candidates if they have any access and support requirements.
- Can you offer a remote option for interview?
- Constantly monitor your progress against any diversity targets you have set. Compare the diversity of candidates at application, short-listing and appointment stages. If diverse candidates are not getting through to short-listing or appointment, does something need to change in the assessment process?

Obviously, the challenge is to hire the person most suitable for the job, so take a long-term view. Things to avoid are tokenism, which is uncomfortable for everyone and can backfire, and stereotypes such as only hiring a person of colour for a diversity/inclusion role, rather than hiring the most qualified person. Some appointments in cultural organisations are rushed through, and candidates chosen largely on the basis that they can 'hit the ground running', because of looming deadlines and other staff taking on extra workload. But staff transitions can provide the opportunity for professional development for others, so try to think of the long-term benefits, rather than short-term fixes (for some appointments, it is the role of the board to persuade the director/CEO and staff to pause and take a longer-term view).

See also:

43. Diversifying staff and visitors/users
45. Accessibility
50. Board diversity and young trustees
55. Succession planning and transition leadership

Notes

1 The Museum of Us in San Diego, California, has explicitly human-centred human resources policies and practices that see team members as people first, rather than means to an end. See museumofus.wixsite.com/human-resources-poli.

2 There are lots of guides and toolkits for equitable and diverse recruitment. The most practically useful for cultural organisations are N. Wreyford, D. O'Brien, and T. Dent, *Creative Majority: An APPG for Creative Diversity Report on 'What Works' to Support, Encourage and Improve Diversity, Equity and Inclusion in the Creative Sector* (report for the All Party Parliamentary Group for Creative Diversity 2021), pp. 120–30, with case studies; L. Mullany and J. Cordell, *Towards Diverse Workforces: Transforming the Language of Exclusion and Bias in Recruitment* (University of Nottingham 2021), on using inclusive language; E. Fox and E. Goff, *We Are Not All The Same: Guidance, Reflections and Actions to Encourage More Equitable Recruitment Practices* (Curating for Change 2022), on reducing barriers for recruitment of disabled people; and *Socio-economic Diversity and Inclusion Toolkit: Creative Industries* (Social Mobility Commission 2021), pp. 58–64, on recruitment and socio-economic diversity.

3 See C. Jansen, 'Do you really need a degree to secure a low paid job in a UK museum?', *Art Newspaper* (15 March 2023), which notes that Historic Royal Palaces advertised for a historic buildings curator with no higher education qualifications required.

4 For example, Cumbria Museum Consortium and Imperial War Museums created short films introducing their teams and collections as part of recruitment materials: see case studies in E. Fox and E. Goff, *We Are Not All The Same: Guidance, Reflections and Actions to Encourage More Equitable Recruitment Practices* (Curating for Change 2022), p. 6.

5 For examples, see L. Mullany and J. Cordell, *Towards Diverse Workforces: Transforming the Language of Exclusion and Bias in Recruitment* (University of Nottingham 2021), p. 11.

6 For example, Black Lives in Music (blim.org.uk) campaigns for the recruitment and career progression of more ethnically diverse musicians.

7 E. Fox and E. Goff, *We Are Not All The Same: Guidance, Reflections and Actions to Encourage More Equitable Recruitment Practices* (Curating for Change 2022), p. 5.

8 Quoted in E. Fox and E. Goff, *We Are Not All The Same: Guidance, Reflections and Actions to Encourage More Equitable Recruitment Practices* (Curating for Change 2022), p. 7.

9 K. McNamee, 'What does a truly equitable recruiting process look like?' American Alliance of Museums blog (25 August 2021): https://www.aam-us.org/2021/08/25/what-does-a-truly-equitable-recruiting-process-look-like/.

10 See P. Parsons, 'Recruitment and retention at the intersections', in B. Barnett and P. Felten (eds.), *Intersectionality in Action: A Guide for Faculty and Campus Leaders for Creating Inclusive Classrooms and Institutions* (Routledge 2016), pp. 15–24.

11 For example, Amgueddfa Cymru/National Museum Wales undertook collaborative recruitment with community partners, which involved jointly drafting the job advert, job description, person specification and then short-listing, interviewing and sharing the final decision (see ourmuseum.org.uk/collaborative-recruitment).

40 Using inclusive language

Cultural organisations are notorious for using jargon and acronyms that are obvious, and second nature, to those in the know, but baffling, irritating and, at worst, alienating to others. Even deceptively simple and seemingly helpful things like job titles alongside a person's name in video calls can have the unintended effect of making those with no job feel inferior:

> They were speaking in acronyms. I couldn't de-code what they were saying. At first I thought it was just me who didn't understand.
> They all had job titles with their names on Zoom. I don't think anyone realised how that feels when you don't have a job.[1]

Inclusive language uses words and expressions that avoid assumptions, biases, slang and jargon that may exclude or discriminate against people. It acknowledges diversity, is sensitive to differences and accepting of everyone, conveys respect, is understandable to all and comes across as welcoming. It says a lot more about whether an organisation is truly inclusive and offers support for difference than the existence of written policies about diversity and inclusion. It should apply to all communications used within your organisation: spoken language in meetings, speeches, lectures, podcasts and job interviews; and written language in emails, websites, recruitment packs and marketing materials such as social media, brochures, leaflets and posters.[2]

The language used in policy and organisational documents is important and revealing about where the organisation sees itself. For example, an analysis of the language of such documents from a group of museums, exploring their institutional attitude to engagement and participation, found that community members were too often cast as beneficiaries or 'supplicants' on the periphery, with senior managers and staff as 'carers' in the centre.[3] This imbalance of power was subtly replicated in the wording of policy documents, revealing an underlying philanthropic but patronising bias, using phrases such as 'we have a responsibility' and 'we can make people's lives better', and words like 'provide' and 'tell', rather than more inclusive and collaborative language. It is a useful reminder for those writing strategy and policy to think carefully about the words they are using, how they reflect the values that the organisation is aspiring to and the assumptions behind and implications of wording. Ideally, such strategic documents should always be produced collaboratively, ensuring maximum understanding and buy-in from staff, volunteers and community partners.

DOI: 10.4324/9781003415886-45

Actions you can take

- Carry out an inclusive language audit of your existing written materials. Review the language for assumptions, jargon, acronyms and hidden barriers that might exclude, puzzle or even offend some people.[4]
- Always be aware of the context in which particular language or words are used and consider the perspective of the user or speaker, and whether they are reflecting any implicit value judgements or unconscious bias (see Chapter 38).
- Use gender-neutral language and words in descriptions and role profiles. Avoid terms like 'guys' to refer to everyone and instead use neutral terms like staff members, folks, or visitors, and so on.
- Be inclusive in pronoun usage, especially regarding gender identity.
- Don't make assumptions about family members or units, like biological fathers and mothers, or wives and husbands. Instead, use terms like carer, guardian, parent and partner.
- Some terms regularly used by cultural organisations when referring to diversity can be perceived as negative and unhelpful, such as 'disadvantaged', 'less affluent', 'hard to reach', 'under-served', 'under-represented' or 'at risk'.[5] These imply a deficit or lack compared to a hypothetical norm and send a message that the organisation thinks it has a mission to 'improve' these groups in some way. They also often mask, or distract from, the organisation's failure to engage with these groups.
- Ensure that job titles are meaningful outside your own specific sector. For example, a 'House Manager' in theatres can be confusing, but 'Customer Service' is not.
- Avoid idioms peculiar to the English language, or even to specific forms like UK English, which is full of odd expressions and metaphors, and which may not be understandable to everyone.
- Finally, be aware of how quickly language, and how it is understood and experienced, can evolve. Meanings and connotations of words change rapidly as society changes, so keep your language under constant review. For example, the acronym BAME (Black, Asian and Minority Ethnic) has been regularly used in the United Kingdom as a catch-all term for all ethnic groups, except white, similar to BIPOC (Black, Indigenous and People of Colour) in the United States. But it is now acknowledged that one term cannot encompass very different groups with their own identities, so it is better to be specific rather than use an umbrella term. If in doubt, ask how people wish to be referred to. Similarly, increasingly the terms 'third world' and 'developing countries' are avoided, especially by third-sector agencies like Oxfam, in favour of 'Global Majority' or 'Global South' to refer to people who are Black, Asian, Brown, dual-heritage, indigenous to the global south, and/or have been characterised as 'ethnic minorities'.[6]

See also:

13. The emotionally intelligent leader: listening, empathy, sensitivity, care and compassion
31. Internal communications
37. Why valuing and respecting difference makes your organisation better
38. Identifying and dealing with racism and bias

Notes

1 Both quotes from project participants in *It's All about Power* (Sheila McKechnie Foundation 2022), p. 37.

2 An excellent resource is *Inclusive Language Guide* (Oxfam International 2023), divided into thematic sections, each with an alphabetical list of terms, describing the term, why it is to be preferred and what terms to avoid. See also Appendix B: Use of Language, in *Socio-economic Diversity and Inclusion in the Arts: Toolkit for Employers* (Jerwood Arts 2019), with a glossary of terms.

3 B. Lynch, *Whose Cake Is It Anyway? A Collaborative Investigation into Engagement and Participation in 12 Museums and Galleries in the UK* (Paul Hamlyn Foundation 2011), pp. 15–16.

4 See, for example, the recommendations on specific words and phrases to deploy and avoid in S. Lingayah and N. Kelly, *Contains Strong Language: A Guide to Talking about Racism* (Reframing Race 2023), pp. 24–5.

5 In 2020, California changed the term 'at-risk' to 'at-promise' in its state educational and penal codes. 'At-risk' was regarded as negative and stigmatising, while 'at-promise' was positive and implied great potential.

6 Globally, these groups currently represent approximately 80 per cent of the world's population: R. Campbell-Stephens, *Educational Leadership and the Global Majority: Decolonising Narratives* (Palgrave Macmillan 2021).

41 Building a diverse leadership team

Having a diverse leadership team is one of the most effective ways of demonstrating that you are a truly inclusive organisation. It inspires confidence in staff, visitors, communities and funders that your commitment to diversity is real and practical and not merely theoretical or aspirational. The more visibly a leadership team showcases difference, and their commitment to equity—whether through gender, ethnicity, disability, socio-economic background or sexuality—the more included different groups in the organisation will tend to feel.

Six actions to diversify your leadership team

- **Don't pick people who are 'like you'**, but be open to, and encourage, difference. Look at your existing leadership team: check if it is representative of your staff and ideally of your community, with a diverse demographic and experience. But ensure that the people you pick are themselves champions of equity, diversity and inclusion (see Chapter 42). Building an effective diverse team is also about building trust (see Chapter 19), and having confidence that diverse team members will be supported and that any structural inequity in the organisation will be addressed (see Chapter 38): otherwise, this is no more than tokenism.
- **Avoid 'the way things are done here'**: be open to new perspectives and cultural approaches to all aspects of the organisation's work, and be prepared to shake things up in response to changes in society. Bringing in different people will change the dynamic and culture of the team, so allow space for this to happen, and be aware of and tackle behavioural responses from existing team members that stifle and resist difference.
- **Encourage diversity of opinion within the leadership team**, rather than seeking validation of your own approach. Everyone's voice counts, even—or especially—if they disagree with you, so make sure everyone on the team feels confident to share thoughts and opinions without fear of blame or censure. Leadership meetings should be genuine dialogues of opinions and experiences. Value the likelihood that probably everyone on your leadership team has different experiences and is better at some things than you are.[1]
- **Don't pigeonhole diversity** by assigning people, for example, from minoritised groups or those with a disability, solely to roles related to those characteristics. Distribute roles and projects fairly and always consider how individuals on your leadership team might develop professionally and take on greater responsibilities.
- **Support, nurture and develop latent leadership talent among your staff**, especially for those from under-represented groups, giving them opportunities for growth (see Chapter 32

DOI: 10.4324/9781003415886-46

for recognising talent and capability through distributed leadership). For example, develop and encourage networking opportunities, especially for meeting leaders in your organisation or others; and provide development support, such as coaching and mentoring, for individuals newly coming into leadership roles (see Chapters 8, 59 and 64 for networks and mentoring).[2]

- **Encourage an inclusive and respectful working culture**. Recognise that people from different backgrounds may have different approaches to—or be unfamiliar with—aspects like office culture, dress codes or after-work social activities. Research has also shown that women leaders who express themselves forcefully or directly at work are often characterised as aggressive or opinionated, reflecting deep-seated, usually male, assumptions.[3] Implicit or unconscious bias training can help to address this (see Chapter 38).

See also:

10. Modelling values and behaviour
21. Effective delegation
32. Developing distributed leadership and sharing decision-making
39. Equitable recruitment
50. Board diversity and young trustees

Notes

1 Mark McCormack, the founder of IMG, the global sports and culture company, hired people who were better than him in certain areas, as he knew they were disrupters who would help him to progress the innovation he was seeking. Such people are challenging to lead and manage but can be a vital catalyst in any organisation: see M.H. McCormack, *What They Don't Teach You at Harvard Business School* (Bantam Dell 1984).

2 For example, the London Theatre Consortium, in partnership with the MOBO organisation, has run several fellowship cohorts for mid-career leaders from Black and minoritised ethnic backgrounds to address the lack of diversity at executive level in UK theatres, offering mentoring, shadowing, access and skill sessions.

3 J. Fletcher, 'The paradox of post heroic leadership: an essay on gender, power and transformational change', *The Leadership Quarterly* 15 (2006), pp. 647–61; also D. Ladkin, 'Creating an aesthetic of inclusivity: a new solution to the "problem" of women leaders', in S. Kay and K. Venner (eds.), *A Cultural Leadership Reader* (Cultural Leadership Programme/Creative Choices 2010), pp. 32–9.

42 Supporting champions of inclusion across the organisation

The most prominent and vocal champion of inclusion must be the director/CEO, who is also ultimately accountable for its delivery across the organisation. Without that vision, active championing and strategic prioritisation from the top, inclusion will not succeed (see Chapter 10). In this sense, leaders are allies: effective allyship means taking notice, listening and using your position, influence and privilege to support those who don't have the same advantages.[1]

The governing body, too, needs to champion inclusion in order for it to be prioritised and sustained when directors move on (see Chapter 50: Board diversity and young trustees).[2] Ideally, progress on inclusion should be monitored as part of organisational targets and milestones.

Who are the champions?

But leaders also need allies within the organisation, and they need to hear different perspectives from a range of staff. Without that broad range of staff champions and advocates across all parts of the organisation, who can alert the director to what is missing or not working, inclusion has little chance of success in the long term. Champions are the staff and volunteers who themselves practise allyship, understand the need for diversity and inclusion, buy into it and enthusiastically support it. It is vital to harness the power of these champions and involve them in making the organisation inclusive and welcoming, because they are the ones who will effectively disseminate it to other staff and bring those other staff on board.

The advantage of working with staff with a positive approach is that it has a ripple effect on colleagues who may be sceptical of the strategic emphasis on equity, diversity and inclusion, and may even dismiss it as a 'politically correct' move by the leadership that will 'blow over' and 'things will get back to normal' (reactions that the authors often encounter in a range of organisations). Ideally, your champions will reflect a cross-section of the cultural organisation, and so all departments will contain enthusiastic advocates. Allies can have many different origins, so the staff or volunteers who are enthusiasts for diversity and inclusion may astonish you. Often, champions will volunteer to be involved in activities connected with diversity and inclusion. So be open-minded about who could be your allies, and welcome any offer of championing, even if you are sceptical as to how effective they may be—prepare to be surprised.

Whoever they are, these champions need appreciating and nurturing. This means being open to constructive criticism from them. Being a champion for diversity and inclusion does not mean agreeing with every aspect of how it is being implemented.

DOI: 10.4324/9781003415886-47

Enthusiastic champions from among the staff and volunteers will often have their ears to the ground and will be in a position to suggest different and better ways of doing things (see Chapter 7: Flexibility: welcoming challenge and different perspectives). Being prepared to listen to their suggestions will boost their morale and confidence and reinvigorate their support.

Depending on the size of the organisation, an effective mechanism is to bring together **a diagonal slice of staff champions** from different roles and levels—and a diversity of backgrounds—across the organisation into an advisory group that reports back to the director/leadership team and maybe the board, with recommendations (in a smaller organisation, this might even involve most employees and volunteers). Such a slice will, ideally, be representative of all levels of staff (and volunteers) across different roles, as well as of the diversity of the staff/volunteer complement. The 'diagonal' element means that the more junior staff will not be present alongside their direct line managers, and so should be free to contribute more readily and be honest about potential solutions, impacts or problems. Remember, though, that if you do not heed their recommendations, you may not retain their support and advocacy for long. If you disagree with any suggestions or recommendations, take the time to explain your reasons to them.

Spreading and embedding the message beyond the champions

Realistically, however, having a network of champions is not enough. The ultimate aim is to change the organisational culture so that it is more welcoming and helps everyone feel they belong and are valued, irrespective of their background. For inclusion to be firmly embedded, it must become part of everyone's values, job and responsibilities, which requires a change of behaviours across the whole organisation. This means you need to spread the message across the organisation. A single email, presentation or policy document is insufficient to change behaviours: you need to be repeating the message constantly.

- Have frequent conversations about diversity and inclusion at all levels: board, leadership team, staff meetings and online in blogs and webinars. Focus especially on practical suggestions and solutions.[3]
- Encourage networks of staff from similar backgrounds, who will support each other. This is also a good way of finding out if some people feel excluded or sidelined and have a limited voice and role in decision-making.
- Use your staff champions to create a network of mentors and allies across the organisation, who will support staff from different backgrounds with practical suggestions and help them to feel integrated—and will feed back any problems and barriers they are encountering.
- Encourage mixing and sharing of ideas across staff and teams. Silos are the enemy of inclusion (see Chapter 30 for the problem of silo-working).
- Use the regular staff appraisal mechanism to explicitly discuss each individual's role in creating an inclusive working environment. Ideally, include practical commitment to inclusion in everyone's job description, to make it clear that it is an integral part of what is expected of every member of staff and volunteer.[4]
- Support the commitment in the previous bullet point by developing training on equity, diversity and inclusion for all staff, so they can learn how to implement them practically into the way they work and create a genuinely inclusive organisation.

See also:

59. How to harness internal networks
64. Strategic peer networks and mentoring

Notes

1 See P. Luthra, '7 ways to practice active allyship', *Harvard Business Review* (8 November 2022).

2 For the common problems and solutions regarding sustaining strategic change when a director leaves, applicable to all cultural organisations, see P. Bienkowski and H. McGowan, *Managing Change in Museums and Galleries* (Routledge 2021), pp. 77–80.

3 See *Socio-economic Diversity and Inclusion in the Arts: Toolkit for Employers* (Jerwood Arts 2019), pp. 18–19.

4 For changing job descriptions to describe roles in terms of responsibilities and expectations rather than tasks, with sample documents, see ourmuseum.org.uk/structures-and-job-descriptions.

43 Diversifying staff and visitors/users

In order to diversify staff and visitors/users, the principle of what a cultural organisation needs to do seems fairly straightforward—although the practicalities are less so. To diversify staff, recruitment processes must reach all potential candidates, whatever their background, and must be equitable; furthermore, the organisation must be a welcoming place for all individuals, where they will feel valued and have opportunities to progress. To attract diverse visitors/users, the organisation must also be a place where they feel welcome, and you need to figure out how to reach and appeal to those diverse potential visitors/users, and what benefits you have to offer them.

The tasks of diversifying staff and visitors/users are separate but connected. If people from different parts of society see themselves reflected among the staff of your organisation, they are more likely to feel comfortable visiting it and see this as an organisation 'for them', that reflects them and their values. This is not just about current visitors, but about future audiences, and the long-term reach and impact of your organisation. The perennial question is: who doesn't visit and why? Are you just an organisation catering to a particular demographic—sadly, some cultural organisations still are[1]—and can you survive financially by just being that?

Below are some practical actions to consider, to ensure that your commitment to diversity is not just rhetoric—a 'box-ticking' exercise to meet stakeholder and funder expectations and achieve success in grant applications—but is backed up by action and change.

> Organisations focusing on ethnicity and feeling that covers diversity…it annoys me to think people are being tokenistic and box-ticking to fulfil the criteria without actually addressing or changing their practice.[2]

DOI: 10.4324/9781003415886-48

Actions to diversify staff

Research shows that marginalised and under-represented groups have higher rates of leaving the cultural and creative sectors.[3] To achieve and *sustain* diversity, it is therefore vital to ensure that working practices, cultures and behaviours, as well as recruitment/assessment processes, are inclusive and equitable, and that policies and procedures are explicit on these points. Some aspects of how to address these are covered in other chapters in this book: diversity and implicit/unconscious bias training and diversity policies (Chapter 38); equitable recruitment processes (Chapter 39); using inclusive language (Chapter 41); building a diverse leadership team (Chapter 41); supporting champions of inclusion (Chapter 42); and accessibility to cater for the range of disabilities (Chapter 45).[4] In addition:

- Have specific, paid positions whose responsibility is to ensure that diversity goals are achieved. Organisations across all sectors with such roles have been shown to be the most effective at increasing and sustaining the diversity of their workforce. These can be individual (e.g., a diversity officer) or group roles (e.g., a task force). When these roles have sufficient seniority to wield agency and decision-making power, they are able to translate an organisation's vocal commitment to diversity into action and change on the ground.[5]
- Where possible and realistic, offer flexible working, job sharing, working from home and part-time work as default, or give clear reasons why this is not possible. It is helpful to have a policy on this topic and to be transparent when advertising/recruiting for a role if flexible working can be part of it: then prospective candidates are clear whether it is a good fit for them.
- Be transparent about pay and possible promotions, and have clear promotion pathways with transparent criteria.
- Don't assume that certain groups—such as part-time or flexible workers, or carers/single parents—do not want or are not suitable for promotion.
- Diversify your pool of volunteers to reflect your community's demographic, particularly those under-represented in your organisation. For example, St Fagans National Museum of History, in Wales, moved from 11 volunteers from the same socio-economic background (well educated, retired, female) in just one area of the museum, to 120 active and diverse volunteers across all departments. They targeted those who normally would not think of volunteering: unemployed young males, homeless people, disabled people, people with mental health issues and those going through drug and alcohol rehabilitation. These volunteers play an active role in making decisions alongside paid staff.[6]
- The performing arts have regular opportunities to cast actors and performers, and commission writers, directors and conductors representing all types of diversity.[7] For example, the Royal Shakespeare Company has a track record of casting diverse actors and commissioning new writers and writers-in-residence, including the first Black Hamlet.[8] 'Gender-bending' casting is now relatively common, such as female King Lears or Prosperos in Shakespeare's plays or a female Peter Pan—and in Shakespeare's time it was standard for boys and young men to play female roles.[9]
- Involve external critical friends, diversity organisations and agencies in the charitable and voluntary sectors, who will prompt you to ask challenging questions about your structures and processes and will help find solutions. These sorts of agencies make ideal strategic partners for cultural organisations, as they are professional and adaptable in their approach and have their own wide community networks—especially reaching

those under-represented communities that cultural organisations often tend to struggle with (see Chapter 67 for external voices and critical friends; Chapter 64 for community partners as peers; and the section on community organisations in Chapter 66: Developing partnerships).

- Run a regular equity audit to track your progress. An equity audit measures both the presence/absence of different groups among your staff and volunteers, and the workplace experiences of those groups. Its purpose is to monitor the effectiveness of current practices and processes, address gaps and identify opportunities. Much of this will be based on data you already hold: representation, recruitment, diversity statistics for applicants vs. hires, retention/attrition, absenteeism, development and training, promotion, pay and benefits. Process the data, identify any inequities between groups and individuals, and take action to mitigate them. Unless you take meaningful action, the process will be perceived as a waste of time. It is useful to set diversity targets to measure yourself against, but be honest about progress or 'failure'. It is important to set aside time, funding and staff resources for this, and to include external voices as advisers and critical friends.[10]
- As well as, or as part of, an equity audit, run an annual, anonymous employee survey to get regular feedback. Ensure you report back to staff about resulting actions.[11]

Actions to diversify visitors/users

> The act of diversifying audiences requires an internal effort to adapt the current offering and make it available, relatable, participatory, and connected to as many people as possible, especially to the new audiences the institution wants to reach.[12]

- A recommended first step is to explicitly map your communities.[13] Who are they, where are they, what are their needs, priorities and assets, and what do you have to offer each other? Otherwise, there is a temptation to continue marketing to existing audiences or engage with whoever it seems easiest to attract. But the best long-term results come if you take time to carefully map who your communities are and how best to engage each one.[14]
- Work with external third sector agencies and networks to find out what their communities/clients are interested in, and how best to engage them (see above, and Chapters 64 and 66 for such agencies as strategic partners).
- Go out into the communities, rather than staying inside your venue and waiting for them to come to you. Community walks and listening sessions—by all staff, not just outreach officers—build confidence and promote empathy, creating better understanding of what is going on and how to engage them. They are also a good way of making media contacts, so you can go into the communities and let them know the latest developments, and, vice versa, hear about their current concerns. They can then post updates in their newsletters/social media or announce them on community radio stations.[15]
- Generate ideas for programming jointly with people from your communities. For example, Science Gallery Melbourne invites open calls to propose installations and research projects for their exhibition seasons. Glasgow Museums ran regular Creative Cafés where community members participated alongside staff in workshops to generate ideas

for programming and partnership working. This encouraged a diverse range of people to share what they were interested in, get involved even before the start of a programme, and be actively engaged in developing it. It is an effective mechanism for getting community voices integrated into an organisation's planning processes at an early stage.[16]

- Undertake an equality impact assessment, an evidence-based approach to help organisations ensure that their policies, practices, events and decision-making processes promote equality, diversity and inclusion and do not create barriers to participation or disadvantage any groups. In some countries, such assessments are a legal requirement for public organisations.[17]
- Introduce mechanisms to include and encourage young people's views—this will provide insight into the concerns of an important demographic (see also Chapter 50 on young trustees). For example, the Royal Shakespeare Company has a Youth Advisory Board that has hosted a wider Young Creatives' Convention, bringing together over 400 young people to focus on access, opportunities and inclusion in the arts:

> [Young people] told us that arts and creative subjects were the only spaces where they had permission to try out new ideas, get things wrong, appreciate and respect difference, articulate new ideas and problem solve.[18]

- Extend inclusion to procurement for cafés within cultural venues, to accommodate dietary requirements for people of diverse backgrounds and preferences. This can become a potent marketing tool and attract more diverse visitors.[19] To be even more inclusive, allow visitors to bring their own food (for health and hygiene reasons this would have to be consumed in restricted areas).
- If your venue charges for admission, consider special rates for under-represented groups and those from lower socio-economic backgrounds. For example, the Zoological Society of London, which runs London and Whipsnade Zoos, offered heavily discounted tickets to anyone on benefits, resulting in tens of thousands of new visitors, and an overall increase in visitor numbers, engagement and income.[20] Many cultural organisations also offer special rates for young people or, especially in the United States, a couple of museum/gallery memberships that can be borrowed from a local library like a book.
- Particularly if you are a rural or out-of-the-way organisation, making access and transport to your venue cheap and easy is an incentive to new audiences, especially those from lower socio-economic backgrounds—not everyone drives, prefers to drive or has a car. Talk to local transport companies and negotiate discounts for your visitors.[21]
- Adapt and tailor your marketing accordingly to reach all the different groups you have identified. Find out from your community and strategic partners which methods of communication work best for which communities (see Chapter 63 on external communications).

Notes

1 For diversity, or its lack, in cultural organisations, and references with statistics, see Chapter 37.
2 Quoted in D. Cameron, *How Diverse Are We, Really?* (Creative People and Places 2021), p. 29.
3 C. Herring and I. Henderson, *Diversity in Organizations: A Critical Examination* (Routledge 2015), chapter 4; on the experiences and problems of diversity in organisations, particularly in

higher education, see S. Ahmed, *On Being Included: Racism and Diversity in Institutional Life* (Duke University Press 2012).

4 For further practical tips on accessibility, recruitment, retention and monitoring, some included in the actions listed below, see N. Wreyford, D. O'Brien, and T. Dent, *Creative Majority: An APPG for Creative Diversity report on 'What Works' to Support, Encourage and Improve Diversity, Equity and Inclusion in the Creative Sector* (report for the All Party Parliamentary Group for Creative Diversity 2021), pp. 88–162.

5 S. Kang and S. Kaplan, 'Working towards gender diversity and inclusion in medicine: myths and solutions', *The Lancet* 393 (10171) (2019), pp. 579–86; S. Ahmed, "You end up doing the document rather than doing the doing": diversity, race equity and the politics of documentation', *Ethnic and Racial Studies* 30/4 (2007), pp. 590–609.

6 S. Burge, O. Rhys and N. Williams, 'Democratic culture: participation at St Fagans National History Museum', in K. McSweeney and J. Kavanagh (eds.), *Museum Participation: New Directions for Audience Collaboration* (MuseumsEtc 2016), pp. 421–2.

7 For example, for the staging of works by overlooked women composers, see R. Franks, 'Opera heroines', *BBC Music Magazine* 31/12 (2023), pp. 40–43; for the severe under-representation of women conductors in classical music, see J. Duchen, 'Closing the gap', *BBC Music Magazine* 32/5 (2024), pp. 48–51.

8 S. Freeman, 'The first black actor to play Hamlet on the RSC on why the arts needs more than tokenism', *Yorkshire Post* (15 January 2018).

9 M. Shapiro, *Gender in Play on the Shakespearean Stage: Boy Heroines and Female Pages* (University of Michigan Press 1995).

10 For an example of an equity audit template, which can be adapted to any cultural organisation, see https://projects.skeo.com/wp-content/uploads/2020/05/DEI-Audit-Template.pdf.

11 See also the link to an inequality self-assessment spider diagram to plot where you sit among the (UK) protected characteristics, which can be used by individuals or teams, in *Power and Privilege in the 21st Century Museum* (Museums Association 2019), p. 18.

12 A. Leyman Pino, 'Breaking the silos: science communication for everyone', in E. Rasekoala (ed.), *Race and Sociocultural Inclusion in Science Communication: Innovation, Decolonization, and Transformation* (Bristol University Press 2023), p. 51.

13 Each cultural organisation needs to define who its communities are. Typically, they can be divided into communities of place, interest, identity (including First Nations peoples), and practice—but of course these categories can and do overlap.

14 For mapping communities, and what works and what doesn't, see ourmuseum.org.uk/wp-content/uploads/Mapping-to-engage.pdf.

15 See the video at ourmuseum.org.uk/staff-tours.

16 M. Craig et al., 'Moving the margins: reflecting on collaboration and consultation', in K. McSweeney and J. Kavanagh (eds), *Museum Participation: New Directions for Audience Collaboration* (MuseumsEtc 2016), p. 291.

17 There are many guides and templates for equality impact assessments available online.

18 J. O'Hanlon, 'Time to be heard', *Arts Professional* (19 July 2023); see also *Time to Listen* (report by Royal Shakespeare Company, Tate and University of Nottingham, 2018); M. Miller, R. Moilliet and E. Daly (eds), *Circuit – Test, Risk, Change: Young People, Youth Organisations and Galleries Working Together* (Tate and Paul Hamlyn Foundation 2019).

19 J. Turtle, *Valuing Diversity: The Case for Inclusive Museums* (Museums Association 2016), p. 15.

20 For the resource implications, risks, benefits and downsides, see M. Gould, 'Letting thousands of poorer families into London Zoo for £3 has changed us for ever', *The Guardian* (3 March 2023).

21 E. Glasgow, 'Rural arts fail to engage diverse audiences', *Arts Professional* (3 May 2023). It is useful to consider a visit as part of an accessibility chain, which begins with the decision to visit, followed by the journey to a venue (e.g. public/community transport, and accessible car parking/drop-off for individuals and groups), then the experience itself, and ends with the visitor's safe return home. If any link in the chain is broken, the experience can be a disappointment or may never happen. See A.M. Petit et al., 'The Accessibility Chain: a challenge and an opportunity for cities and people with disabilities', *The Journal of Public Space* 7/2 (2022), pp. 205–22; for a practical guide to planning using an accessibility chain, see sensorytrust.org.uk.

44 Building a participatory organisation

There are different understandings and definitions of what constitutes participatory practice in cultural organisations. For some, it may be no more than audiences taking active part in artistic events or performances that have been pre-designed by an artist or the organisation; or it may be some form of co-creation of an exhibition or programme. At the other end of the spectrum, participation involves cultural organisations and communities working together as equal partners, sharing authority and making decisions jointly on programming and strategy (and even on aspects such as recruitment and, in museums and galleries, collecting and disposal policy): this can be defined as doing things 'with' communities rather than 'to' or 'for' them.[1]

Being a participatory organisation is not a binary condition, yes or no. Participatory practice is a continuum, an ongoing conversation between the organisation and its communities, creating a bond that develops, shifts and changes. Organisations will be at different stages, or better at some aspects than others, and some may have good reasons for not going as far as equal power sharing or handing over control to communities. Table 44.1 provides a simplified framework that benchmarks two ends of the participatory spectrum, from starting out to best practice, to help organisations work out where they are now, where they want to be and how to get there.[2]

Barriers to participation

The barriers to becoming a truly participatory cultural organisation are now well known, though not always easily recognised or overcome. These barriers cut right across all activities of cultural organisations and their external relationships. Typically, it is not just one barrier, in one place: there are lots of barriers across the whole organisation (Figure 44.1).[3]

These barriers involve everyone in a cultural organisation, from the top to the bottom, inside and out: trustees, directors, staff, volunteers, community partners and funders. To address all of them, and to become a truly participatory organisation, means that participation must be everyone's job, not just that of a single outreach/community engagement officer or department (which are often the first posts to be cut when there are financial pressures). It takes time, patience and commitment from all of those groups; the challenge is usually to explore how, in practice, each individual role contributes to participatory practice and to welcoming community voices into all aspects of running the organisation. A useful mechanism is to include responsibility for participation in everyone's job description, no matter what role, and to use appraisal discussions to explore how that might work in practice.

DOI: 10.4324/9781003415886-49

Table 44.1 Benchmarking framework for participatory practice

	Starting off	*Best practice*
Mission, values and vision (how embedded is it?)	• References to participation in mission statement • Organisational values contain reference to participation	• Mission statement promotes participation and is actively used to guide the work of the whole organisation • Community partners are actively involved in creating and revising the mission statement
Leadership and governance (are those in charge championing it?)	• Passive commitment to participation from the organisation's leadership—but it is mostly led by committed staff • Trustees are aware of participatory work in the organisation	• Leadership team actively champion participatory practice throughout the organisation • Trustees receive training in participatory work and champion it in the organisation • Community partners are represented on the governing body
Commitment to action (is it written into policies and enacted?)	• External project funding is sought to deliver participatory programmes • Participatory work is carried out on a project basis with ad hoc community partners	• Participatory work has a core budget and is embedded in business and strategic plans • The organisation builds and sustains lasting relationships with community partners, who are involved in planning and embedding participatory work
Engagement in decision making (who has a say in which areas?)	• Participatory work is planned by staff • Community partners are consulted on pre-determined programmes and activities • Community partners are engaged on a project-by-project basis	• Leadership, staff and community partners are involved in participatory work as part of overall strategic planning • Mechanisms are in place for community partners to have a say in decision-making at the highest level in the organisation, including strategic and business plans • Community partners have a long-term relationship with the organisation and work on both core and project-based activities
Workforce and professional development (are we confident and capable?)	• Staff, contractors and consultants know about participatory practice through internal communications and meetings, and there is reference to it in training sessions • Recruitment materials for community and other related posts reference participatory practice	• Trustees, leadership and staff take part in training and professional development in participatory practice • Community partners deliver training for staff on aspects they are more expert in • Community partners are involved in the recruitment process, including job descriptions, person specifications, shortlisting and interviewing • All members of staff have participatory practice in their job descriptions

Source: adapted from the Museums Association's *Power to the People: A self-assessment framework for participatory practice*, 2018

Leadership and governance
- Lack of active championing and support by directors and trustees

Conflicting strategic agendas
- Weighing up participation against generating income and increasing audiences

It's someone else's job
- Responsibility for participatory work is localised and not shared

The usual suspects
- Working with a restricted pool of communities

Staff resistance and skills
- Poor understanding of participatory practice and anxiety about expertise

Fear
- Fear of change can lead to avoidance

Figure 44.1 Barriers to participation

Effective and sustainable relationships with communities

True participation is more than just community consultation, which can occasionally be tokenistic. Each organisation must identify a diverse range of voices from its own communities (for mapping communities, see Chapter 43), decide how far it is prepared to go in terms of sharing authority and decision-making and, of course, assess how far its communities would like it to go. Some communities and individuals might want to be more actively and strategically involved, others less so. Participation does not necessarily mean all the time and can vary between intense and light touch, and long- and short-term.

> Community partnerships start where the communities mingle.[4]

Don't assume communities will come to you. You need to go out to them: these are the places where cultural practitioners need to show up, interact, engage, and gain the trust of their local communities as partners (see also Chapter 43 on diversifying audiences).

There are common elements in creating sustainable and dynamic relationships between cultural organisations and communities:[5]

- Relationships often begin with open conversations about what organisations and communities might want to do together. Ideas are then jointly developed, rather than fixed projects imposed by the cultural organisation.
- Long-term relationships can develop from a single or annual event into something ongoing and deeper that is not just about performance or exhibition but about fostering creativity across the community.[6] But such relationships require care when transitioning

into something longer: always be aware of the interests and time constraints of the participants, as all partners may not be equally committed.

- Reflecting on how successful relationships have developed, community partners single out the building of trust, the knowledge that it is not tokenistic but for the long-term and constantly developing. But building trust takes time and patience: it is a process that cannot be rushed or fast-tracked (see Chapter 19). Time needs to be built in to allow for trust to grow at its own pace. The authors' experience is that it takes at least a year for trust to develop in such relationships.
- Programming is designed around the needs and interests of community partners.
- The partners feel they have agency in decision-making, they feel valued and the relationship with the organisation is creative and mutually beneficial.
- The expertise of community partners is recognised and respected. They bring useful knowledge, skills and experience to the organisation, and might run training workshops for staff on aspects where they are more expert.
- Some projects/programmes are led by community partners.
- Community partners feel able to challenge the organisation and have the freedom to raise all sorts of issues—although there is acknowledgement that trust is required before partners feel able to challenge.
- Community partners should always be kept informed, sent notes of meetings and what was discussed and decided (not necessarily formal minutes) and given feedback about the progress of the project/relationship, the impact of the partnership on the organisation and aspirations for the future.
- Always consider some form of financial compensation/honorarium for community partners to show that you value their contribution and set aside budgets and/or add a line into your grant submission to cover this.

Be aware, however, of taking short cuts by working with one group and creating programmes specifically aimed at them that are short-lived and have limited, narrow impact. This can create silos, instead of engendering a sense of community and an opportunity for diverse groups to learn from one another.[7]

Involving community partners in strategy

Probably the deepest form of participatory practice is involving communities in developing longer-term strategy, working with the organisation in setting policy, targets, monitoring and evaluation rather than just on short-term projects.

There are different mechanisms through which communities can be involved in wider strategy (see also Table 44.1):[8]

- Community partners sit on the governing body. Their role is not to 'represent' the community or their own organisation, but to bring particular skills and knowledge to contribute to the governance of the cultural organisation. Appointing community partners helps diversify a governing body, especially by including voices that haven't been heard, brings in different skills and perspectives and is one way of keeping track of changing community agendas (see Chapter 50: Board diversity and young trustees). Of course, not all community partners want to be involved in an organisation's governance: some prefer to continue to work on short-term projects that reflect their own interests, and it is always important to ask about their routines and time commitment.

- Community partners can contribute to strategic discussions through advisory panels or participatory forums that focus on different areas of work. For example, Amgueddfa Cymru/National Museum Wales worked with eight participatory forums around areas of work and demographic groups they needed to target in order to be fully inclusive (Diversity, Craft and Creativity, Volunteering, Young Ambassadors, Primary & Special Schools, Secondary Schools, Informal Learners and Academics); these were drawn from a range of organisations from the public and third sector and the diversity of communities in Wales.[9] While these may not always be formal layers of decision-making, they bring new expertise and perspectives into the organisation, especially if they report regularly to the governing body.
- Community partners can participate in workshops with the organisation to develop long-term strategy, in a collaborative process alongside staff, volunteers, trustees and stakeholders. When this works well, everyone has the opportunity to contribute and reach consensus, and to decide how far, if at all, to be further involved in developing and managing programmes. In some cases, this might lead to other jobs and a pipeline to diversify the workforce from the ground up.

Pitfalls to avoid

Two common pitfalls in relationships between cultural organisations and communities are reported by community partners. These pitfalls have been termed 'false consensus' and 'rubber-stamping', in which cultural organisations deliberately over-emphasise the level of buy-in from communities in order to carry out their own plans and avoid differences of opinion and conflict.[10]

False consensus is where the organisation deliberately, or even subconsciously, works with communities that are less challenging, more in keeping with the organisation's priorities and more willing to accede to its goals. The organisation convinces the participants that their interests align, leaving no room for robust challenge or dialogue about aims. The effect on partners is to make them feel disempowered and not listened to, and unlikely to want to sustain the relationship.

Rubber-stamping is when communities are brought in simply as a means of agreeing and signing off existing plans already drawn up by the organisation, that they have had little or no involvement in shaping. The organisation then claims that it has consulted and has community support for its 'participatory' plans.

False consensus and rubber-stamping are not participation: they are tokenistic consultation, in which communities have no real voice or agency.

See also:

64. Strategic peer networks and mentoring
65. How to involve stakeholders
66. Developing partnerships

Notes

1 S. Arnstein, 'The ladder of citizen participation', *Journal of the American Institute of Planners* 35/4 (1969), pp. 216–24; D. Wilcox, *The Guide to Effective Participation* (Partnership 1994).

2 Table 44.1 is an edited version of the Museums Association's 2018 more detailed framework, *Power to the People: A self-assessment Framework for Participatory Practice*, which one of the authors (PB) was instrumental in developing. For other tools for self-assessment and reflection

around participatory and inclusive practice that work well for any cultural organisation, you can download the Inclusion Wheel and Inclusion Handbook, prepared by the UK Association for Science and Discovery Centres, from sciencecentres.org.uk; or the table on building relationships with partners, showing a progression from transactional (largely one-way) to transformational engagement (with deeper community sense of belonging and ownership), on p. 22 in A. Jackson, C. Nguyen and V. Nuñez, *Diversity, Equity, Access, and Inclusion Booklet: Tools for Engaging Communities and Incorporating DEAI practices into Informal STEM Projects* (Sciencenter 2022), at nisenet.org/DEAI-tools.

3 For more detail on these barriers, and how to overcome them, see P. Bienkowski, *No Longer Us and Them: How to Change into a Participatory Museum and Gallery – Learning from the Our Museum Programme* (Paul Hamlyn Foundation 2016); see also N. Simon, *The Participatory Museum* (Museum 2.0 2010).

4 A. Leyman Pino, 'Breaking the silos: science communication for everyone', in E. Rasekoala (ed.), *Race and Sociocultural Inclusion in Science Communication: Innovation, Decolonization, and Transformation* (Bristol University Press 2023), p. 59.

5 P. Bienkowski, *Our Museum: What Happened Next? A Review and Further Learning Two Years On* (Paul Hamlyn Foundation 2018), pp. 22–3, and the audio-visual resources on participatory practice in ourmuseum.org.uk, applicable to all cultural organisations not just museums; S. Lee and K. Gean, *The Engagement Revolution: A Study of Strategic Organizational Transformation in 10 California Arts Nonprofits* (James Irvine Foundation 2017), pp. 44–6; N. Sim, 'Findings from the field: partnership working between galleries and youth organisations', in M. Miller, R. Moilliet and E. Daly (eds), Circuit – *Test, Risk, Change: Young People, Youth Organisations and Galleries Working Together* (Tate and Paul Hamlyn Foundation 2019), pp. 40–8. See also ofbyforall.org.

6 For example, Cumnock Tryst in Ayrshire, Scotland, developed from an annual music festival to ongoing work by orchestras and professional musicians and composers with schools, community groups across the region and groups with learning disabilities, who compose and perform their own music alongside professional musicians. See thecumnocktryst.com and J. MacMillan and J. Martin, *Creative Composition for the Classroom* (Trinity College London Press 2021).

7 A. Leyman Pino, 'Breaking the silos: science communication for everyone', in E. Rasekoala (ed.), *Race and Sociocultural Inclusion in Science Communication: Innovation, Decolonization, and Transformation* (Bristol University Press 2023), pp. 48–62.

8 M. Strauss, *Democracy at the Top: Embedding Community Participation in Governance and Strategic Decision-making in Museums and Heritage* (Clore Leadership/Arts and Humanities Research Council 2022).

9 S. Burge, O. Rhys and N. Williams, 'Democratic culture: participation at St Fagans National History Museum', in K. McSweeney and J. Kavanagh (eds.), *Museum Participation: New Directions for Audience Collaboration* (MuseumsEtc 2016), pp. 417–20.

10 B. Lynch, *Whose Cake Is It Anyway? A Collaborative Investigation into Engagement and Participation in 12 Museums and Galleries in the UK* (Paul Hamlyn Foundation 2011), pp. 11–13.

45 Accessibility

The aim of an inclusive organisation is to make its physical and virtual spaces, programmes and events accessible to everyone.[1] A particular challenge for many cultural organisations is how to identify and remove barriers for disabled people. There are two elements to this challenge: one is understanding the physical barriers and what constitutes accessible design, but equally important are attitudes towards disabled people (for digital inclusivity, see Chapter 46).

Attitudes: ableism and anti-ableism

'Ableism' is the term for bias, prejudice or discrimination in favour of non-disabled people. This attitude marginalises disabled people, defining them by impairments and medical conditions, and by inference categorises disabled people as inferior and of less worth than the non-disabled, at most worthy of pity.[2] While equalities legislation in many countries makes disability discrimination unlawful, there is nevertheless evidence of continuing (or even increasing) social prejudice against people with physical or mental disabilities, seen in the level of abuse faced by disabled people.[3] In some cases—for example, in the music industry—there is a culture of fear around disclosing disabilities in case it might negatively impact opportunities for being hired.[4]

On a practical level, ableism often makes large parts of the world—including some cultural organisations—inaccessible to disabled people. It is the responsibility of any organisation that regards itself as inclusive, or strives towards inclusivity, to challenge and counter ableism, inequalities, prejudice and discrimination based on developmental, emotional, physical and psychiatric disability—a strategy termed 'anti-ableism'. Failure to acknowledge the types of disabilities that people can experience, not all of which are visible, or ignorance of what people with disabilities can or cannot do or what skills they might have, are forms of unintentional ableism. Certainly within most cultural organisations, unintentional ableism stems from lack of disability awareness and assumptions about what people need or don't need.[5]

A necessary first step, therefore, is to incorporate training for all staff on awareness of the range of disabilities and the consequences of ableism, ideally delivered by disability agencies who have first-hand experience of negative attitudes and practical problems.[6] Such training should also include awareness of the social model of disability:

> The Social Model of Disability holds that people with impairments are 'disabled' by the barriers operating in society that exclude and discriminate against them.[7]

DOI: 10.4324/9781003415886-50

The social model makes a distinction between an impairment—an individual's physical, sensory or cognitive difference—and disability, which is the social consequence of having an impairment, and which can be changed or removed. It is the removal of barriers that ensures equity and independence for disabled people, and therefore, in an inclusive organisation, it is the leader's responsibility to take action to remove those barriers.

Addressing the physical barriers

If you are already working with disability agencies to deliver staff training, the next step is to ask if they can carry out an accessibility audit, with recommendations for changes.[8] Typically, these are the sorts of problems they will pick up:

Physical space:

- Badly designed public and office spaces, with narrow corridors and passageways.
- Stairs not ramps and lack of lifts.
- Lack of step-free access to office, public and backstage spaces.
- Inaccessible toilets.
- No parking places (and/or inaccessible transport).
- Poor lighting.
- Poor seating (too high, too low or not enough).

Information:

- Lack of information in different accessible formats, for example, Easy Read or simply large font.
- Lack of information about access, for example, location of lifts, ramps, level entrances, accessible toilets and parking.
- Few or no sign language interpreters: for example, the Royal Shakespeare Company have at least one performance of each production with an integrated British Sign Language interpreter on stage alongside the actors.
- Information or display panels are not provided at eye level for wheelchair users.
- Lack of audio-described displays, such as alt (alternative) text: this makes images or objects accessible to blind and partially sighted people. It is a written description read aloud by a reader to help people with sight loss understand the context of the image/object and to engage with it.[9] Many theatre companies also have audio description available for their plays.

In terms of programming, too, the most inclusive approaches involve:

- Strategic partnerships with disability agencies (see Chapter 66).
- Co-production with disabled people.[10]
- Commissioning of disabled artists—this includes having an open conversation around disability, asking about their needs, and being open to additional requests like changes to lighting in a show, adapted seating, or help with travel arrangements.[11]
- Availability of free or discounted companion tickets.
- Displays related to disabled people.

- Programmes or spaces aimed specifically at neurodivergent audiences. Many venues now offer regular 'relaxed', low stimulus performances and events, with natural or low lighting, minimal announcements, and hand-dryers in toilets switched off, although how this works in practice is dependent on the art form.[12]

You might also consider the Seven Principles of Universal Design, which are useful guidelines for designing inclusive experiences to avoid segregation and stigmatisation of users. The seven principles are: equitable use; flexibility of use; simple and intuitive use; perceptible information; tolerance for error; low physical effort; and size and space for approach.[13]

See also:

37. Why valuing and respecting difference makes your organisation better
39. Equitable recruitment
40. Using inclusive language

Notes

1 Four specific types of access—physical, cognitive/intellectual, financial and linguistic—are identified by P. Moore, R. Paquet and A. Wittman, *Transforming Inclusion in Museums: The Power of Collaborative Inquiry* (Rowman & Littlefield 2022), p. 65.
2 P.D. Harpur, *Ableism at Work: Disablement and Hierarchies of Impairment* (Cambridge University Press 2022); M.R. Nario-Redmond, *Ableism: The Causes and Consequences of Disability Prejudice* (Wiley-Blackwell 2019).
3 E. Gibbs, 'The constant abuse and harassment from non-disabled people isn't changing – in fact it's getting worse', *The Guardian* (14 October 2022).
4 See R. Rowntree, 'A change of tune', *BBC Music Magazine* 31/4 (2023), pp. 44–6, on the constraints and opportunities for disabled musicians.
5 See *Time to Act: How Lack of Knowledge in the Cultural Sector Creates Barriers for Disabled Artists and Audiences* (British Council 2021).
6 E. Ladau, *Demystifying Disability: What to Know, What to Say, and How to Be an Ally* (Ten Speed Press 2021).
7 *Factsheet: The Social Model of Disability* (Inclusion London 2015), p. 7.
8 See the best practice case studies at disabilityartsinternational.org. Touring companies have little control over venues, some of which can be old and unsuitable for adaptation. In those cases, the challenge and choice—which may have financial implications—are whether to only tour to fully accessible venues or to compromise on accessibility.
9 For example, in 2024 Turner Contemporary in Margate partnered with the Royal National Institute of Blind People to start including alt text in its exhibitions.
10 For disabled people taking ownership and shaping displays, see N.R. Johnson-Symington and H.A. Robertson, 'Pioneering partnerships at the Riverside Museum', in K. McSweeney and J. Kavanagh (eds.), *Museum Participation: New Directions for Audience Collaboration* (MuseumsEtc 2016), pp. 344–61.
11 For example, the Aurora Orchestra in London sends an 'Additional Needs' document to all players before a project begins, which gives an opportunity for support requests to be worked into plans at an early stage.
12 For example, T. Jonze, 'Wigmore Hall addresses neurodiversity with "low stimulus" concerts', *The Guardian* (29 March 2023).
13 From the Centre for Excellence in Universal Design (universaldesign.ie).

46 Digital inclusivity

Most, if not all, cultural organisations have for years used digital tools and technologies[1] for marketing and are active on the main social media platforms. Digital tools are useful for communicating with audiences and strategic partners, presenting work (e.g., through live streaming) and collecting data about audiences and for evaluation purposes.

The COVID-19 lockdowns of 2020/21 led to a step-change in digital engagement by cultural organisations, with widespread realisation that creative projects could be delivered online and that digital tools and online engagement were vital for maintaining communication and connection. The sudden and accelerated pace of change in that short period of time resulted in progress in digital engagement that may have taken years under more normal circumstances and created a wealth of learning about what works, what doesn't and what to look out for. In subsequent years, digital engagement has remained key for many cultural organisations, at least in hybrid form alongside in-person engagement.[2]

The advantages of digital engagement

Digital tools and technologies have huge potential for reaching a broader audience and extending or deepening community engagement and participation:

- They help connect with new people, who may not have visited your venue.
- They enable engagement with those who, for whatever reason, are unable to participate in person and so can stimulate and shape community consultation and co-production—people can participate in ways that best suit them.
- Online video meetings can be more accessible than in-person—they enable participation to be fitted in around work, caring commitments, disability, distance, accessibility, transport and parking.
- WhatsApp or Facebook (or equivalent) groups can link participants (as well as staff and volunteers) to share experiences, check in and support each other.

> Decision making meetings have shifted very successfully online with no obvious barriers to participation, although we are very much aware of digital exclusion in the borough. We must continue to offer this as an option long term as it enables the involvement of a range of people who struggle to leave home for meetings.[3]

DOI: 10.4324/9781003415886-51

The digital divide and exclusion

Digital tools and technologies also have the potential to exclude. While in the European Union and the United States, c. 93 per cent of households have internet access,[4] digital exclusion is more complex than internet access or its lack. It is rooted in wider social inequalities, and evidence shows that those who are socially excluded—for example, in social housing, on lower wages, unemployed, disabled and older people—are less likely to use the internet.[5]

There are numerous factors in digital exclusion:

- Many families have limited digital capacity, often referred to as 'data poverty', that is, not being able to afford sufficient access to broadband or mobile data; not having data on mobile phones switched on all the time because of cost; and not having access to digital devices.[6]
- Problems of connectivity, especially in rural areas or at times of high local internet use.
- Lack of digital literacy, skills and confidence, particularly for people new to the technology, for example, how to download an app or take part in a video call.
- One of the largest groups of non-users of the internet is the 'not for me' camp, those unwilling to engage with digital, based on fear or nervousness, a sense that it is irrelevant to their lives or lack of awareness of its potential.[7]
- Concerns around personal data/identity safety online (especially if you have to log-in and register to use a digital service).
- Lack of confidence in showing what your home looks like in video calls.
- Access problems for people who struggle with speech or are not fluent in the country's main language.
- Increasingly, some people are withdrawing from close engagement with the internet because of the negative impacts on their mental and physical health, and the abuse and personal attacks prevalent on social media.[8]
- Simple fatigue with video calls—the feeling that staring at a screen is no substitute for real human connection and can exacerbate its absence.

> We've never relied solely on digital because as an area we have a higher than average level of digital exclusion as well as issues such as data poverty or in many households lack of access and/or shared devices.[9]

Digital accessibility

Digital spaces, such as websites and videos, often have barriers that limit the access of visually and hearing impaired and neurodivergent people: they can be just as inaccessible as physical spaces (see Chapter 45). Many of the accommodations to improve access for these groups often benefit a wider audience:[10]

- Subtitles/closed captions as standard.
- Audio descriptions (a form of narration describing key visual elements for the visually impaired).
- Films with BSL (or equivalent) sign language.
- Accessible text on your website.

- Colour on websites:[11] high colour contrast between content and background; do not rely on colour to communicate anything (e.g., 'click the red button'); use white or black space to help break up low contrasts.
- Content and layouts that don't overstimulate: arrange text and information in a way that isn't cluttered and avoid unexpected noises or sudden visual changes.
- Clear visual cues to enhance content (e.g., a phone icon next to contact information).

Some practical tips

Be aware of what is missing by having digital-only events:

- Face-to-face interaction: digital technology can reduce direct human contact.
- Unexpected encounters and conversations (e.g., over coffee or lunch).
- It is less easy for facilitators to 'read the room' online in the same way as for a live group activity.
- Public events can attract passers-by and enliven an area.

> These passing moments, that often happen on the sidelines of a creative event or with those who hadn't planned to participate in any formal way, can be absolutely at the heart of community creativity—but have proved enormously difficult to replicate online.[12]

In addition:

- Staff digital skills (and confidence) need regular updating, as digital platforms constantly evolve and digital behaviours, especially among younger generations, are always shifting.
- Demystify 'digital': using non-technical language can make the difference between communities feeling put off ('it's not for me') and excited and engaged (see Chapter 40 on inclusive language).
- It can be a slow process moving participants onto a specific app and taking them through its features—don't expect everyone to catch on straight away.
- In social media group chats or video meetings with external participants, ensure you have clear guidelines for respectful behaviour and be prepared to expel anyone who transgresses them, especially for using abusive language and personal attacks. People need to feel that these are safe spaces. It is good practice to have a digital safeguarding policy to protect everyone using your digital services from online harm, such as discrimination, harassment, disinformation and sharing personal information.
- Don't assume that digital is an easy, cheap solution to accessing low cultural engagers. It is not always the most appropriate way to reach some audiences.

For an organisation striving to be inclusive, it is important for digital to be not just one-way emails, blogs, webpages or videos, but a means of facilitating and encouraging two-way engagement. In most cases, the ideal approach is a hybrid model, with some in-person activities supported by digital for further engagement. Each half of the model offers something unique. In-person activity offers deeper personal connections and can more effectively reach those who do not typically participate, including those with limited digital access or skills. A digital offer helps more people to get involved and enables collaborative work, ongoing feedback, interaction and communication, but it is important to take the time to ensure participants are comfortable with the technology.[13]

Notes

1 We define 'digital' as platforms and channels such as websites, social media and email marketing; digital tools such as apps; technologies such as digital videos, interactive art and participatory games; and digital devices such as computers, tablets and smartphones.

2 A valuable case study that takes into account the experiences and learning of the COVID-19 lockdowns is K. Welch, *The Role of Digital Engagement in Place-based Projects* (Creative People and Places 2020). Also useful, although pre-COVID-19 and slightly overtaken by the explosion of digital engagement strategies during and since lockdown, are J. Visser and J. Richardson, *Digital Engagement in Culture, Heritage and the Arts* (2013, a toolkit for arts and heritage organisations, see digitalengagementframework.com); and *Digital Engagement and Opportunities* (The Audience Agency 2019).

3 Creative People and Places, Hounslow, quoted in K. Welch, *The Role of Digital Engagement in Place-based Projects* (Creative People and Places 2020), p. 3.

4 'Digital economy and society statistics – households and individuals' (December 2022, on ec.europa.eu); Pew Research Center, 'Mobile Technology and Home Broadband' (2021).

5 C. Martin, S. Hope and S. Zubairi, *The Role of Digital Exclusion in Social Exclusion* (Carnegie UK Trust 2016), p. 28.

6 In the United Kingdom, in 2023, eight million households had problems affording communications services, a figure that had doubled since 2021—source: annual Communications Affordability Tracker (ofcom.org.uk).

7 *Digital Engagement and Opportunities* (The Audience Agency 2019), pp. 36–7.

8 N. Pennington, 'Quitting social media: a qualitative exploration of communication outcomes', *Qualitative Research Reports in Communication* 22/1 (2021), pp. 30–38.

9 East Durham Creates, quoted in K. Welch, *The Role of Digital Engagement in Place-based Projects* (Creative People and Places 2020), p. 4.

10 See the useful pointers in E. Powell, 'Do you cater for neurodiversity?', *Arts Professional* (25 May 2023).

11 About 300 million people worldwide (c. 3.8 per cent of the global population) are affected by some form of 'colour blindness'.

12 K. Welch, *The Role of Digital Engagement in Place-based Projects* (Creative People and Places 2020), p. 5.

13 K. Welch, *The Role of Digital Engagement in Place-based Projects* (Creative People and Places 2020), p. 6.

Part 5

Governance for an inclusive and sustainable organisation

A governing body should be the strategic leaders of any organisation. The differences between a strategic leader and an executive are highlighted, drawing clear distinctions between those who plan and those who do. This also applies to smaller organisations where the executive may be volunteers.

The roles of board members will vary according to their skills and particular responsibilities, but the role of the chair is discussed in some detail. The principles of a skills-based board and of open recruitment for trustees are now well established, though not implemented everywhere. Open recruitment is time consuming to administer, and tips are given of key things to ensure success. Attracting younger trustees is also a challenge and some examples are given.

'Founder's Syndrome' is a recognised problem that particularly affects the cultural sector, especially for smaller organisations or those created in the last 40 years. How an executive leader can influence and build a strong partnership with their board is explored, particularly the relationship between the director/CEO and chair.

In the last 25 years, standards of ethical behaviour of leaders in public life have been closely scrutinised. Conflicts of interest are analysed and the phrase *conflicts of loyalty* is used for preference. Finally, a key role of a governing body is to manage leadership succession smoothly: this is rarely done effectively, and there are common reasons for this failure.

DOI: 10.4324/9781003415886-52

47 The strategic role of the board

The board[1] is the ultimate leader in any charitable/non-profit organisation and as such must always take the longer view for the good of the organisation. As outlined in this part, the board should always be strategic in their thinking and not be distracted by discussions about detailed, operational matters. Their leadership should focus on ensuring that the direction and success of the organisation is in line with any objectives, charitable or otherwise, and any current strategic plans. They will always have collective responsibility.

The director or chief executive, here called Chief Executive Officer (CEO) as is often the practice now, is the link between the strategic thinking and policymaking of the board, and the executive and staff, whether paid or voluntary or a combination of both. The CEO has a role to play in interpreting and explaining both sides to each other. They put into practice the policies of the board, but also use their experience and knowledge to ensure that board decisions are not fanciful, will be effective and pragmatic, and will support the drive towards being an inclusive and sustainable organisation.

Ensure that your board (if you are the CEO or the chair) is discussing the right things in the right way. Some boards tend to focus, often quite eagerly, on day-to-day operational matters, and their meetings might even be a bit unstructured—this can be the case in small, locally based organisations, which are often largely or completely volunteer-run. It is vital that the board pays most of its attention to the more strategic matters that are its responsibility—such as the longer-term strategic direction of the organisation—and to structure its meetings accordingly (see *Successful meetings* in Chapter 48).

In many sections of this book, the authors have assumed that the CEO is either the initiator of strategic shifts in policy to build an inclusive and sustainable organisation or is delivering them with enthusiasm and belief. However, on occasion, it is possible that this is not the case and that the CEO themselves needs to be changed. If this is so, then the board must take the lead, as they are the key player in the shift in strategic direction to be a more inclusive, diverse and resilient organisation. It is also their role to challenge their executive.

Understanding the difference between executive and non-executive directors is important for the success of any cultural organisation. It matters as it supports both sides in doing their jobs correctly. The board's strategic focus should make the demarcation between executive and non-executive very clear. Even if an organisation is entirely run by volunteers, the executive role will be fulfilled by someone. If staff are employed, then the line should always be obvious: the board sets policy and standards, with staff implementing them. However, a board should also monitor the executive and be confident in challenging them as necessary.

DOI: 10.4324/9781003415886-53

Note

1 In this part, the governing body is called 'the board' even though they may not be trustees of a charity. Whatever their name, they are in a position of governance and leadership of the organisation, even if the organisation is not an independent charity. Trustee is used throughout for ease to mean anyone: trustee, director, member or governor.

48 Roles of board members in leadership

To survive, all cultural organisations must adapt and bend in the wind to ensure they can remain relevant to the public. Periodically, therefore, they will all need to reinvent themselves, just as leading brands in the consumer world relaunch and refresh their image and products.

If a shift in policy to be more inclusive and sustainable has been initiated by the board themselves, it is likely that the trustees may have already recognised that some fundamental rethinking is required to build a resilient organisation. But if the change has been introduced from an external source, by another person or organisation—for example, a new appointment of a CEO or by a government body—then the board themselves may have to take an active part in the process and change themselves too. Becoming an inclusive and sustainable organisation does not happen through evolution but through conscious leadership.

Each trustee is an equal member of the board, even if they are in a nominated seat; they share collective responsibility as a board, so dissension can only be expressed round the boardroom table, not afterwards or in public. Sadly, there are recent examples in Europe of political appointments and interference in major museums and other cultural organisations around appointments of chief executives because of their affiliations to a political party/government. This has resulted in inexperienced CEOs who are incapable of leading the organisation, with consequent spectacular failures, or introducing change which was not needed or successful.

There may (or should) be individuals on the board who have particular experience and knowledge of many of the challenges of creating and leading an inclusive and sustainable organisation. These individuals should be given a clear mandate to lead the more detailed work of the board in some of these key areas, with delegated powers to keep the process moving forward. Milestones must be agreed on for this group to report back to the board, and everyone should be kept up to date in between, without overwhelming one and all in endless email threads.

The role of the chair

One of the board should be appointed as the chairperson—however you address them.

The chair will have three statutory duties:[1]

- Chair the full board meetings, ensuring clear decisions are made and all voices are heard.
- Ensure the organisation is fully accountable in terms of submitting statutory returns.
- Be the organisation's public face in times of triumph and disaster.

DOI: 10.4324/9781003415886-54

The chair must be a person who is appointed by the board to be a trustee initially and—at least in the United Kingdom—only then can they be appointed as the chair. They may or may not be new to the board at this point. There is no rule for this. Any actions that the chair undertakes beyond the statutory duties listed above must be agreed by the board: the chair cannot act unilaterally. The board should be aware of everything and the chair should not presume on their approval for any individual actions. Collective responsibility should always continue to be the over-riding culture.

It is practical for the CEO or equivalent and the chair to work closely together, especially in times of crisis, for example, taking the decision when to close at the start of the 2020 pandemic. They should meet regularly and be able to talk confidentially. Good practice is that the CEO 'checks in' with the chair when fast decision-making is crucial or when a media enquiry may lead to publicity (either good or bad). So this is a crucial relationship which should be built on mutual trust and support and professional conduct and is one which is essential to a smooth-running and successful cultural organisation.

If there is an inter-regnum between chairs, then a temporary appointment can be made by the board of one of their members to chair meetings. Or, the chair of the board meeting can be shared and rotated, selected prior to each board meeting. If there is a vice or deputy chair, this is ideal as they can step into the role to fill the gap and take the lead in the recruitment process (see Chapter 55 on succession planning).

Successful meetings

The traditional start to a meeting, with the minutes of last time, and then matters arising, does not inspire a feeling of action and urgency, indeed it makes most attendees want to switch off immediately and go to sleep. So right from the start, the meeting has to work hard to create momentum. Putting the most important items after lots of standard/routine stuff means that most participants are exhausted or disengaged by the time serious decisions need to be made.

This makes your board meetings, in particular, and any other internal meetings, appear to be tedious, too long and therefore not an effective use of time. It prevents good engagement by the people round the table, and where you might have external advisers or experts, you cannot risk losing their full attention as they will have limited intellectual time to support you. Particularly if you are a smaller organisation, you can ill afford to waste staff time in a talking shop where nothing happens as a result. Especially if you are trying to diversify your board and recruit younger people, then this becomes even more vital.

Ensure that meetings do not last more than two hours; at most, two and a half hours is the maximum anyone can be expected to concentrate (unless it is an away day when it should be structured differently). Build in comfort breaks and ensure there is plenty of water/tea/coffee freely available. Start on time and do not backtrack if someone is late.

Minutes should be issued once the chair has agreed them. Members must be instructed to read them when they are issued, and query or correct anything which needs doing. So once they appear on the agenda, they are agreed and everyone has read them. Put them at the *end* of the agenda under the heading *To Be Noted.* Along with any panel, committee or working group notes, these should then simply be noted, and do not need to be discussed.

Hybrid meetings are often a challenge if some participants are present in the room but some are virtually present on a video call screen. CEOs may have to diplomatically advise their chairs about how best to handle these, but remember to follow their own advice if chairing an internal meeting!

Concentration is key to having a productive meeting, so there should be an agreement that everyone is listened to without interruption (unless they deviate from the subject in hand). No-one should leap in without the chair inviting them to speak, or those who are lined up to speak could be cut off unfairly. In return for agreeing not to interrupt others, when you yourself are speaking, you should agree to be succinct. This way, everyone's contribution is valued equally. Everyone should keep their eyes on the speaker, and the chair should ensure that the meeting's focus doesn't wander down rabbit holes, so participants start checking emails on their phones.

The CEO should maintain an annual calendar for board business with key topics which must be dealt with at certain times of the year, for example, the strategic plan, or the revenue budget.

Issue your papers (by email) at a minimum of 10 days' notice, but ensure recipients will have at least one weekend within that timescale.

Allocate sufficient time for each topic, perhaps indicating timings alongside the agenda item which allow participants to understand the relative weight of each one. In addition, you can mark each agenda item as 'for noting', 'for discussion' or 'for decision', which clarifies what response is being asked for from the board.

Agenda items should not ordinarily be tabled at the meeting itself, as participants cannot make considered judgements if they have not had time to think about them. But anything which has just arisen or requires an emergency response can be presented, with a written summary circulated at the time recording the main points and the recommendation.

Create agendas for meetings to focus on assessing key topics which are important to the organisation and making decisions to progress them. Do not have a meeting just for the sake of it, simply *because it's in the diary*. Standard agendas and routine items do not interest participants who are of the right calibre and who need to be engaged to keep their interest and support.

The chair and the leadership team should address the agenda in advance, answering questions such as:

- What is the main purpose of this meeting?
- Which items need discussion or have short deadlines?
- Are there topics which need additional work before putting them onto an agenda?
- Do these topics require flagging up with participants; do they need to prepare or think about anything in particular so as to be able to contribute to the discussion?

Practitioners may think that they do this now, but many start from the position of discussing the next meeting. Start from the other end of the telescope and consider what you need to decide/discuss to see if you need a meeting at all, then go from there. It seems a small point but can give you a completely different point of view.

Note

1 This is true of UK charities. In the United States, for example, not-for-profit board roles and responsibilities can vary from state to state.

49 It shouldn't be who you know

A skills-based board

If an organisation is changing the emphasis of its programmes in order to be more inclusive and sustainable, then the outlook of the board and staff, in particular their skills, will need to be transformed too in order for any strategic change to be introduced and successfully implemented.

If an independent museum, for example, was initially created in the late twentieth century (as many industrial archaeology museums in the United Kingdom were from the late 1970s to 1990s), then the board is likely to be full of experts in the subject matter, site and collections of that museum. When cultural organisations are bumping along the bottom and worried they may go bankrupt, the board is likely to be peopled by financial and legal experts, as many were in the early years of the twenty-first century. Of course, these skills are needed on any governing body to some extent, but not to the exclusion of those who have a background in a cultural organisation, in learning, experience of running a visitor attraction or a theatre, or developing trading and income streams.

The concept of the participatory and inclusive cultural organisation may be a new one[1] to a trustee from a more traditional background; the majority of consumers of culture in general, certainly in much of Europe and the United States, are still middle class, middle aged and well educated. Consequently, if broadening the audience and involving them directly in the work of the organisation is a new development, then experience of this way of working must be represented on the board to guide and oversee the change in emphasis, and reassure (or persuade) more reluctant board members. For reluctant many may remain, despite the deliberate shift in policy which led to the decision.

An evaluation of change at 10 museums and arts organisations in California noted that such cases inspired the most fraught discussions between staff and board, and sometimes resulted in the organisation having to slow down or scale back its ambitions.[2] This was particularly true where some long-serving board members regarded engagement as a sideshow and not part of the core activities of the organisation.

This all underlines the crucial importance of ensuring your board is not only appointing people they already know—i.e. like themselves, so regarded as safer—but filling the gaps in order to achieve a balance of skills and knowledge suitable to implement the board's strategic aims of being inclusive and sustainable.

Therefore a regular skills analysis is a starting point for diversifying your board. The analysis should focus on several time periods: what skills and knowledge do you need when? Examining the needs of medium- and longer-term timescales will also help you to focus your succession plan for both trustees and senior staff (see below and Chapter 53).

DOI: 10.4324/9781003415886-55

However, it should not only be skills and background that you consider but what impact you need appointees to make. Impact is now a key indicator for funders to assess an organisation's suitability. If you are leading your organisation towards being more inclusive and sustainable, that should be one of the main focuses of your recruitment.

Recruitment

Open board recruitment is very time consuming, but it is the most effective way of taking a significant step towards being more inclusive and sustainable. You will meet people whom you would not otherwise meet with more traditional forms of board recruitment (see also Chapter 39 on equitable recruitment).

However, many boards still recruit from among people the existing trustees know personally; in these circumstances, they always get more of the same. Some feel uncertain about going outside their comfort zone, and open recruitment is still often seen as risky, especially in smaller organisations. However, if you are going to be more inclusive, you as the leader will need to grasp the open recruitment nettle. You will be unlikely to be able to introduce new skills and a new outlook onto the board without it. This, however, does not completely exclude approaching those whom you already know have the right skills and approach for what you need.

Following a skills and impact audit to assess exactly what knowledge, skills and experience the board needs and when, ensure that a role description is prepared, listing the skills and impacts you are seeking. This is similar to the job description and person specification you would prepare for recruiting a member of staff. It should describe not only the organisation and the duties of a trustee but also what qualities you expect applicants to have.

A paper assessment against the role description of the potential candidates should be followed by something face-to-face (or virtual) for your shortlist. This should be similar to a job interview, but more relaxed and informal with a view to both parties learning about each other.

Increasingly, open board recruitment is accepted as best practice and it is becoming more frequent not only in the cultural sector but throughout the public sector, with even the chair of UK Sport being selected through this process in 2017. Open recruitment is also a perfect opportunity for the organisation to generate some positive publicity for itself: for local and social media, a cultural organisation shifting emphasis, wanting to engage more with its public and seeking fresh blood to help them to do so, is a terrific news story. If you are particularly recruiting locally, holding an open evening or day could also assist recruitment and involve as many of the current board as possible.

Time commitment for governing bodies

Often the most significant barrier in becoming a trustee is the fact that it is a voluntary role which may demand a substantial amount of time. Estimating how much time would be required in your role description may make it sound daunting, but being honest will support you in recruiting the right people. There are always options here, as attending events and representing the organisation at various meetings can be shared amongst all trustees and senior staff. Some will be more able to put more time in than others, but time should not be a major stumbling block if the candidate is otherwise ideal.

One of the topics to stress in the role description, and in conversations, is to ensure that any applicant understands that attending board and other meetings is not only about the time of the actual meeting. It is also about preparing by reading the papers, thinking about the decisions that will be needed and raising queries in advance to clarify your position and opinion. In addition, attending relevant events to represent the organisation will also be an important part of a trustee's role.

Trustees must always act in the interests of the charity and not be swayed by personal opinions of little or no relevance. In order to do this, it is essential that any prospective trustee is confident that they would be supportive of the organisation's mission as this will always encourage them to spend time in assisting the cause.

Nominated trustees

Many cultural organisations have one or more nominated trustees, mostly dating back to their foundation and often linked to financial support. Local authorities, universities or learned societies who founded an institution may have the right to nominate trustees. During the early years of this century, for example, many UK local authorities established charitable trusts for some of their discretionary services, such as museums, arts centres or community arts. They usually built into the governing documents the right to nominate at least one, and often two, seats on the board. Often this was in the mistaken belief that their interests would be protected and represented by these nominated people. Usually, one seat for each of the main political parties was required, but the individuals selected were usually elected members and some of the 'old guard', often near the end of their active political careers; it was seen as a sort of reward for loyal service.

If your board (if you are the chair or the CEO) has nominated trustees, it is vital that you, and they, understand the following:

- Ensure that the nominated trustee has a full induction and doesn't put you off by saying they are an experienced trustee or are too busy to attend; many trustees never have an induction!
- A nominated trustee does not represent the interests of their nominating body; they are standard trustees in their own right, as are their colleagues, so must always act for the good of the organisation.
- They are able to advise the board how their nominating body may react to a decision, but cannot directly lobby for their interests.
- If the nominated trustee is not actively engaged in the business of the board and regularly sending apologies or comments in advance if they are unable to attend a meeting, you must challenge them. If their engagement does not improve, then you can request that they be replaced.
- If it is a (UK) local authority nominating, the trustee does not have to be an elected member but could be anyone appropriate, such as, an officer, a former officer or councillor or an interested member of the public, such as a member of a civic society, local history group or a director of a theatre company.

Notes

1 See, for example, N. Simon, *The Participatory Museum* (Museum 2.0 2010).
2 S. Lee and K. Gean, *The Engagement Revolution: A Study of Strategic Organizational Transformation in 10 California Arts Nonprofits* (James Irvine Foundation 2017).

50 Board diversity and young trustees

Diversity is a challenging word for many cultural organisations, especially the smaller ones or those with a military connection (such as regimental museums in the United Kingdom) (for definition of diversity, see Introduction). Many organisations are appointing more diverse people onto their boards with voices and life experiences which add to the rich mix of views round the boardroom table. While Part 4 addresses diversity and inclusion in some detail, this chapter looks specifically at diversity with reference to board recruitment (see also Chapter 39 on equitable recruitment).

In the cultural sector, probably the three most significant barriers against more diversity in board recruitment are:

- Trustees are volunteers, so are not paid for their work.
- The majority of trustees are currently over 55.[1]
- Board meetings are traditional and bureaucratic in format, timing and content (see Chapter 48).

These barriers naturally discriminate against age diversity, as younger generations cannot afford to give so much time to a voluntary role. The sight of 10 or 12 people over 55 round a table will not automatically inspire someone under 25 to want to join them. Equally, the sight of 10 or 12 white people over 55 may be a barrier to recruiting people of colour. Nor do the format and timing of meetings attract younger people, who are likely not to have experienced working in a professional capacity with the formality of board meetings.

Currently less than 3 per cent of trustees in the United Kingdom are under 30 years of age.[2] The UK's Young Trustees movement grew out of Young Charity Trustees founded in 2011. It is not only age which is a barrier against young people joining boards, but a combination of geography, education, income, race, religion, social class and culture which are all stopping young people deciding to become involved. The British Youth Council is a rare example in the UK with all trustees under 25. They support young people to get involved in their communities and democracy locally, nationally and internationally, making a difference as volunteers, campaigners, decision-makers and leaders. Historic Buildings and Places (formerly The Ancient Monuments Society) held an open recruitment drive in late 2022, recruiting six first-time trustees, all under 40. Several of them said they were encouraged to apply as a result of the advertisement stating that you did not have to have experience of being a trustee.

It is no longer unusual for cultural organisations to have youth advisory boards. While these are not necessarily 'trustees' with a decision-making remit, they are a valuable source of advice on young people's concerns and hopes. For example, the Global Opportunity

DOI: 10.4324/9781003415886-56

Youth Network, working across nine countries in Latin America, Africa and Asia, has youth advisory groups that help set priorities, contribute to strategic planning and give feedback. In Mexico City, every member of the group represents different causes and priorities. Also in Mexico City, a children's council at the Papalote Museo del Niño consists of children 9–11 years old, invited through schools, whose ideas, opinions, desires and preoccupations inform the development of programmes and the whole museum.[3]

What else can cultural organisations do to address these imbalances? Examining timings and format of board meetings will help (see also *Successful meetings* in Chapter 48). If you are employed, then taking time off to attend a meeting on a regular basis, in the middle of the day, is not an option. Early evening meetings may be easier, but this can often conflict with the demands of family life. Flexibility in timings for board and working group meetings in addition to addressing their format will undoubtedly help; and nowadays many of them can take place virtually, eliminating the need for travel time.

However, most important of all is to discuss frankly with the prospective trustees (whether young or otherwise) what the challenges might be in advance, create an open and honest culture where the trustee could raise problems without feeling guilty or being blamed, and where the existing trustees welcome the newcomer and do not feel awkward as though they should be treated differently from anyone else. Ideally, there needs to be a particular focus or task to help a diverse trustee—someone who stands out as being 'different' and may as a result feel self-conscious—to settle in quickly, although this applies equally to any new trustee joining an existing board. A good rule of thumb is not to automatically assign a 'diverse' trustee to be solely responsible for diversity on the board: this is classic pigeon-holing, and all board members need to take collective responsibility for how diversity and inclusion impact their organisation.

Younger and more diverse trustees will bring an injection of fresh energy and perspectives to your organisation, so it is worthwhile to spend time and effort adjusting how your organisation works to welcome and accommodate them and make them feel that they belong.

Notes

1 Research shows that 92 per cent of trustees in England and Wales have an average age of 55–64, rising to 65–74 in smaller charities, with 92 per cent white, two-thirds male, and 75 per cent with higher-than-average income and levels of education. See *Taken on Trust: The awareness and effectiveness of charity trustees in England and Wales* (Charity Commission 2017). In the United States, the average age of board members is 52, 76 per cent are white, with a 55/45 per cent male/female ratio. Source: Board of Directors Member Demographics and Statistics in the United States, by Zippia (zippia.com).

2 *Taken on Trust* (see previous note), p. 18, Table 4.

3 The Consejo de Niñas y Niños Papalote was originally created in 2001 under Executive Director Marinela Servitje and Deputy Director Maribel Ibarra and continues today.

51 Ethical behaviour

Recent political interference in appointments and programming decisions (see Chapter 48) has put ethical behaviour in the governance spotlight. In addition, increasingly those in public life are not conducting themselves ethically and in a responsible way. This makes it even more important for the leader of a cultural organisation to ensure that they, their staff and the board behave to high ethical standards (see Chapter 10).

In 1977, the UK's Museums Association became the first in their sector to adopt a Code of Ethics. Still admired round the world by those aspiring to work ethically, the Code will have its third review and refresh by 2025. It is built into the UK's Museums Accreditation regulations, and those aiming for the professional membership level must formally agree to abide by the Code in their future work.

It is now usual for cultural organisations to develop and publish their values, as part of their vision, mission and values trilogy. Ethical behaviour should be part of this. Charities were first founded in the medieval period to provide alms for the poor and educate those who wanted to enter the Church; still today, they all must have public benefit. High profile scandals of recent years have shown the importance of ethical behaviour, particularly in influencing public opinion of charities/non-profits.

If, as a leader, your cultural organisation does not have published vision, mission and values, you should take the lead on developing them, involving everyone in your organisation, and ideally external voices too, such as your communities. They should be reviewed and refreshed regularly. The conversations you will have with your board, leadership team and staff will contribute not only to a robust code of ethics/values but will enhance the impact of the organisation and cement relationships (see Chapter 26 on finding common purpose).

DOI: 10.4324/9781003415886-57

52 'Founder's Syndrome'

Succession planning (see Chapter 55) will remain a sensitive subject as you strive to ensure both continuity and fresh thinking. Current, longstanding trustees may feel that their colleagues don't want them anymore. They may be out of touch with your audience, or they may be up to date and still a valuable member of the board. Whichever is the case, the chair's conversation about them moving on must respect their past commitment to the organisation.

However, for many smaller organisations, such a trustee may have been one of your founders. Likely to be well respected in their community, they may be former mayors or local politicians who championed the establishment of your organisation. Many community arts organisations or industrial heritage sites, locally based and focused on a local audience, will have at least one trustee like this. They will constantly judge ideas and new developments against a yardstick of the past and the standards of the time when you were founded. So they are often a barrier to change and new ways of thinking and working.

In a similar way to a long-established family business, loyalty to a founder's ideas and too much respect for past achievements can be very dangerous. Typically, if a new investor or owner was assessing a business, they would break the family stranglehold and appoint directors or staff on the basis of merit, not family ties.

In order to implement a succession plan, these blockers must be removed if your organisation is to adapt and thrive. But this should be done with care and respect for their past achievements. The rest of the board and the CEO should confidentially discuss appropriate rewards and future status, while being aware that you are creating a precedent for the future. Creating 'vice patrons', 'ambassadors' or 'champions' are the type of title it might be appropriate to award to such luminaries from your past.

Recurrence can be prevented by adopting a board resolution to ensure that trustees are always appointed for a fixed term, by confirming your succession plan as a policy and ensuring it is implemented.

DOI: 10.4324/9781003415886-58

53 Working with, and influencing, your governing body, and the relationship between chair and CEO

Influencing upwards is a key skill for leaders (see Chapter 22). Many of the approaches described are appropriate for influencing your board, but maybe the most significant relationship is that between the CEO and the chair. Every governing body must have a chair (even if they are called something different).

It is important for the chair and CEO to work closely together. If there are challenges in the relationship between the chair and the CEO, then the board will need to sort it out, but if there is no natural leader, other than the chair, then the deputy or vice chair, the treasurer or the most senior member of the board should take the lead. The most important thing to remember is that the organisation must be your focus of attention, as all board members are collectively responsible for its future.

In the 2010s, a large cultural organisation had a chair who was developing dementia. He was aware he was struggling, but told the CEO that he wanted to serve out his term of office. One of the authors was contacted by the CEO to advise on this situation, confidentially. The advice was to work with the deputy chair to mitigate the impact of the illness, taking over as many meetings and events as possible, and to encourage him to resign. Some of the other trustees were reluctant to 'get involved', despite already being involved. But with some persuasion, he did agree for the organisation to begin to recruit his successor and then handed over to them. This is an example of members of a governing body not wanting to rock the boat, as such a situation needed careful, discreet handling. However, it was imperative that it *was* addressed to protect the organisation's reputation and charitable status; in such circumstances, personal discomfort should be forgotten.

Because the chair and CEO relationship is so crucial, if the board is recruiting a new chair, it is good practice for the CEO to be involved. There are two ways of doing this:

- The recruitment panel selects who they wish to appoint and invites them to meet the CEO for a confidential but informal conversation. Afterwards, the chair of the panel listens to the CEO's honest opinion in addition to hearing from the chosen candidate. If the feedback is positive, the panel then recommends the candidate to the whole board; if not, the panel look at their second choice, and so on.
- The CEO observes the 'interviews', but takes no active part in asking questions, only contributing to discussions afterwards. Having a silent observer can be off-putting for some but, if there are two rounds of interviews, one may be virtual so the CEO can observe more discreetly.

DOI: 10.4324/9781003415886-59

If your appointment as the CEO was a signal that there needed to be a change of emphasis within the strategy of an organisation, then it is logical that the board will support your proposals for any change in direction. However, in these circumstances, boards are often slower to play an active leadership role and might even show resistance, especially where a change measurably affects the organisation's core or traditional programming, and when it starts to affect its business model. For example, a move to a more democratic outlook, with participation and wider community connections, may mean a psychological shift for many boards. As a new leader, you will need to work to influence your board to support your proposals and the new way of working that they represent. There will come a time when you can no longer remind them that they appointed you on the basis of your ideas, so you should continue to woo them to wholeheartedly support your thinking.

All these suggestions assume that the CEO has the full support of the board; if they do not, then a more nuanced approach will be needed. In these circumstances, the chair should take the lead in sorting it out. Needless to say, being aware of employment law and professional human resources procedures would be essential. If the CEO has been in post for some time, then new members of the board may struggle to create a good working relationship with them. All governing bodies should take time to get to know each other, maybe having dinner prior to an away day, for example.[1] Once people feel they know each other, they will be able to work more effectively together. The chair and CEO should both encourage this approach.

When the CEO's appraisal takes place, the chair is the natural person to carry this out, but when such formal reviews are due, there should always be two trustees present: ideally, the chair and the deputy/vice-chair if you have one, or the treasurer or other senior member of the board. If one of them has a background in human resources or leadership, then they may be the most appropriate second person. But like any appraisal, this session should be a two-way conversation.

Of course, if you are not a registered charity, you have more freedom about what powers you give to your chair. Cooperative or mutual societies are not charities but often behave in similar ways as they have philanthropic motives. But beware appointing an inspiring chair who may develop dictatorial tendencies; collective responsibility is one of your weapons here if this shows signs of happening.

Note

1 H. McGowan, *Successful Away Days for Boards of Museums and Heritage Organisations*, www.aim-museums.co.uk/for-trustees/. Although this was written for museums, it is applicable to the wider cultural sector.

54 Conflicts of loyalty

At the start of any formal meeting, whether board, committee or working group, there should be an item requesting declarations of conflicts of loyalty or interest. These happen when, for other reasons, a trustee might not be able to make decisions that are the best for the organisation. *Conflict of interest* appears to (although doesn't always) focus on financial interests, so using *conflict of loyalty* may be more useful and easier to manage.

This can happen if the organisation's decision involves a person or organisation linked to a trustee. For example:

- The trustee's employer.
- Another organisation where they are a trustee.
- The organisation that nominated them as a trustee.
- Their relatives or friends.

Annually, the CEO should ensure that the register of trustee interests is updated and accurate. This should therefore highlight any obvious conflicts in advance but may not be applicable in every case. Follow any rules in your organisation's governing document about conflicts of loyalty.

You should also create a policy to tell trustees:

- When conflicts of interest/loyalty commonly happen.
- How to declare them.
- What all of the trustees need to do about them.
- Review your policy regularly, discussing it with new trustees as part of their induction.

There are four steps to handling conflicts of loyalty:[1]

Step 1

Do not ignore something that might be a conflict for any trustee. Individuals should talk to the chair. All the board should identify and declare conflicts at the start of meetings so any potential conflict declared can be recorded.

DOI: 10.4324/9781003415886-60

Step 2

As trustees, you all have to take action to stop the conflict from affecting your decision:

- Consider if it is best for the organisation to remove the conflict. This is particularly important if it is a serious conflict.
- If you decide that you do not need to remove the conflict, you must prevent it from affecting your decision.

Step 3

Follow any specific rules for managing the conflict. So check and follow:

- Your organisation's governing document.
- Any directions from a charity/non-profit governing body, for example, the Charity Commission in England and Wales.
- Any other legal rules that apply to your organisation.

If you do not have any of these rules to follow, make sure you set some before you make a decision affected by a conflict of loyalty.

As a minimum, these rules should require that the conflicted person:

- Leaves the relevant discussions.
- Does not take part in any decision or votes.
- Is not counted in the quorum for the meeting.
- If your organisation is a company, you must add the rules to its governing document before you make your decision.

You are all legally responsible for making sure you manage the conflict, so the chair must be clear on how to limit its impact.

Step 4

Record:

- What the conflict was.
- Who or what it affected.
- When it was declared.
- How you managed it.

This will show that you have acted properly.

Note

1 With thanks to the English Charity Commission for some of this four-step guidance: www.gov.uk/guidance/managingconflictsofinterest.

55 Succession planning and transition leadership

A board succession plan is an action plan for recruiting future trustees, to ensure continuity on your board. It considers the skills, knowledge and experience of your current board members, and acknowledges what attributes your organisation needs and what you might look for in subsequent trustees in the event someone steps down or their term of office ends.

A succession plan is useful because:

- Now is never too early.
- Those who may be suitable are likely to be in demand elsewhere or existing trustees already, so not immediately available.
- A long lead time will be needed as the right candidates are worth waiting for.
- Risk of upsetting current/longstanding trustees ('you don't want me anymore!').
- Risk of dipping below minimum number if many leave at once, or having too many for too long (and out of touch with what the public will respond to).
- Allows you to recruit additional/new skills as required.
- The same people being associated with the organisation for a long time runs the risk of projecting the wrong image locally and puts potential new trustees off because they will assume it's a very long-term commitment.

If an organisation has not had terms of office specified before, the topic of long-serving trustees moving on is a sensitive one, so needs to be handled with care. The chair and deputy/vice-chair (if there is one) should take the lead in these conversations, as it is inappropriate for the CEO to carry out alone (see also Chapter 52 on 'Founder's Syndrome').

However, the CEO should encourage the board to adopt a policy of setting maximum terms for trustee appointments as part of the succession plan, even if the governing document does not specify them. A succession plan should be adopted as a policy by the board, so all trustees will be aware of their own terms of office.

For many of the same reasons, a succession plan for senior and key staff will also be useful for maintaining operations and continuity of planning. In these cases, **transition leadership** can assist in maintaining both momentum and focus. Senior posts are usually a minimum of two months' notice and are often three. Three months or longer can be a significant length of time, especially if it is a sensitive time of year, particularly for seasonal or tourist-related businesses.

There are leaders who specialise in this area, as the style and content in being a transitional leader can be radically different from a longer-term appointment. It is a fine line to tread between keeping things going and introducing new, more effective ways of working.

DOI: 10.4324/9781003415886-61

Interim leaders, however, can be very effective following the departure of a successful and admired CEO; they can provide a period of calm after significant upheaval and change; or occasionally they can be brought in for a short period with a specific brief to put an organisation back on a sound financial footing. Sometimes it is better to have a short-term appointment while the board debates what type of CEO they need and what their priorities should be, than to rush into advertising the post. The Royal Exchange Theatre in Manchester took some time to consider whether they wanted to replace their Artistic Director in 2023, and the following year, having made a decision to do things differently, appointed a triumvirate of creatives to fulfil the role (see Chapter 25).

Equally, if a chair suddenly has to leave, for whatever reason, an acting/interim chair could support the CEO and help keep the organisation on track while the organisation waits for the right candidate to be available.

Part 6

Leading a learning organisation

A sustainable organisation is one that is constantly learning from what went well and not so well, and what could be done differently, and welcomes challenge and new perspectives: it is a learning organisation because it is constantly adapting. It is important for a leader to ensure that the mechanisms for organisational learning are present and embedded in day-to-day practice—too often, cultural organisations claim to be 'learning organisations', but lack any mechanism through which that learning occurs.

The two most important learning mechanisms are evaluation and reflective practice. Evaluation should not just be a tick-box exercise at the end of a project to placate funders, but an opportunity for everyone to learn from successes and mistakes and to grow. Organisational reflective practice is ideally built into everyday working practices involving all staff and is the moment of stepping back to see what worked and how, and thinking about and questioning one's actions and considering alternatives. This helps the organisation to address uncomfortable topics—because if things aren't aired and discussed, they don't change—and to build a culture of trust and openness which is essential if the organisation is to be inclusive and grow.

Another mechanism for learning are internal networks, which encourage the development and sharing of ideas and innovation, and help create links that allow things to happen within the organisation. All these mechanisms together can ensure that the learning becomes part of organisational memory—a clear understanding of how it all began and why, what the organisation has learned, how it got to here from there and where it is heading.

DOI: 10.4324/9781003415886-62

56 What is a 'learning organisation'?

How does an organisation improve and change? Put another way, how does an organisation learn? In the absence of learning, organisations (and individuals) simply repeat old practices and mistakes and are incapable of change.

A learning organisation can be defined as

> an organization skilled at creating, acquiring and transferring knowledge, and at modifying its behavior to reflect new knowledge and insights.[1]

A learning organisation is open to new ideas: these might be reflections on past activities and performance and what might be done differently, ideas from outside the organisation or flashes of insight and creativity. These can be the trigger to organisational improvement, but in order for that to happen, there must be mechanisms in place to apply the knowledge and learning to current activities and guide decision-making and new ways of behaving.

There are five characteristics of successful learning organisations:

- **Systematic problem solving**, based on data not assumptions.
- **Experimentation with new approaches**—being prepared to take risks and to value and learn from mistakes rather than assign blame.
- **Learning from their own experience and past history**—recording and reviewing successes and failures, documenting and sharing the lessons in an accessible format.
- **Learning from the experiences and best practice of others**—being open to new perspectives and criticism.
- **Transferring knowledge quickly and efficiently throughout the organisation**—mechanisms include written, oral and visual reports, tours, training programmes, lunchtime talks and workshops, mentoring, job swaps and reflective practice sessions.

Building a true learning organisation takes time, but there are simple first steps you can take:

- Agree your shared goals, as well as a shared language, for example, what do we mean by 'inclusive' or 'participatory' (see Chapter 26 on finding common purpose).
- Foster an environment that is conducive to learning—free up staff time for reflection, analysis and sharing. This is not time wasted: learning and improvement are essential activities in cultural organisations.

DOI: 10.4324/9781003415886-63

- Stimulate exchange of ideas across different teams and individuals, through reflective sessions, talks and workshops.
- Build in ongoing reflective practice, so that analysis and knowledge sharing become integral to daily working and part of the culture of the organisation.
- As a leader, be aware of how the changing social, political and economic environment affects staff morale, motivation and capacity for learning and change, positively or negatively (see also Chapter 12 on political antennae and horizon scanning).[2]

The following chapters in Part 6 build on these steps to creating a learning organisation.[3]

See also:

57. Evaluation as learning
58. Organisational reflective practice
61. The importance of organisational memory – and how to sustain it
64. Strategic peer networks and mentoring
67. External voices and critical friends

Notes

1 D.A. Garvin, 'Building a learning organization', *Harvard Business Review* (July-August 1993). The five characteristics are also drawn from this paper. For a longer definition, see L. Varbanova, *Strategic Management in the Arts* (Routledge 2013), p. 214.

2 For example, the impetus for racial equity many cultural organisations experienced after the Black Lives Matter protests in 2020, or in campaigning against climate change.

3 See also *Creative Health Quality Framework* produced by the Culture Health & Wellbeing Alliance, at culturehealthandwellbeing.org.uk, which sets out principles for equitable and inclusive practice that stress learning, reflection and well-being.

57 Evaluation as learning

Evaluation is the ideal mechanism for an organisation to learn together, to share that learning and to use it to change ways of working and make them better. Unfortunately, many organisations regard evaluation as a necessary evil, as something to be compiled at the end of a project and sent to a funder or stakeholder, typically reporting how brilliantly everything went, admitting no mistakes and registering no useful learning at all. Research shows that many evaluations in cultural organisations say little that is useful, are rarely acted on and have little impact and are not well enough understood by the organisations themselves, policymakers and funders: they are simply treated as part of the chore of accountability to funders, rather than as an opportunity for reflection and learning.[1]

But if evaluation is understood as being primarily about learning, then its function is to help the organisation to develop even further. Its primary role should be to help an organisation find out what is going well, what could have gone better and what it might do differently as a result of those findings, not to 'spin' information for advocacy, funding or public relations purposes.

Collaborative discussion across the cultural sector has proposed 12 shared principles that should inform evaluation.[2] Evaluation should be:

Beneficial
- Committed to learning and/or change
- Ethical
- Applicable

Robust
- Rigorous
- Open-minded
- Proportionate

People-centred
- Empathetic
- Many-voiced
- Socially engaged

Connected
- Transparent
- Aware (e.g., of context and existing research)
- Shared

DOI: 10.4324/9781003415886-64

These principles particularly stress prioritising learning over monitoring or number-crunching, incorporating different voices and perspectives, including those from outside the organisation,[3] exploring why and how things happen, not creating a false consensus, learning what to do differently, and making recommendations and incorporating the learning into activities.

Different types of evaluation

Conventionally, evaluation is divided into three types: front-end, formative and summative.

Front-end evaluation is undertaken before a programme begins, in order to find out the expectations of visitors/users/audiences, non-users, staff and stakeholders. Formative evaluation is the process of testing a programme while it is ongoing, to find out what is going well or not so well and to adapt it as you go along before it is too late to change anything. Summative evaluation occurs at the end of a programme and is used to gauge whether you have achieved its aims and objectives.

It is particularly useful to include a baseline, which gives you a clear understanding of 'before, during and after'. A baseline measures where you are starting from, so that you are monitoring your own journey, and not measuring against objective criteria or against other organisations. It is often possible to recreate a baseline using existing data.

There is a real benefit to starting the evaluation process at the baseline, before the start of an activity or programme (e.g., a three- or five-year programme for the whole organisation). It enables everyone involved to agree where the organisation is starting from, and to share what it is trying to achieve, what outcomes are being looked for and what success might look like. When undertaking baseline evaluation, it is important to measure the same things you will be measuring later. You can then say, 'this is where we were at the beginning of our journey', and it will be possible to look back and say, 'this is how far we have come—this is the progress we made on our journey'.

The most effective evaluation methods, that ensure you learn and adapt along the way, avoid a hard division between front-end, formative and summative evaluation, but, starting with baseline evaluation, run a formative evaluation throughout a whole programme, which helps you to learn and to change things as they go along, constantly tracking and feeding back and taking action.[4] This iterative reflective practice is a key part of the monitoring and learning process and that is covered in detail in Chapter 58. Through ongoing evaluation and reflection, you are constantly measuring your current position against what you hope is your destination.

It is useful to develop a clear framework to track the activities and progress of the whole organisation as well as individual programmes.[5] This should state what outcomes you are trying to achieve (such as progress on equity, diversity and inclusion initiatives and targets), alongside indicators of success.[6] The indicators of success are how you will track whether or not you are achieving the outcomes—they are the sort of evidence of organisational behaviour you would expect to see if the outcomes were being achieved. Indicators—and the data that will be measured against them—can be either quantitative or qualitative. Quantitative indicators help to answer questions about things that are inherently expressed in numbers: how many? how often? how much? Qualitative indicators help to demonstrate, describe or detect that something has happened and its impact on people: how? when? who? where? which? what? why? [7]

Types of evidence to demonstrate change

Evidence that things are changing—or not changing—comes in many forms.[8]

Known and easily shared: this is the sort of evidence that cultural organisations regularly collect and disseminate for other purposes, such as annual reports, board/committee reports, vision statements, business plans and visitor/user profiles.

Known but not necessarily shared: this is evidence that is known but not always written down and shared, such as how values are expressed and made visible, or how experience and learning are shared and passed on within the organisation. This evidence might be gathered through questionnaires and interviews.

Emergent or avoided: this is evidence that those involved in a programme might not yet be consciously aware of or are deliberately avoiding because it is uncomfortable, or evidence that is only just beginning to surface. An example might be what happens when there are setbacks, problems, conflicts or challenges, and how these are addressed. Evaluators will usually use observation and non-verbal techniques to surface this kind of evidence. It is a valuable source of learning, as it often holds the spark of a new idea or insight, and can shine a light on a difficult barrier, challenge or tension within the organisation.

Unexpected discoveries: these are problems, actions, events and consequences that cannot be foreseen at the outset, and one never knows when or where they might emerge. It is useful to record ideas, insights, frustrations and questions as they arise and share and discuss them within the organisation and with evaluators. Such evidence can be very revealing and might occasionally lead to the overall programme being amended.

Any programme, particularly larger-scale change (see Chapter 27), will rarely go completely to plan or smoothly, and the blend of these different types of evidence helps unearth underlying reasons why things go well or not so well: for example, how someone got involved in a particular activity, how something came about, who made the decisions and with what assumptions, or why a particular event happened at a particular time. There is an enormous amount of learning and insight about change to be gained from gathering and exploring the 'who, what and why?' elements of the process, which helps the organisation to overcome barriers to change.

See also:

58. Organisational reflective practice

Notes

1 M. Davies and C. Heath, *Evaluating Evaluation: Increasing the Impact of Summative Evaluation in Museums and Galleries* (King's College London, November 2013), p. 3.

2 *Evaluation Principles* (Centre for Cultural Value 2021). This publication offers useful pointers to organisations, evaluators and funders on how to apply these principles in practice when undertaking evaluation.

3 For involving participants and community partners in evaluation, see: E. Pringle, 'Evaluating *Circuit*', in M. Miller, R. Moilliet and E. Daly (eds), Circuit – *Test, Risk, Change: Young People, Youth Organisations and Galleries Working Together* (Tate and Paul Hamlyn Foundation 2019), pp. 430–5; A. Diakopoulou, 'Challenges of the *Circuit* evaluation process', in M. Miller, R. Moilliet and E. Daly (eds), Circuit – *Test, Risk, Change: Young People, Youth Organisations and Galleries Working Together* (Tate and Paul Hamlyn Foundation 2019), pp. 483–5; A. Wandersman *et al.*, 'The principles of empowerment evaluation', in D. Fetterman and A. Wandersman (eds), *Empowerment Evaluation Principles in Practice* (Guilford Press 2005), p. 27.

4 R. Moilliet *et al.*, 'Creative evaluation methods', in M. Miller, R. Moilliet and E. Daly (eds), Circuit – *Test, Risk, Change: Young People, Youth Organisations and Galleries Working Together* (Tate and Paul Hamlyn Foundation 2019), pp. 471–80.

5 For the six most common change models used in cultural organisations, see P. Bienkowski and H. McGowan, *Managing Change in Museums and Galleries* (Routledge 2021), pp. 35–8.

6 For example, the Monterey Bay Aquarium in the United States monitors the demographic shifts and its achievements and improvements regarding the diversification of its audiences and includes the analysis in an annual report (see montereybayaquarium.org).

7 For the benefits of qualitative evaluation, see P. Bienkowski and H. McGowan, *Managing Change in Museums and Galleries* (Routledge 2021), pp. 168–73.

8 See ourmuseum.org.uk/evaluation-for-change.

58 Organisational reflective practice

Reflection is an essential tool in learning, and arguably you cannot claim to be a 'learning organisation' unless you have rigorous, and regular, mechanisms for that reflection.

Reflective practice is the moment of stepping back to see what worked and what didn't; thinking about and questioning one's actions; being self-critical; and constantly learning from what went well, what could have gone better, and what might be done differently. It can be defined as the examination of reasons for acting and is the process through which an organisation learns how to work better, what needs to change and whether the changes it has already made are successful or not. It includes the skill to listen, to have an honest dialogue that is about learning not blame, and being open to challenge, alternative values and working methods.[1]

Ideally, reflection is built into everyday working practices and involves not only staff but also external voices such as community partners and other stakeholders. Indeed, one of the first reflective questions to ask is: 'who else should be involved in this discussion so that we capture all perspectives?'

However, building reflection into daily practice is still a challenge for many cultural organisations, who acknowledge its importance but struggle to find time for it. Yet the common response that it takes time out of normal working is not an excuse for not doing it: reflection should be central to normal working—otherwise, how does the organisation learn?

Some cultural practitioners, when they first try a reflective process, dismiss it as navel-gazing. But to be able to reflect honestly, without assigning blame, and genuinely listen to other perspectives and question assumptions, is a skill to be learned, like any other. It requires the development of trust, so that participants feel safe and secure in being open and honest (see Chapter 19). One might compare it with the process of raising children, with parents getting them used to talking about the 'easy' topics, slowly building trust and eventually enabling conversations about the more difficult subjects. It is an essential organisational learning process that feeds back into planning and action, and answers the key question: are there things we need to address? It is also an ongoing, iterative process that should not be limited to a discussion at the end of a project.

Too often, cultural organisations claim that they do reflect, but admit they have no formal, robust mechanisms for that reflection. In those cases, what tends to happen is that any reflection and learning sits with individuals, where it can be a valuable aid to self-awareness and processing feelings and emotions. However, if it is not shared with colleagues, it does not influence the learning of the whole organisation. For reflection to be systematic, in depth and effective, it should be formalised into identifiable mechanisms.[2]

DOI: 10.4324/9781003415886-65

The most successful approaches integrate reflection into regular meeting agendas, providing space to reflect and evaluate together, challenge assumptions and working practices and help with problem solving. Some of these can move away from a traditional meeting structure, instead encouraging a more participatory and relaxed, even playful, approach by including practical mini-workshops, Open Space and group discussions, either facilitated externally or led by a group member.

The ideal situation is when several processes overlap and encourage continual reflection and learning. Here are some models of reflection that can be built into daily practice.

Set aside five minutes at the end of each meeting to reflect on what just happened: what did you learn; how does it impact the rest of the organisation; what could you do differently; was everyone there who should have been there; were there people present who didn't need to be there and/or didn't or couldn't contribute; were all voices heard equally?

Create a regular forum for debate, including staff, community partners and peers from other cultural organisations. Use it to bring in new perspectives, share, feedback and reflect on practice. In some organisations, each 'best practice' session has a specific focus and consists of brainstorming ideas whose overall aim is to discuss different methods of working tested through various programmes, so that all staff feel confident using them.

Use formal debriefs of projects and programmes—ideally with community partners and external stakeholders—to focus on lessons learned and what the organisation is trying to achieve, learning from both positives and negatives and bringing assumptions to the surface. Sometimes referred to as a 'wash-up meeting', this is a vital part of the reflective process whose rather domestic name belies its importance.

Use regular meetings with staff and volunteers (i.e., weekly or monthly meetings) to focus not only on operational matters but to include reflection by asking questions and sharing learning: for example, in the last week/month, what went well and what could have gone better? It is important to create an atmosphere that is not about blame but about shared learning.

Empowering staff frees up time for reflection. When staff understand and buy into the strategic aims of the organisation, it allows managers to give them more freedom to make decisions within that strategic framework (see Chapter 32: Developing distributed leadership and sharing decision-making). As a result, meetings no longer need to focus as much on operational details and should become more philosophical and reflective (for structuring successful meetings, see Chapter 48).

Many cultural organisations around the world support joint reflection by creating opportunities for staff to share fresh perspectives on ways of working, which might also challenge them to think differently. This can be through regular seminars where invited practitioners present new and emerging practice, or 'cultural competency conversations' in which staff explore and discuss ideas provoked by resources such as books, papers, reports, videos or podcasts. This is an ideal way to keep abreast of new developments and encourage collaborative learning and deeper understanding throughout the organisation.

See also:

57. Evaluation as learning
60. Don't avoid uncomfortable issues
61. The importance of organisational memory—and how to sustain it

Notes

1 For an in-depth guide, see B. Bassot, *The Reflective Practice Guide: An Interdisciplinary Approach to Critical Reflection* (second edition, Routledge 2023).
2 For an evaluation of the benefits and challenges of reflective practice sessions in participatory arts, see N. Naismith, *Flourishing Lives: Reflective Practice Groups* (Baring Foundation 2022).

59 How to harness internal networks

Organisations are often poor at sharing learning and innovation, over time tending to become dominated by bureaucracy, and perhaps even compartmentalised into silos (see Chapter 30). This can stifle innovation, effective working and sharing of experiences and learning across organisational boundaries and hierarchies. A good antidote to this are internal networks, which people join of their own free will, bringing with them their talents, resources, time and enthusiasms. They can be a great way of sharing, encouraging learning from each other and producing fresh ideas.

It is important to recognise the range of different experiences typically found in a cultural organisation. Even relatively small ones employ people (in both paid and voluntary roles) with a wide range of different skills: not only acting, music or curating, but educational, marketing, design, construction, interpretation, human resources, ICT, managerial, administrative and financial. It is not uncommon for staff and volunteers in individual departments—especially in larger organisations—not to know what their colleagues in other departments really do, and to have no idea at all what knowledge, skills, experience and expertise they have. Yet, many of them will have worked outside the cultural sector in diverse environments such as schools and colleges, local and national government, and in the private sector. Similarly, trustees (or equivalent members of a governing body) have a wide range of skills and experience across the whole range of running a cultural organisation as a business and a public venue; often, they have worked in the financial, legal, visitor attraction/tourism and educational sectors and bring considerable experience of running and leading an organisation. It is useful to harness all this readily available experience and expertise.

An internal network can be defined as connecting with colleagues within your organisation even if your job does not require you to do so. Such networks are usually informal and organic, consisting of people you might work with or meet informally during working hours or socially. Research on networks at the Royal Shakespeare Company concluded that informal networks had a measurable impact on the way the organisation worked and how it adapted to change, helped build a common culture and shared values and were a major way to get things done.[1] Significantly, senior managers were central to these networks—including social ones—and therefore were seen by members of staff as accessible and approachable, rather than being remote at the top of a hierarchical pyramid.

In 2024, the Royal Shakespeare Company went further and established three, more formal 'colleague networks': Pride (LGBTIQA+), Equity (race and ethnicity) and Access (deafness, disabilities and neurodivergence). Each of these has a leadership team, with an elected chair, and a sponsor from the senior leadership team. The networks are tasked to deliver action plans that have an impact on these topics across the organisation. There are also three 'community groups': Parents and carers, Interfaith, and Menopause. These are

DOI: 10.4324/9781003415886-66

support groups providing a simple space for people to connect and share within a community (see also Chapters 32 and 33).

The advantages of internal networks are that they encourage:

- Collegiality.
- A sense of connection to the work of the organisation and insight into what others do.
- Collaboration.
- Effective working across departments and hierarchies.
- Sharing of knowledge and ideas.
- Problem solving and innovation.
- Support for individuals.
- Staff retention, because people feel connected and have a clearer picture of the organisation's values and purpose.
- Above all, a sense of inclusion: that everyone belongs and has an important role to play.

It is therefore important to create an environment within which internal networks can grow and flourish. Here are some actions leaders can take:

- Start at induction: new staff and volunteers meet colleagues across the organisation and find out what they do.
- Facilitate opportunities for staff and volunteers to meet informally.
- Organise social activities, with refreshments.
- Encourage lunchtime gatherings and informal talks.
- Make physical spaces available for informal gatherings.
- In larger or dispersed organisations, encourage informal virtual connections, such as online chat forums.
- Encourage senior managers to take part.
- Don't see internal networks as a threat.

Despite that last point, however, be aware that networks are not always positive and benign. Existing channels of communication and alliances can also be used in subversive ways, as staff use their contacts both internally and externally to lobby and try to influence. So leaders should be aware of the existing relationships between staff or between staff and a Friends group, for example, as these channels may be a route for undermining the strategic direction of an organisation.

See also:

8. The power of a personal network
19. Building trust
30. Leading a specialist workforce and the problem of silo-working
32. Developing distributed leadership and sharing decision-making
33. Staff morale and well-being
64. Strategic peer networks and mentoring

Note

1 R. Hewison, J. Holden and S. Jones, *All Together: A Creative Approach to Organisational Change* (Demos 2010), pp. 81–93, 121–4.

60 Don't avoid uncomfortable issues

Part of the skill set of a leader is to be able to deal with uncomfortable subjects and have difficult conversations (Chapter 24). For an organisation to constantly learn and work effectively, it is essential that uncomfortable or sensitive topics are acknowledged and confronted, and that staff, volunteers and external stakeholders feel free to speak openly to managers about problems without being branded disloyal or a troublemaker.

In many organisations of all kinds, including the cultural sector, there are problems that are off limits, things that cannot be said, that are too uncomfortable to raise and discuss, and so they do not get discussed; there might also be conflicts between individuals or teams. These might include a reluctance to admit failure or report inappropriate behaviour, or a tacit moratorium on voicing doubt about decisions or strategic direction (the authors regularly work with cultural organisations whose default setting is 'we're really very good at this' and do not allow staff to question this gung ho attitude, even in closed meetings).

> [F]ailure is a very difficult word for cultural professionals to use in a public context, especially when the discussion relates directly to their own projects, practices, and policies.[1]

In those cases, the organisation is not able to learn, improve or change.

Unacknowledged uncomfortable subjects or unresolved conflict lead to:

- Increased tension between staff.
- Lack of trust in leadership.
- Confusion, rumours and distortion, leading to creation of factions within the organisation, with their own agendas and territories.
- Poor morale and staff retention.
- Slow or poor decision-making.
- Stifling of creativity (which can become a particular problem for cultural organisations).
- Lack of engagement with the wider work of the organisation.

Avoiding uncomfortable topics or conflict holds an organisation back from working effectively, and confronting and dealing with such issues is a normal, healthy and inevitable part of leadership. It is the leader's role to tell the difficult, sometimes scary, story, no matter what.

DOI: 10.4324/9781003415886-67

Here are some steps you can take:

- Avoid trying to smooth over or ignore uncomfortable subjects or conflict.
- Welcome challenge and feedback, even (or especially) if it concerns your own behaviour or decisions, or those of your senior team.
- Don't close down or ignore uncomfortable conversations in meetings—as a leader, you must acknowledge that these issues exist and be seen to address them.
- Encourage anonymous feedback—for example, through a password-protected portal—which will help you spot difficult issues early on and act on them. Always report back to staff on what actions you have taken, so they know their concerns are being taken seriously; this will increase trust in the process.
- Don't be afraid to show vulnerability—this fosters an atmosphere of trust and safety and sends a strong message that you value honest feedback.
- Make mistakes and admit them—this shifts the focus from the mistake (and why it was made) to what the organisation can learn from it.
- Be transparent and firm—tell staff, governing bodies and stakeholders what they need to hear, rather than a more comfortable, sanitised version.

It is not easy to create an environment of trust, within which everyone can speak honestly about the work of the organisation. Two approaches, described in detail elsewhere in this book, can help: reflective practice and the external voice.

Reflective practice (Chapter 58) is thinking about and questioning one's actions, being self-critical, and constantly learning from what went well, what could have gone better and what might be done differently. It includes the ability to listen, to have an honest dialogue that is about learning not blame, and being open to challenge, alternative values and working methods.

The external voice (Chapter 67) is someone from outside the organisation who brings a fresh and independent perspective, encourages reflection and helps ensure that difficult subjects are addressed and not avoided. One of the most useful external voices is the critical friend. A critical friend can ask provocative questions, or bring the question into the open that others are avoiding, and ensure that everyone's voice is heard and given value. It is a balance between being positive and constructive, and teasing out the real challenges an organisation is facing but may be too nervous to acknowledge.

See also:

7. Flexibility: welcoming challenge and different perspectives
10. Modelling values and behaviour
19. Building trust
24. How to have difficult conversations and deal with uncomfortable issues

Note

1 L. Jancovich and D. Stevenson, *Failures in Cultural Participation* (Palgrave Macmillan 2023), p. 41; see also id., 'Failure seems to be the hardest word to say', *International Journal of Cultural Policy* 27/7 (2021), pp. 967–81.

61 The importance of organisational memory—and how to sustain it

'Organisational memory' is an important, and often underestimated, aspect of being an effective learning organisation. It is the memory, experience and learning of the whole organisation, and not of one individual member of staff or volunteer, one team, a group of senior managers or a governing body. It is memory, learning and experiences that are acquired, retained and passed on to current and future generations of the organisation. In effect, it is how an organisation continues to learn over a long period of time, integrating past learning into present and future work. It has an important informational role, contributing to efficient and effective decision-making and ensuring that the same mistakes are not repeated.

Particularly if you are a leader, knowing your predecessors and their contribution to the organisation's development (for good or ill) can be crucial in understanding how it came to be as it is today: how it all began and why, what the organisation has learned, how it got to here from there and where it is heading. Decisions explained and justified through the prism of the organisation's history are less likely to meet with resistance, even or especially if you are taking a radical new direction.

Cultural organisations are often poor at organisational memory. It is not easy to achieve or sustain and is increasingly difficult in an environment of funding cuts and staff changes, as people move on or are re-assigned, and roles are re-structured. The challenge is essentially how to transmit learning within the organisation over a long period, so that it sits within the whole organisation and not with one particular member of staff (whose learning is lost when they leave).

There are three stages in the organisational memory process: acquisition, retention and retrieval.[1] First, the memory or learning must be generated; then, for that learning to impact future behaviour, it must be stored in organisational memory, and later retrieved. Yet, if the organisation succeeds in developing ongoing evaluation that is truly about learning, and manages to embed reflection into daily practice (Chapters 57 and 58), then the core of these three stages can be effectively subsumed into a smooth, iterative and reflective process that becomes part of normal working (Figure 61.1).

Acquisition

Acquisition of learning in an organisation is ideally a shared process that does not sit just with individuals in isolation. It is accumulated data and feedback on past decisions and their consequences, what went well, what could have gone better, what could be done differently, the contexts and constraints of programmes, why certain decisions were made, by whom and on what assumptions. The mechanisms for generating, reflecting on and sharing such learning are detailed elsewhere in this book (Chapter 57 on evaluation as learning;

DOI: 10.4324/9781003415886-68

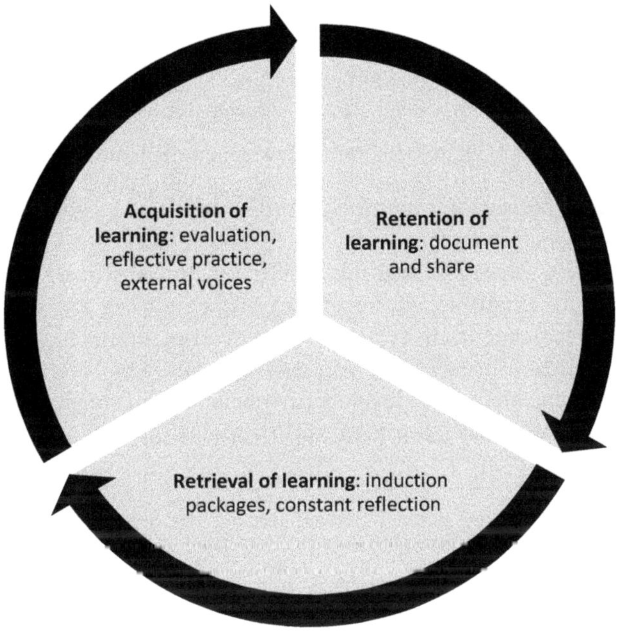

Figure 61.1 Constant learning: a reflective practice model of organisational memory in cultural organisations.

Chapter 58 on organisational reflective practice; and Chapter 67 on external voices and critical friends). These mechanisms for gathering learning and memory are particularly appropriate for cultural organisations, because they bring in diverse voices and perspectives and are able to respond to the concerns of their communities.

Retention

The learning, knowledge and memories of an organisation sit in two locations: individual people's memories and the organisation's archives (both paper/hard copy and digital). Unless the learning and knowledge are documented and shared, though, they become ephemeral and risk being lost and forgotten. So it is vital to document any learning: this can be done effectively in evaluation documents (which should be widely shared internally and externally), and in written policies, strategies, business plans and annual reports, which can be made available on a website.

It is common nowadays for staff in cultural organisations to share ideas and learning through various social media platforms, and this can be a great way to stimulate new thinking. The danger is that the messages and even the platforms themselves can be ephemeral: so make sure any new insights are documented separately and shared within the organisation, for example, in regular reflective sessions, newsletters, lunchtime talks or online blogs.

Retrieval

Probably the biggest challenge to effective organisational memory is remembering and efficiently retrieving previous learning and knowledge, so that it aids current problem solving and decision-making. In the heat and stress of the moment, you and your staff can easily forget that you have gathered previous learning that can help you with whatever problem you are facing and avoid making the same mistakes.

Two mechanisms can help this process of remembering and retrieval. First, documents such as annual reports and business plans show progression over a period of time; they are not just a form of accountability or advocacy but should be a guide to working practices and a record of the organisation's memory. Made available as part of induction packages for new staff, volunteers, governing body members and stakeholders, they can help newcomers understand why the organisation is where it is and how it has been changing.

Secondly, ideally, an organisation never stops learning but embeds previous learning into its continual development. If reflective practice becomes part of the organisation's working culture, then literally every day you will be looking back at what you have learned and exploring how it can help you develop further and do things better or differently. In this way, learning is always foregrounded and becomes an organic part of the organisation's memory.

See also:

57. Evaluation as learning
58. Organisational reflective practice
67. External voices and critical friends

Note

1 J.P. Walsh and G.R. Ungson, 'Organizational memory', *Academy of Management Review* 16/1 (1991), pp. 62–70.

Part 7

Advocacy and external networks

Advocacy and public pressures are an intrinsic part of leading a cultural organisation, but there are plenty of sources of external support available to leaders. External activities include how to advocate effectively with politicians—speaking their language and learning how to align the priorities of your organisation with theirs. External communications are about marketing your organisation, but also about anticipating what the media and public reaction might be to certain programmes, and being proactive in addressing any concerns or backlash.

External relationships include those with peers in other organisations—who can provide moral support but also potentially mentoring by a more experienced leader—and with stakeholders, some of whom might have a financial stake in your organisation, and who can be involved in strategy and planning through carefully managed consultation. There is also an increasing popularity of formal partnerships between cultural organisations, and there are practical tips on the pros and cons of these and what to look out for.

Important sources of support and of different perspectives on your organisation's work are external voices and critical friends, who come from several sources and help encourage reflection and ensure that difficult topics are addressed and not avoided. The final chapter looks at how leaders of cultural organisations can best navigate popular issues and campaigns and their political reverberations.

DOI: 10.4324/9781003415886-69

62 Advocacy with politicians

Cultural organisations rarely work in a political vacuum, even when they are not directly funded by local or national government. In order to attract funding, almost invariably they need to address priorities developed by governments or government agencies.[1] Often they need the support or facilitation of elected politicians who control or have access to resources or who can use their influence to get things done or to mediate relationships.

Where cultural organisations are funded by government, the relationship can be especially challenging, as political authority can change and expectations shift. Particular tensions can arise where cultural organisations are socially engaged and working for change with their communities—communities that politicians have been elected to represent and who claim to speak on behalf of those communities—and, in these situations, there may be an uncomfortable overlap with the political arena. Particularly in such cases, it is useful to understand the basis of political authority and what role elected members play.

The basis of political authority

The claims to authority of political leaders in democratic societies—defined as those who hold formal political authority acquired through election—can be understood as:[2]

- Democratically elected
- Representatives of the community
- Vulnerable to deselection
- Operating within, as well as influencing, a constitutional and legal framework
- Wielding authority based on a mandate officially granted by an electorate
- Requiring the consent of those they govern and serve.

In these ways, political leaders in democracies differ from other leaders such as chief executives and managers of cultural organisations, who are usually appointed by the organisation's governing body rather than elected by a wider constituency. The pressure on political leaders is that their authority is subject to challenge on a daily basis, from their political party, opposition politicians, the media, their constituents, and bodies such as charities, lobby groups and business confederations. It is such pressures that leaders of cultural organisations need to be aware of when advocating with politicians, as the immediate political response will vary according to the current political environment.

The nature of advocacy must necessarily adapt in non-democratic or authoritarian societies, and it needs to function within the bounds set by those regimes.[3] Nevertheless, case studies show that civil society can effectively lobby and advocate inside such societies,

DOI: 10.4324/9781003415886-70

despite constant threat and uncertainty. In those cases, an effective approach is a question of balance, experience and judgement: having just the right amount of acquiescence and assertiveness with non-elected politicians, a mix of private persuasion and public pressure, and the flexibility to change quickly to adapt to different situations.[4]

What are you advocating for?

One of the first rules of advocacy with politicians is to be very clear and targeted about what you are advocating for. Typical reasons that cultural organisations have for approaching politicians are:

- Funding and other resources
- Political support and championing of the organisation
- Brokering links and facilitating partnerships with other organisations, agencies, government departments or influential individuals
- Personal support/appearance through speeches, event launches or membership of governing body
- Facilitating elected members' understanding of the needs of the organisation and its communities
- Lobbying for policy change affecting the cultural organisation.

In democratic societies, it is usually illegal for non-profit or charitable organisations to engage in partisan political activity. They can take part in political activity that supports their purpose (e.g., lobbying for a particular policy change) and are permitted to engage in non-partisan voter registration and civic engagement activities, but may not give support to a political party.[5]

Advocacy strategy

Effective advocacy with politicians is a process, requiring careful research and preparation and relentless follow-up.

Before:

- Ensure clarity of your message and what you need. Be clear about your objective, its impact and cost. Choose your battles: being targeted about what you ask for is always better than a scattergun approach.
- Prepare back-up data, case studies and evidence (and why your organisation is worth supporting and investing in).
- Be clear about what action you want from a politician.
- Research and identify the best politician to approach, ideally someone who aligns with the values of your organisation and who will be the most effective in addressing your needs.
- Identify what motivates that politician—who has been elected to support a particular political platform—and as far as possible align your message with their aims and objectives, to demonstrate that your organisation can deliver against them. Your personal political views should be put to one side and must not compromise this advocacy work.
- Identify how you will approach them (telephone, letter, email, WhatsApp message and face-to-face meeting), and who is the best person from your organisation to carry this out.

- Be aware of when policy decisions will be voted on and get in touch with elected members beforehand.
- Consider coordinating with allied organisations to hold events to have conversations at a senior level with politicians (e.g., at a national level, at places like Westminster or Washington).
- Create photo opportunities for politicians.

After:

- Make yourself available for follow-up, and follow up relentlessly. Politicians are busy people with many calls on their time and diverse issues vying for their attention: make sure you push your concerns to the top of their in-tray.
- Tag elected members in your social media posts.

Engaging in regular advocacy means you are in a better position to have an impact on politicians affecting your organisation:

> Many arts leaders express frustration at having to repeat the messages about the benefits that the arts provide as local government councillors come and go and funder priorities change, but as a leader it is your job to be out there talking to funders on a continuous basis, making contacts, giving formal presentations and socializing.[6]

Ideally, develop a personal, ongoing relationship with political champions who understand and support your organisation.

See also:

12. Political antennae and horizon scanning

Notes

1 For example, the strategies of Arts Council England, funded by central government and the National Lottery, or the National Endowment for the Arts in the USA, funded annually by Congress.

2 K. Morrell and J. Hartley, 'A model of political leadership,' *Human Relations* 59/4 (2006), pp. 484–5; summarised in M. Broussine and R.F. Callahan, 'Public leadership,' in T. Bovaird and E. Loeffler (eds), *Public Management and Governance* (third edition, Routledge 2016), p. 284.

3 For politics, politicians and civil rights in non-democratic states, see A. Dadze-Arthur and C. Skelcher, 'Democratic governance: the role of politics and politicians', in T. Bovaird and E. Loeffler (eds), *Public Management and Governance* (third edition, Routledge 2016), pp. 227–9.

4 See case studies in M. Grömping and J.C. Teets (eds), *Lobbying the Autocrat: The Dynamics of Policy Advocacy in Non-democracies* (University of Michigan Press 2023).

5 M. Avner, *The Lobbying and Advocacy Handbook for Nonprofit Organizations* (second edition, Fieldstone Alliance 2013) gives excellent practical advice, albeit within a US political and legal context.

6 R. Hewison and J. Holden, *The Cultural Leadership Handbook: How to Run a Creative Organization* (Routledge 2011), p. 126.

63 External communications as advocacy

It is no accident that this chapter on external communications is in Part 7 on advocacy, and not in Part 3 on leading a sustainable organisation, alongside internal communications (Chapter 31). All external communications are about advocacy—about how you want your organisation to be perceived by the outside world. They are not simply a means of marketing or sharing information about programmes and events but are an opportunity to reflect your organisational values and culture, to ensure that everyone knows what you are and what you do, particularly if you are a socially engaged organisation committed to, and working towards, equity, diversity and inclusion.

The key theme of this chapter is: use all external communications to champion your values and hammer home that message of inclusivity, to mould the way your organisation is perceived. This will help different audiences understand what you are about, build trust and connections and assist in achieving your aims and objectives. Make external communications the equivalent of standing on the rooftop of your building (if you have one) and proclaiming to everyone that your organisation is all about diversity and inclusion. Don't shy away from repeating the message constantly and consistently.

The difference between internal and external communications

External communications have different audiences and messages from internal communications. Internal communications are mostly about knowledge sharing, ensuring that everyone in the organisation has the appropriate information to do their job effectively and is on the same page. Nevertheless, you should think carefully if there is to be a difference between the information given to staff and volunteers and that provided to an external body. For example, in situations where internal structural change is being discussed, and where staff may be feeling anxious about change and their jobs, it is difficult to keep matters confidential. In these circumstances, beware of betraying confidential assessments to an external body—never tell a stakeholder anything that is not readily available elsewhere.[1]

Ideally, you should develop a strategy to cover both internal and external communications, to ensure that all communications are consistent, set the right tone and send the message you want to send. This reduces the risk of damaging or ineffective communication: using the wrong tone or word can send the wrong message and could harm your organisation's reputation.

DOI: 10.4324/9781003415886-71

External communications: who, what and how

External communications are the processes used to communicate with people and entities outside your organisation. These include visitors, supporters, Friends' groups, your communities, the wider public, tourists, funders, sponsors, partners and the media. Typical topics that cultural organisations communicate externally about are their impact, programmes, projects and events, news and announcements and annual reviews. The methods of communication, which have altered drastically in recent years, are now mostly through a website, email, social media, videos and podcasts, and blog posts, but still include press releases to the mainstream media, brochures and newsletters, and—targeted at individuals—letters and telephone.

As the section below explains, it is essential to tailor the communication mechanism (e.g., a social media platform or a hard-copy brochure) to your audience: one size does not fit all. It may be simpler and cheaper to base external communication largely on Facebook or other social media posts or e-newsletters, but these won't reach everyone, and have the potential to exclude certain groups and communities (see Chapter 46: Digital inclusivity).[2]

Six steps towards a strategy

There are lots of examples of communications strategies in cultural organisations available online, and it is easy to search and find one to use as a template and adapt to your own needs. This section focuses primarily on the thinking, preparation and actions that underpin a communications strategy, that require careful research and consideration relating to your organisation's environment and audiences and that cannot be cut and pasted from another source.

- *Know your audience and tailor your communications*: Communications needs or preferences will vary with different segments of your audience; for example, between funders and your communities, or between ages or genders. You need to know what those communication needs/preferences are and choose the appropriate communication method or platform for each one.[3]
- *Involve your communities and partners*: To ensure you are reaching everyone in the most appropriate way, ask your communities and partners what communications or social media platforms their groups use and prefer. Ask how you can best target and reach those groups—in some cases, you may find that community partners acting as intermediaries is a better solution than direct communication (but be aware of community 'gatekeepers' who control the flow of information to their communities, which has both advantages and disadvantages).
- *Establish the tone of your external communications*: How do you want to be perceived as an organisation? Use external communications as a way of emphasising, spreading and repeating your message. Try to make your style and voice unique, rather than repeating overused platitudes that are not distinctive.
- *Establish clear responsibility for communications*: Who in your organisation is responsible for what sort of communications? Everyone should be aware of the principles, strategy and overarching message, and elements like brand guidelines and use of logos, from

members of the governing body/trustees and leadership team to staff and volunteers. Most of this can be covered during an induction process. Trustees—brought in from the outside for limited terms and with particular skills, knowledge and experience—can sometimes be loose cannons, and it is important that you ensure they promote your organisation through consistent external communications, rather than voice their own opinions. Either they should refer complex or difficult questions to the director/CEO or the relevant member of staff, or be given a prepared statement on any sensitive topic that they can use in a tight spot with staff or the media.

- *Anticipate adverse reactions and be proactive*: Certain programmes or actions by cultural organisations, particularly those committed to equity, diversity and inclusion, can cause controversy and a media backlash.[4] If possible, try to anticipate adverse reactions beforehand; if you wait until the backlash, you will be on the back foot, firefighting negative headlines. Prepare briefings for the media *before* the programme launch, explaining why it is within your remit and necessary to achieve your organisation's aims and objectives, and what you hope to achieve.
- *Evaluate your communications regularly to ensure you are reaching everyone effectively*: Use feedback to assess the reach and impact of your external communications. Ask your community partners and gather statistics from your social media platforms.

See also:

10. Modelling roles and behaviour
31. Internal communications
65. How to involve stakeholders
68. How to respond to popular causes and campaigns and survive 'culture wars'

Notes

1 P. Bienkowski and H. McGowan, *Managing Change in Museums and Galleries* (Routledge 2021), pp. 129–31.

2 For the problems of a 'digital divide' and social exclusion, see C. Bellamy and D. Campbell, 'Digital technology, information policy and social media in public services', in T. Bovaird and E. Loeffler (eds), *Public Management and Governance* (third edition, Routledge 2016), pp. 134–47.

3 For example, in 2022, 42 per cent of the world's population used social media—which means that the majority did not. 86 per cent of 18–29-year-olds used Facebook, but only 34 per cent of 65+-year-olds; 38 per cent of 18–29-year-olds used X/Twitter (the largest age demographic), but only 7 per cent of 65+-year-olds; and over 70 per cent of X/Twitter users were male (source: Khoros 2022 Social Media Demographics Guide—khoros.com/resources/social-media-demographics-guide).

4 For example, decolonisation research by the National Trust in the United Kingdom, which came under attack from the media and right-wing politicians (for a brief case study, see Chapter 68).

64 Strategic peer networks and mentoring

The three levels of networking, with different aims and objectives, were defined in Chapter 8—personal, internal (or operational, see Chapter 59) and strategic. This chapter focuses on the third of these, strategic peer networking. This is not really about the individual leader's personal and professional development, but concerns the strategic context and organisational environment, cultivating contacts through which a leader looks to the future direction of the organisation, imagining and creating new opportunities. This sort of networking has been succinctly described as

Figuring out future priorities and challenges; getting stakeholder support for them.[1]

Understood that way, strategic networking is an essential part of forward-thinking leadership. Its purpose is to:

- Create new opportunities
- Solve problems
- Build relationships and strategic alliances
- Explore new ideas
- Marshal support and resources
- Influence others to take action

As a first step, it is useful to think about the scale at which you are networking: is it local, regional, national, international or a mix of these?[2] Networking takes time and effort, so think strategically about the context of your organisation, and develop shared goals with peers, even if you are in different sectors. Be realistic: international networks and peers can seem impressive, even exotic (and with today's video conferencing technologies such international networking has never been easier),[3] but, unless you are a large organisation with a wide remit, often peers closer to home understand your context better and can offer more practical opportunities for mutual support, influencing and strategic alliances.[4]

DOI: 10.4324/9781003415886-72

Who are your peers?

External peers can be divided into three types—community partners, other organisations and universities—each of which offers something distinctive.

Community partners who work with a cultural organisation should be regarded as peers and not as outsiders. They bring the skills and experiences of their own environments and workplaces but, as partners, they have also developed an understanding of the challenges facing the organisation and are a valuable source of peer support and learning. If you don't have formal community partners, reach out to local community groups and umbrella agencies, and attend local meetings and events. Being seen as part of the community is key to local networking and is increasingly regarded as essential by stakeholders and funders.

Many community partners work in community organisations and agencies in the voluntary and charitable sectors, often operating in the same environment as the cultural organisation, and so are an excellent source of strategic alliances. This is a fast-changing sector, always vulnerable to even slight financial and social fluctuations, and so these agencies tend to be extremely adaptable and fleet of foot in how they operate. They are used to responding to events rapidly, in more streamlined and less traditional ways, and have much to teach cultural organisations about, for example, diversity and up-to-date methods of recruitment, relying more on competency-based frameworks than on formal qualifications. Such approaches are essential if cultural organisations are to diversify their staff to better reflect the make-up of their communities.

A good way of sharing this learning is for community partners to deliver training to staff, especially on how to work with more diverse audiences, for example, up-skilling staff on awareness of homelessness, unemployment, disabilities, mental health problems or substance misuse. This can have a massive impact on how the organisation is perceived by its communities and stakeholders.

Peers in other cultural organisations, or even organisations in a different sector, will often have had similar experiences to you, and you may have stakeholders and funders in common. Don't be shy about picking their brains and sharing experiences, and perhaps even setting up a mentoring relationship (see below and Chapter 67 for peers as external voices). Contact them, visit them, invite them to give talks to your staff, volunteers and board about their experiences, read their blogs and reports and listen to their conference presentations. The learning will almost certainly be reciprocal, and a longer-term networking relationship may well develop.

Many *universities* have courses on cultural studies in some form, and are natural partners and peers for cultural organisations—many of their academic staff have worked in a cultural organisation at some point in their careers. Much of the research that university academics working in the cultural sphere undertake and publish is heavily informed by theory and covers wider issues such as social justice or diversity and is often less applicable to the day-to-day practice of cultural organisations. However, they can be interested in longer-term research on cultural programmes—often across a group of organisations—especially if there is potential for learning that is innovative, transformative, has lessons for the cultural sector as a whole and has a wider societal impact.[5] Several universities also run research centres that carry out action research with cultural organisations, often concerned with change, experimentation, the value of culture, audience attitudes, diversity, and health and well-being.[6] University academics can therefore offer different perspectives on a cultural organisation's work, often placing it within a wider societal context and asking challenging questions about why you are doing what you are doing.

Peer networks

Cultural leadership development courses such as Clore Leadership and Oxford Cultural Leaders aim to encourage more effective leadership and innovative practice and encourage each cohort to build upon friendships created at their residential sessions and sustain them through peer networks afterwards to support development beyond the formal courses. These form confidential, safe and supportive forums to share experiences and learning and provide personal support for sometimes less experienced leaders. For example, the Cultural Leadership Programme (CLP) Network brings together a wide range of cultural leaders to communicate online. A similar international peer network is Of/By/For All, which helps connect cultural organisations with their communities in effective ways, and offers an online programme that provides tools and coaching.[7] Museum Hue in the United States and Museum Detox in the United Kingdom are networks for people of colour who work in the museum, heritage and cultural sectors, and are particularly focused on addressing issues of diversity and equality.

Mentoring

Mentoring can be understood as a form of peer support and networking, through guidance, advice and support from someone with more experience. Mentoring and coaching are different. Mentoring is a non-commercial relationship that usually helps with longer-term development with a focus on the future, whereas a coach is paid to help with shorter-term problems or moments of particular difficulty.

The origin of the term 'mentor' helps to define its meaning and purpose. In Homer's *Odyssey*, probably composed between 750 and 650 BCE, Mentor is left in charge of the household on Ithaca when Odysseus leaves to fight the Trojan War. On several occasions, the goddess Athena appears to Odysseus's son, Telemachus, in the guise of Mentor to offer advice—hence the idea of a 'mentor' as a protective, guiding and supportive figure who acts as a wise and trusted counsellor.[8] Today's mentor shares their experiences, provides regular support, feedback, practical tips, an external perspective, helps with pitfalls to avoid and with problem solving and also challenges you to think innovatively and possibly outside your comfort zone.[9]

A good local source of business mentors is a chamber of commerce, a form of local business network found all over the world. Many countries also have specific organisations that act as a bridge between the business and arts sectors, and which broker appropriate mentoring relationships. For example, there are independent Arts and Business teams for England, Scotland, Wales and Northern Ireland; Americans for the Arts in the United States; Business/Arts in Canada; and Creative Partnerships Australia. The role of these bridge organisations is to broker and strengthen partnerships between business and arts organisations, to source business people for the boards of arts organisations and to host events at which arts and business professionals can meet to exchange ideas, address challenges and share best practices. Although some cultural professionals may consider their members too commercially minded, many cultural organisations lack business skills.

To ensure a beneficial mentoring relationship, both parties must have a clear understanding of the process and shared expectations of the relationship, for example, how often you meet, what sort of support and advice you might expect, and a mutual commitment to confidentiality.

See also:

8. The power of a personal network
59. How to harness internal networks
66. Developing partnerships
67. External voices and critical friends

Notes

1 See table in H. Ibarra and M.L. Hunter, 'How leaders create and use networks', *Harvard Business Review* (January 2007).
2 L. Varbanova, *Strategic Management in the Arts* (Routledge 2013), p. 131.
3 For a case study on ICOM (the International Council of Museums), a global network of institutions and museum professionals, see L. Varbanova, *Strategic Management in the Arts* (Routledge 2013), pp. 73–8. ICOM is a classic case of an international network that has little impact on the majority of museums with a local or regional remit, and which has minimal influence on local stakeholders.
4 Performing and visual arts organisations, especially, can earn substantial revenue from international activity such as touring. However, in England, international projects more than halved between 2018/19 and 2021/22, due to the complexities of the United Kingdom leaving the European Union and the COVID-19 pandemic; see L. Parker, B. Corriette and R. Naylor, *International Activity Supported by Arts Council England* (Arts Council England/BOP Consulting 2023).
5 For example, research on decolonisation at the National Trust: S.-A. Huxtable, C. Fowler, C. Kefalas and C. Slocombe (eds), *Interim Report on the Connections between Colonialism and Properties now in the Care of the National Trust, including Links with Historic Slavery* (National Trust 2020).
6 For example, the Institute for Cultural Practices at the University of Manchester, or the Research Centre for Museums and Galleries at the University of Leicester.
7 ofbyforall.org.
8 A. Roberts, in 'The origins of the term mentor', *History of Education Society Bulletin* 64 (1999), pp. 313–29, notes that the word 'mentor' was first recorded in the English language in 1750 due to the popularity of François Fénélon's *Les aventures de Télémaque*, published in 1699, and its many reprints and translations.
9 D. Clutterbuck, *Everyone Needs a Mentor* (fifth edition, Chartered Institute of Personnel and Development 2014).

65 How to involve stakeholders

Stakeholders and cultural organisations

The first usage of the term 'stakeholder' was in 1963 in an internal memo of the Stanford Research Institute, where it was defined as a member of

> groups without whose support the organization would cease to exist.[1]

The term has since developed to mean more broadly a person, group or institution with an interest or concern in an organisation, or affected by it, though not necessarily in financial or governance terms. Irrespective of the type of organisation, its sustainability and success depend on its ability to meet stakeholders' interests and aims. But cultural organisations are distinctive in that they often have overlapping objectives which can be local, regional, national or international, and which appeal to the interests of many different stakeholders and types of stakeholders. Cultural organisations tend to be embedded in their communities and are open to many varied external partnerships, and therefore may have a multiplicity of stakeholders whose interests need to be taken into account. It can sometimes be complex to find ways forward that are acceptable to all.[2]

In practice, not all stakeholders are always benign and supportive or necessarily have aims and objectives aligned with those of the cultural organisation. It may be that the interests and aims of some stakeholders will need to be prioritised over those of others. For example, in performing arts, there may be conflict between artistic excellence and innovation, entertainment, audience numbers and income.[3]

The first step is stakeholder analysis, to identify and evaluate your stakeholders and prioritise those most crucial to your success:

- What are the nature and level of their interest in your organisation?
- What is their power to affect the organisation (positively or negatively)?
- What are the mutual benefits to the stakeholder and the cultural organisation?
- What are the relations between stakeholders and are their aims complementary or in competition?
- What is the potential for collaboration between stakeholders?

DOI: 10.4324/9781003415886-73

Who are my stakeholders?

The nature of stakeholders will vary depending on your organisation, as will the level of their interest, motivation, potential involvement and impact. There are critical or key stakeholders, whose support (usually financial or political) is needed for the organisation to exist and to continue to function. Some stakeholders will have a financial stake in cultural organisations, sites and buildings and may even ultimately own them.[4] Some may be sponsors or funders for particular projects or developments, or even core funders of an organisation over many years, such as Arts Council England. Some, like the National Lottery Heritage Fund in the United Kingdom, which grant-aids a wide range of cultural projects, will ask that the receiving organisation signs a contract not only for the duration of the project, but for many years ahead. Others, like the Art Fund, would want a contract if they grant-aided the purchase of a particular object by a museum, to ensure it would not be disposed of in future without consulting them, and potentially paying back the grant monies.

Other stakeholders may not have a direct financial stake in your organisation, but often their support is necessary to demonstrate your reach and impact and to unlock financial or political resources. Community groups, small organisations or individuals might not have a lot of capacity or resources on their own, but collectively they can generate interest and momentum and attract investment and funding.

Here are some typical stakeholders of cultural organisations:

- Investors, funders, donors and sponsors
- Financial institutions
- Private developers
- Cultural policymakers
- Politicians and governments (local and national)
- Your town, city or region
- Audience members (both in-person and virtual)
- Staff and volunteers
- Governing bodies
- Trades unions
- Artists and scholars
- Friends' organisations and corporate members
- Learned societies which may have founded your organisation
- Local residents
- Community members and organisations
- Indigenous/First Nations peoples
- Third-sector agencies
- Neighbourhood associations
- Local schools
- Special interest groups
- Creative organisations

Why engage stakeholders?

At the most basic level, you need to know what each stakeholder wants from your organisation, how their priorities align with yours and what you can do for each other. Do they know what you really do and how it can impact them (and vice versa)? Many cultural organisations find that simple steps like having an open day, or giving stakeholders and potential partners tours of their buildings and activities, especially 'back-of-house', can be a real eye-opener. The opposite is also true: staff tours outside your building can give insights into what is going on in the community.[5]

Once you have that basic understanding of a stakeholder's interests and motivations, continued engagement with them is an ongoing process, which:

- Improves communication between parties and helps the organisation understand who is affected by your programmes.
- Creates and maintains support for the organisation.
- Helps develop shared priorities.
- Gathers information for the organisation.
- Helps find solutions to challenges.
- Reduces the potential for conflict and helps you to identify groups who may not support your activities and to understand their motives.
- Ensures all voices are regularly heard.
- Can set the stage for broader and deeper engagement, especially with communities.

How to engage stakeholders

Once you have carried out your stakeholder analysis, the next step is to decide what level of communication and engagement is appropriate for each stakeholder. This will probably vary according to the level of their impact on your organisation—it is unlikely that one size will fit all. Does a particular stakeholder need to be persuaded, expect to be consulted or actively engaged in your work, or merely kept informed? If practical, ask what their communication preferences are.

There are essentially four models of stakeholder engagement to choose from: lobbying, information, consultation and shared decision-making. In all four, the key is effective communication. It is vital that the parameters of the relationship are clearly established at the start and are fully understood by all parties. Particularly where financial support is concerned, there is considerable scope for stakeholders to believe they can influence the direction, style and programming of the organisation. So if you are involving them in consultations or programmes, it must be clear that meddling and interference is not part of the involvement once the programme has been agreed by the governing body.

Lobbying

Aimed particularly at influential policymakers and funders—often governments or government-funded agencies such as Arts Council England—this activity stresses the contribution of the organisation to the stakeholder's aims and objectives in order to elicit support or advocate for a change of policy priorities. It is usually a key role of leaders—CEOs or trustees—occasionally supported by commissioned public relations companies (see Chapter 62: Advocacy with politicians).[6]

Information

This model of engagement is a simple one-way flow of information from the organisation to the stakeholder. It can be achieved through newsletters, blogs, updates on social media and reports (some less involved stakeholders will be satisfied to receive just an annual report). If a stakeholder is working with you on a particular programme, make sure that the information sent relates to that programme, rather than being something generic.

Consultation

This model involves two-way dialogue between the organisation and the stakeholder through some form of consultation, via formal meetings, surveys, interviews, workshops, focus groups or a mix of these. This process can also include multiple stakeholders and is an opportunity to bring together diverse stakeholders to explore a shared vision.

Managing expectations of a consultation process is important. It is vital to provide clarity at the outset about the role of consultees, and who will make any final decision. Consultations can spark conflict when there is lack of clarity about decision-making, as participants might feel they have not been listened to. If the process is just about your organisation seeking the views of its stakeholders, but any final decision is to be taken by itself (or by its governing body), you must be transparent about this from the start.

Shared decision-making

This involves active engagement by stakeholders in the decision-making processes of the organisation, extending from programme development and delivery to wider strategy.[7] Usually, this level of engagement relates to community groups and partners, including Indigenous/ First Nations peoples, rather than financial or political stakeholders, but could involve schools, third-sector agencies, special interest groups or partner creative organisations.

Mechanisms for shared decision-making include workshops, forums and panels. Especially when bringing together diverse groups and individuals, identify beforehand who should be in the room and who is excluded and why. The group should agree up front if decisions are to be by consensus or some form of voting.[8]

Involvement in wider strategy can be through stakeholders sitting on a trustee board, advisory panels or taking part in strategy workshops with staff.[9] Tyne & Wear Archives & Museums, a large multi-site service in north-east England, experimented with an annual People's Parliament, bringing together a wide range of people to find out more about the needs of communities and how it might respond to these and involve people in key decisions. A similar approach is citizens' assemblies at the Bundeskunsthalle in Bonn and SKD in Dresden: comprising about 30 people over four days, selected by lottery to be broadly representative of local communities, these explored how the organisations could become more democratic and relevant. Glasgow Museums ran a regular Creative Café for community partners and stakeholders, a discussion forum to share and collaboratively generate ideas to develop programmes and potentially be involved in delivery. Ongoing communication in this sort of active engagement is vital to keep everyone informed and on board, and many cultural organisations use online platforms to connect with stakeholders, such as Teamwork that can hold emails, reports and calendars, and capture everything in one place.

See also:

12. Political antennae and horizon scanning
20. Understanding users' needs and agendas
26. Finding common purpose

28. Balancing conflicting priorities
32. Developing distributed leadership and sharing decision-making
44. Building a participatory organisation

Notes

1 R.E. Freeman and D.I. Reed, 'Stockholders and stakeholders: a new perspective on corporate governance', *California Management Review* 25/3 (1983), pp. 88–106.

2 For stakeholders in cultural and not-for-profit organisations, see particularly L. Varbanova, *Strategic Management in the Arts* (Routledge 2013), pp. 100–01; M.C. Giorgino, 'Stakeholder engagement in cultural organizations: an explorative study on participatory theatre', *International Journal of Business and Management* 11/9 (2016), pp. 21–35; P. Dziurski, 'Stakeholder management in cultural organizations', *Cultural Management: Science and Education* 1/2 (2017), pp. 65–78.

3 S. Boerner and J. Jobst, 'Stakeholder management and program planning in German public theatres', *Nonprofit Management and Leadership* 22/1 (2011), p. 76.

4 For example, in the case of local authorities in the United Kingdom where trusts operate their sites, so they are in effect a client, or some sites will have a private landowner from which a cultural organisation operates, for example, Creswell Crags Museum and Heritage Centre in England.

5 See the video at ourmuseum.org.uk/staff-tours.

6 L. Varbanova, *Strategic Management in the Arts* (Routledge 2013), p. 131.

7 In museums, increasingly there is shared decision-making with stakeholders around repatriation, deaccessioning and decolonisation.

8 For practical tips, see L. White, *Shared Decision-making: Tips, Tools and Case Studies from Creative People and Places Projects* (MB Associates 2017), pp. 25–39.

9 P. Bienkowski, *Our Museum: What Happened Next? A Review and Further Learning Two Years On* (Paul Hamlyn Foundation 2018), p. 24.

66 Developing partnerships

A partnership is a way of doing something that you can't do alone, or that you can do better, differently or more economically in formal collaboration with another organisation. It enables organisations to make the most of each other's strengths and resources, combining their efforts and expertise to achieve greater, and often more cost-effective, impact. This might be through sharing costs and resources (including staff), adding expertise or skills that you don't have, doing something at a larger scale or with wider reach and impact, or to leverage stakeholder and financial support. All partners have resources and assets, and an effective partnership creates a resource pool that every partner can draw on. In recent years, concerns about future financial sustainability have prompted many cultural organisations to consider formal partnerships to enhance resilience. Some worry about loss of identity and independence, but a partnership is not a merger.[1] It can range from something focused on a particular area of work or even one specific programme, to a broader strategic alliance that shares staff and resources.

Who are your partners?

There are various natural strategic partners for cultural organisations.

Other cultural organisations

Usually located in the same city, town or region, such partnerships can share staff and resources, co-produce programmes and undertake joint fund-raising, marketing, audience development or administrative activities like IT, payroll, human resources and health and safety. The advantage is that organisations working in a related field do not duplicate basic tasks and can save considerable amounts of money.

In Tennessee, four cultural organisations located near one another in Chattanooga formed a cost-saving consortium, comprising the Tennessee Aquarium, the Creative Discovery Museum, the Hunter Museum of American Art and the Chattanooga History Center. The consortium shared services in five main areas of operation: human resources, finance and accounting, IT, marketing and joint retail purchasing.[2]

A similar UK example is the Cumbria Museum Consortium, a group of three individual organisations, operating six museum, gallery and cultural sites in north-west England, that are treated as a single 'major partner museum' by Arts Council England for the purposes of funding.[3] Such approaches are becoming more common to combat reduced income and rising costs. A group of major theatres in Scotland commissioned a report that recommended close collaboration through the creation of a new company, as well as sharing services.[4]

DOI: 10.4324/9781003415886-74

Other sectors

These can include tourism, health and social care, environmental and religious organisations. Such partnerships can help with marketing and audience development, wider reach and impact (addressing issues of importance to stakeholders) and provision of space. For example, in Massachusetts, West Concord Union Church, empty most days and with high maintenance costs, partnered with Concord Conservatory of Music, which needed space for teaching, administration and performance.[5]

Community organisations

Agencies in the voluntary and charitable sectors make excellent strategic partners for cultural organisations. They have their own wide community networks and can involve their clients in cultural programmes and volunteering (see also Chapter 64 for community partners as peers). Amgueddfa Cymru/National Museum Wales works strategically with organisations across Wales in the public, voluntary and charitable sectors, including agencies covering homelessness, unemployment, disability, ethnic minorities, substance misuse, mental health issues and working with non-English speakers.[6] Such partnerships can impact on different roles in an organisation, like making joint funding bids, involving community partners in the development of policies and programmes, having community voices on the governing body, or community partners delivering training to staff on topics where they have more expertise—for example, working with audiences with mental health problems, or non-English speakers. For what makes effective partnerships with communities, see Chapter 44.

Education sector

Cultural organisations have partnered across the whole range of the education sector. In higher education, partnerships involve:[7]

- Research—producing or commissioning cultural research alongside academic staff
- Teaching—running workshops, co-developing degrees and acting as mentors in universities
- Placements—hosting students for work experience or collaborative doctoral work
- Public and community engagement—such as co-producing festivals
- Collaborative programming/commissioning—developing and curating exhibitions and performances
- Artist/company-in-residence—embedding the individual or organisation within the university with access to space and resources, or alternatively placing a researcher-in-residence within a cultural space.

For example, Northumbria University in Newcastle has partnerships with many different cultural organisations—museums and galleries, a writing development agency, a theatre and a cinema—for collaborative teaching and learning, reports on impact and public engagement.[8]

Partnerships between cultural organisations and young people's education are particularly popular. In the United Kingdom, Local Cultural Education Partnerships (LCEPs) support children and young people to access cultural experiences, with partners coming from the cultural, education, youth, health, criminal justice, voluntary and creative sectors, alongside local government. Cultural organisations act as 'bridge organisations' connecting the cultural and education sectors to develop a network of cultural provision.[9] They can also have a partnership role in responding to crisis situations, such as gallery education linking with schools creatively to foster communication and connection of refugee Ukrainian school-age children forced out of their homes by the 2022 Russian invasion and now living in Poland and helping to form a bridge with Polish children.[10]

What to look out for when considering a partnership[11]

- What will be the benefits, and how will you measure the success of the partnership? Will it achieve a positive synergy—a better result than acting alone?
- Are your potential partner's goals compatible with yours? (They don't have to be the same goals, as long as they don't conflict)
- Will the partnership be equal, or lop-sided, with more benefits accruing to one partner than others?
- A certain amount of decision-making and accountability will become shared, so you will need to build a relationship of trust with the partner, and agree in advance on a mechanism for shared decision-making.
- What will be the impact on your staff, in terms of their roles and responsibilities? If the partnership is about saving money and sharing resources, including staff, some of your staff might be worried about increased workloads on the one hand, or losing their job on the other (see Chapter 34 for how to deal with restructures, redundancies and cuts).
- Do you share values and ethos with the potential partner, for example, in your commitment to diversity, inclusion and transparency?
- Are you in competition with your partner(s) for the same audiences?
- Does the potential partner have a positive reputation that will enhance the partnership?
- What is the legal status of your potential partner? Partnerships with public sector organisations, especially those run by local government, can involve multiple and time-consuming layers of official review and approval—but might also offer greater reach into and impact on the community.
- What is the financial situation of your potential partner—and do the finances work to mutual advantage? Will it save you money, or cost extra? How financially secure are they, especially if they are receiving grants and may be administering the finances for your joint project?
- Will the partnership be formalised through a contract or written agreement (e.g., a consortium), or be looser in form (e.g., a network)?[12] If sharing staff and other resources, any agreement needs to be explicit about costs and time allocation.
- Partnership arrangements should not be indefinite but finite, ideally for a set number of years, potentially renewable. Make sure there is a 'get out' clause, so that if the partnership is not working for you, you can leave relatively easily.

Finally, a note of caution. Partnerships can be extremely useful, but they are not the answer to everything, and at times can be an inefficient use of time and resources and might deflect you from your organisation's mission. It takes time, money and capacity to develop an effective partnership. Research reveals that, for many cultural organisations with limited capacity, the perceived cost and administration of partnership arrangements for staff and volunteers outweigh the benefits.[13] Like marriage, think very carefully before committing to a partnership and be prepared to:

'Say "no" to partnerships, where they don't help!'[14]

See also:

64. Strategic peer networks and mentoring

Notes

1 For mergers, see L. Varbanova, *Strategic Management in the Arts* (Routledge 2013), p. 128.
2 T. Wolf and G. Antoni, *More than the Sum of its Parts: Collaboration and Sustainability in Arts Education* (National Guild for Community Arts Education 2012), p. 24.
3 Another UK example, which reveals some of the problems of these sorts of partnerships, was Cornwall Museums Partnership, a consortium of eight organisations set up in 2015 to provide strategic support to Cornish museums. This closed in 2023 because members felt that museums would have greater flexibility to develop and promote their own work by receiving funding directly rather than through allocation via a consortium.
4 *Disappearing Act? A Data-led Review and Recommendations for Urgent Actions to Safeguard a Credible Producing Theatre Sector in Scotland* (Data Culture Change 2023).
5 T. Wolf and G. Antoni, *More than the Sum of its Parts: Collaboration and Sustainability in Arts Education* (National Guild for Community Arts Education 2012), p. 18.
6 S. Burge, O. Rhys and N. Williams, 'Democratic culture: participation at St Fagans National History Museum', in K. McSweeney and J. Kavanagh (eds.), *Museum Participation: New Directions for Audience Collaboration* (MuseumsEtc 2016), pp. 417–20.
7 E. Wilson and E. Hopkins, 'Ways of working with universities revealed', *Arts Professional* (25 January 2022).
8 K. Shaw and C. Malcolm, 'Arts and higher education: a successful partnership in action', *Arts Professional* (21 October 2021).
9 Arts Council England, *Research into Local Cultural Education Partnerships* (report by BOP Consulting, July 2019). For a different type of US example, T. Wolf and G. Antoni cite the case study of a ballet company that worked with teachers on a curriculum, using dance to help children with mathematical concepts and to develop imagination skills: see *More than the Sum of its Parts: Collaboration and Sustainability in Arts Education* (National Guild for Community Arts Education 2012), p. 12.
10 The Bridge (*Most*) project at U-jazdowski Castle Centre for Contemporary Art in Warsaw (see u-jazdowski.pl).
11 This section draws partly from the questions posed by L Varbanova, *Strategic Management in the Arts* (Routledge 2013), pp. 128–9; and T. Wolf and G. Antoni, *More than the Sum of its Parts: Collaboration and Sustainability in Arts Education* (National Guild for Community Arts Education 2012), p. 22. For the pros and cons of partnerships, see T. Bovaird and E.-H. Klijn, 'Partnership working across public and private sectors', in T. Bovaird and E. Loeffler (eds.), *Public Management and Governance* (third edition, Routledge 2016), pp. 238–44.
12 For example, Sydney Cultural Network was formed in 2017 against a backdrop of cuts to cultural funding. Its 26 members comprise arts, educational and cultural organisations, with a view to enhancing collaboration and to create a platform for joint programming, shared resources, professional development and knowledge exchange. For a European network example, the RuhrKunstMuseen (Ruhr Art Museums), a network representing 20 museums in 14 cities around the Ruhr region of Germany, enables collaboration in collections, exhibitions, education, public art, politics, marketing and public relations. For a typology of partnership forms, with equal/unequal and tightly/loosely formulated types of relation, see T. Bovaird and E.-H. Klijn, 'Partnership working across public and private sectors', in T. Bovaird and E. Loeffler (eds.), *Public Management and Governance* (third edition, Routledge 2016), p. 237.
13 Source: UK Heritage Pulse survey on organisational partnerships, April 2023.
14 T. Bovaird and E.-H. Klijn, 'Partnership working across public and private sectors', in T. Bovaird and E. Loeffler (eds.), *Public Management and Governance* (third edition, Routledge 2016), p. 246.

67 External voices and critical friends

An external voice means involving people from outside the organisation in open and honest conversations about your work, in order to bring fresh and independent perspectives to bear, to encourage reflection and to help ensure that difficult topics are addressed and not avoided.

The external voice can come from several sources, including peers, critical friends, funders, evaluators, community partners and artists. Although they all bring different perspectives, each of these external voices offers something specific, and because of that you should have different expectations of their roles. Think about your needs as an organisation and choose the most effective external voice to meet those needs—is it just a talking shop, or will it have a practical application? What is it that a particular external voice can do, and how can it help your organisation? External voices are a good way of influencing a governing body, which is often more open to external perspectives about the work of its organisation.

Critical friends—fresh perspectives and difficult questions

A critical friend is a trusted person outside the organisation who takes the time to fully understand the context of the work and the outcomes that the organisation wants to achieve, asks difficult questions or brings questions into the open that others are avoiding, provides additional data, evidence or lessons from elsewhere that give a fresh perspective and offers a critique of work. It is a balance between being positive and constructive, and teasing out the real challenges an organisation is facing. It is about listening to what is said, and what is not said, and being alert to the significance of the body language of the participants, which often can be more revealing than words. Crucially, it is about ensuring that everyone's voice is heard and given value and that no-one dominates a conversation or tries to shut it down (including the leader).

In most cases, a critical friend will be commissioned by the organisation to help with a particular piece of work. Although, in principle, peers or community partners can be critical friends, they do need to understand the role and have the skills and experience to carry it out effectively—and they may be too close to the organisation to be properly objective. In some cases, funders and independent evaluators can also be critical friends, although the relationship with funders can be complex because an organisation may not feel able to be totally honest, as its responses may affect current or future grants. Generally, the most effective critical friends are externally commissioned consultants with a wide experience of different organisations who can take a clear and independent viewpoint to assist you.

DOI: 10.4324/9781003415886-75

Pros

- More objective and can help you see things that are hard to see close up.
- Ensures that awkward topics surface and are addressed.
- Ensures everyone's voice is heard.

Cons

- They need time to understand your organisation.
- They cannot affect change, they can only advise, question and prompt.
- If you choose the wrong critical friend, they may be too 'polite' or lack the relevant experience to challenge you effectively.

Peers—mentoring and sharing

Peers from other cultural organisations are an obvious source of an external voice, but generally do not make effective critical friends. The relationship is less about providing structured critique, or even of giving feedback, since often peers can be uncomfortable critiquing each other.

The peer voice is more about mentoring, and the sharing of experience, knowledge, information and learning, or acting as a sounding board. It helps if the peers have a shared area of interest and shared goals, and ideally a relationship of trust built up over several years. Unlike the critical friend, this is a two-way relationship, with everyone on the same level.

Feedback from peers is most effectively done in a structured way. If you want feedback, you need to ask for it explicitly, but for it to work, you need to build trust beforehand with a small group which can safely encourage openness.

Pros

- Peers often understand your work and have the expertise to make useful comments.
- They might, eventually, be very candid, so it can be a very efficient and cost-effective way of learning.

Cons

- Peers often feel constrained from offering proper critique.
- In a peer group, it is important to emphasise that each organisation and its goals are different, so that comparing yourself against a very different organisation can occasionally feel disheartening.
- It takes time to build trust for effective two-way critique.

Community partners—aiding reflection

While it may seem as if community partners could potentially be a good source of critical friends, in practice they can best help an organisation by assisting it to reflect actively and regularly on what has gone well and not so well, on the next steps and on their relationship.

This is quite a different role from that of a critical friend, who is more of an objective facilitator. Indeed, the closer the relationship between an organisation and its community partners, the less able a community partner is to be objective and critical—essentially, and ideally, they become part of the team; but they continue to have a different external perspective which can aid in reflection and new thinking.

Pros

- The views of your community partners are essential if your organisation is to be rooted in local needs and stay relevant.
- Cultural organisations can act as external voices for community partners too.

Cons

- Their perspectives are crucial, but not as objective or as experienced in certain organisational areas as a critical friend might be.
- The longer and closer your relationship becomes, the less objective their perspectives will be.
- Community partners sometimes feel constrained from critiquing a cultural organisation.
- Occasionally it takes the input of a critical friend to bring out the voices of community partners on an equal level.

Artists—a creative perspective

Artists often work with cultural organisations, not just to create something for display or performance, but to provide a different perspective from that of cultural professionals on how the organisation functions. An artist can bring a fresh, creative and open perspective to these topics, unencumbered by layers of professional training and history. Often, they can point out working practices which are outdated or illogical, but have been accepted for years as 'the way it is', and can challenge the organisation to explore new ways of working.

Pros

- Can be a creative and fresh approach, re-invigorating the staff.
- The process can also result in an artistic output, as the artist responds creatively through working with the staff.

Cons

- An artist's intervention will not appeal to all members of staff—some will find it an irrelevant distraction and might respond negatively.
- Like critical friends, an artist cannot effect change: they can only challenge and offer fresh perspectives, and sometimes artists in these roles feel they have had little impact.

Choosing the right external voice

Here is a checklist that summarises which roles are best carried out by particular external voices:

- Teasing out challenges: critical friends
- Mentoring: peers
- Sharing experiences and learning: peers
- Feedback: critical friends, peers, community partners, evaluators and funders
- Reflection: critical friends and community partners
- Fresh perspectives: critical friends and artists

When sourcing an external voice to work with you, be bold and try to avoid playing it safe by choosing someone who is an easy fit, less challenging, and perhaps a 'usual suspect' that you have worked with comfortably before. Consider what perspectives you are currently missing within your organisation, what you need them to do and who is likely to offer something new and challenging (possibly even uncomfortable), but who will be constructive not just critical. Some cultural leaders find external voices a threat, so if you find yourself reacting that way, ask yourself why (see Chapter 5: Recognising your weaknesses and blind spots).

Whoever your external voice is, it is best to have a clear (preferably written) agreement about their role, what is expected from both sides, the duration of their work, and any remuneration. Other than peers, with whom you might have a reciprocal agreement, it is always good practice to try to pay external voices and treat it as a contractual arrangement with defined outputs, not a favour.

See also:

7. Flexibility: welcoming challenge and different perspectives
9. How to respond to criticism
60. Don't avoid uncomfortable issues
64. Strategic peer networks and mentoring

68 How to respond to popular causes and campaigns and survive 'culture wars'

Cultural organisations are perhaps particularly susceptible to pressure to support popular causes and campaigns. This is often driven by demands for empowerment by disenfranchised or marginalised groups for organisations—especially museums and heritage bodies—to change their narratives, include previously silent voices, encourage discussion around 'hidden' histories, challenge assumptions about the often murky moral background of their collections and open negotiations with claimant groups around contested objects and human remains. Sometimes these are driven by the organisation's own staff, who may have the best intentions of being 'inclusive' or may even themselves represent minoritised groups. But such approaches can provoke a backlash—now increasingly on social media, often accompanied by *ad hominem* attacks on staff—from other sectors of the community, who see them as a threat to how they see the world, to how their past is understood, to their values, to their identity and even to the social order.[1]

This is what is meant by 'culture wars', a phrase that emerged in the US media in the late 1980s.[2] It can be defined as confrontations between groups within the same society, often spearheaded by self-appointed moral crusaders, based on polarised or even incompatible worldviews regarding moral values and changing norms, usually expressed as a tension between orthodoxy (often religious) and progressivism (based on the rights of the individual). The topics that cause these conflicts tend to relate to race and ethnicity; gender and sexual orientation; the body and abortion rights; identity politics; religion; the legacies of colonialism and slavery; climate change; and patriotism and national identity. Research indicates, however, that in most cases the debates are deliberately stoked by activists following a particular social or political agenda, and that culture wars are 'primarily a top-down, elite-driven phenomenon' that the wider public cares little about.[3]

How do culture wars affect cultural organisations?

As Steven Dubin has pointed out, culture war controversies have been particularly noticeable at venues such as museums, monuments and heritage sites (or more generally heritage organisations), where history, memory, meaning and feelings of place and belonging are constructed.[4] These are sites which are usually trying to attract a wider, sometimes tourist, market and chasing corporate sponsorship. In such cases, tension and conflict can be created because progressive and inclusive narratives are pursued, to the irritation of some culture warriors; or particular marginalised voices are left unheard or silenced to placate sponsors, to the annoyance of disadvantaged groups; or one particular displayed object causes offence to a specific group and there is pressure to remove it.[5]

DOI: 10.4324/9781003415886-76

However, in recent years, controversies have also affected the performing arts, for example, around the question of which actors should be allowed to play which roles. There has been discussion around colour-blind[6] or colour-conscious casting and accusations of institutional racism in commercial theatre,[7] and whether only LGBTIQA+ actors should play LGBTIQA+ characters.[8]

To give an indication of how such controversies can impact different types of cultural organisations, below are three short case studies, covering museums, heritage organisations and the performing arts.

One of the most notorious museum controversies was in 1994–1995 around the display of the *Enola Gay*, the aeroplane that dropped the first atomic bomb on Hiroshima in 1945. For the 50th anniversary, the National Air and Space Museum in Washington, DC, planned an exhibition that included exploration of the decision to use the bomb and its impact on Japanese cities and people. But the plans created a backlash, especially from military organisations, veterans' groups, politicians and the media, and were labelled a revisionist interpretation, unpatriotic and a betrayal of the war generation, with congressional threats to withhold funding. The exhibition was cancelled—replaced by a smaller exhibition with no interpretation or context—and the museum's director was forced to resign, though the cancellation itself sparked criticism from the academic and museum communities.[9]

In 2020, the National Trust, the UK's biggest and oldest heritage organisation, published a report detailing the connections of some of its properties with slavery and colonialism, to raise awareness of the complexities of their histories.[10] It faced criticism from the media and members of parliament that it was pursuing a 'woke agenda', and threats to withdraw funding. An activist group—which claimed that the Trust's perceived left-wing politicisation was distracting it from the task of looking after heritage—planned a vote of no confidence in the chair, who resigned in 2021.[11] However, the National Trust weathered the storm and successfully fought off critical motions by this group at annual general meetings in both 2022 and 2023.

Culture wars controversies can inadvertently cross international borders. As an example, polarised views regarding the portrayal of ancient Egyptian characters regularly impact film, theatre and opera productions. In 2023, the streaming service Netflix sparked anger in Egypt by casting a Black actor as Cleopatra. There were efforts to ban the series in Egypt: its Supreme Council of Antiquities stated that this was 'a falsification of history', arguing that Cleopatra was of Greek descent, while a government-owned Egyptian broadcaster planned to make a documentary portraying Cleopatra with lighter skin.[12] In 2022, a singer cancelled a performance in Italy in protest at the lead soprano's Blackface makeup when portraying the Ethiopian princess Aida in Verdi's opera;[13] in 2020, producers of a Cleopatra film were accused of 'whitewashing' by casting an Israeli rather than an Arab or African actor in the lead role;[14] and in 2016, a concert performance of *The Prince of Egypt* with a majority white cast was cancelled after diversity complaints.[15]

How you can respond

It is useful to understand that culture war backlashes are usually based on three elements. First, they tend to be challenges to the legitimacy of a progressive or inclusive approach, which is often dismissed as 'political correctness' privileging minority views, or 'misuse of public funds' by a cultural organisation. Second, they are based on an assumption that there is a single (traditional and authorised) interpretation of history ('the facts'), a monument, a building, a work of art or a historical (or even fictional) character. Third, most culture war complaints come from a minority who shout loudest (although admittedly these are sometimes in positions of political or financial influence or even outright control).[16]

There are three steps that cultural organisations can take.

Evidence of community support

Gather evidence that your (potentially controversial) actions are in response to community interest, rather than staff bias or activism. While socially engaged activism by cultural organisations can be positive and even admirable, there is a danger that the organisation (re)casts itself—or is perceived—as the uncontested 'expert' (on a nineteenth-century colonialist model) that knows better and promotes its own values as universally applicable.[17] An inclusive, socially engaged organisation must demonstrate that its actions are responsive to its communities and that it is not the sole arbiter of knowledge.

An effective response to culture warriors is to show that your organisation has close relations with its communities, with robust mechanisms for reflecting, responding to and supporting community agendas, and is a genuinely open to community voices. It is then not so easy to dismiss your actions as 'political correctness'.

Democratic dialogue

Involve all parties in a dialogue, ideally being proactive, not reactive after a backlash when it is too late because you are already on the back foot defending your actions. You may have decided in advance what you want to do—but listen carefully to any concerns, especially from perspectives other than your own. Of course, it can be difficult to decide which voices to include. Are there extreme and undemocratic voices who should be excluded because they do not abide by a code of conduct for respectful dialogue?[18] Maybe: but be very careful before you exclude anyone, as they are precisely the ones who will later launch a coordinated campaign against you and accuse you of being undemocratic and biased.

Cultural organisations sometimes shy away from creating such open opportunities for dialogue because of concerns that bringing together mutually exclusive and contradictory beliefs will lead to radical disagreement and conflict. Yet agreement on all topics is not necessarily the aim of such conversations: rather, the objective is for all those affected or interested to have an opportunity to participate, to communicate, to feel they have been heard and to listen to alternative views.[19]

This sort of dialogue with audiences, communities and stakeholders is useful not only for museums and heritage organisations planning exhibitions but for other cultural organisations such as theatres and music venues—whether staging non-traditional operas, for example, by homeless people, reinterpreting classics from an inclusive modern perspective, or foregrounding authors, composers and performers from diverse backgrounds. Talk it through, listen and do all you can to bring your audience (and stakeholders) with you.

Be prepared for a backlash

Anticipate fallout and be proactive in your external communications (see Chapter 63: External communications as advocacy). Think about the worst-case scenario. Prepare press releases and media briefings beforehand, explaining why you are doing this, why it fits with your organisation's remit and what you hope to achieve.

See also:

12. Political antennae and horizon scanning
20. Understanding users' needs and agendas
44. Building a participatory organisation
62. Advocacy with politicians
65. How to involve stakeholders

Notes

1 See P. Brown, 'Us and them: Who benefits from experimental exhibition making?', *Museum Management and Curatorship* 26/2 (2011), pp. 129–48. For the historical and philosophical background to different cultural worldviews and conceptions of the past, which can lead to exclusion, anger and conflict, see P. Bienkowski, 'Whose past? Archaeological knowledge, community knowledge, and the embracing of conflict', in G. Scarre and R. Coningham (eds.). *Appropriating the Past: Philosophical Perspectives on the Practice of Archaeology* (Cambridge University Press 2013), pp. 42–62.
2 J.D. Hunter, *Culture Wars: The Struggle to Define America* (Basic Books 1991), pp. 42–5; S.C. Dubin, 'Incivilities in civil(-ized) places: "Culture wars" in comparative perspective', in S. Macdonald (ed.), *A Companion to Museum Studies* (Wiley-Blackwell 2011), pp. 477–93.
3 B. Duffy et al., *"Culture Wars" in the UK* (The Policy Institute, King's College London, June 2021), p. 22.
4 S.C. Dubin, 'Incivilities in civil(-ized) places: "Culture wars" in comparative perspective', in S. Macdonald (ed.), *A Companion to Museum Studies* (Wiley-Blackwell 2011), p. 478.
5 For example, K. Malik, 'An art treasure long cherished by Muslims is deemed offensive. But to whom?' *The Guardian* (8 January 2023).
6 Colour-blind casting—the practice of casting without considering the actor's ethnicity or race—and other contested 'culture war' topics are explored through the lens of staging Shakespeare by J. Shapiro, *Shakespeare in a Divided America: What His Plays Tell Us About Our Past and Future* (Penguin 2019).
7 Colour-conscious casting is intentional or race-conscious affirmative action to avoid racially homogeneous casts and requires casting directors and producers to accept growing diversity, so that theatres better reflect the changing demographic make-up of the population. See K.B. Hopkins, 'There's no business like show business: Abandoning color-blind casting and embracing color-conscious casting in American theatre', *Harvard Journal of Sports and Entertainment Law* 9 (2018), pp. 131–55.
8 See C. Kaiser, 'Should straight actors play gay roles? A star TV writer says no', *New York Times* (24 February 2021); L. Bakare, 'UK theatres promise to only cast trans actors in trans roles', *The Guardian* (26 May 2021).
9 For this and other examples, see S.C. Dubin, *Displays of Power: Controversy in the American Museum from Enola Gay to Sensation* (New York University Press 2000); and his examples of museum controversies from South Africa in 'Incivilities in civil(-ized) places: "Culture wars" in comparative perspective', in S. Macdonald (ed.), *A Companion to Museum Studies* (Wiley-Blackwell 2011), pp. 484–91.
10 S.-A. Huxtable, C. Fowler, C. Kefalas and C. Slocombe (eds.), *Interim Report on the Connections between Colonialism and Properties now in the Care of the National Trust, including Links with Historic Slavery* (National Trust 2020).
11 For an assessment of the media and political response, see P. Mitchell, 'The National Trust is under attack because it cares about history, not fantasy', *The Guardian*, 12 November 2020.
12 H. Sherwood, 'Cleopatra was light-skinned, Egypt tells Netflix in row over drama', *The Guardian* (28 April 2023).
13 C. Smith, 'Soprano Angel Blue cancels Arena di Verona debut in response to Anna Netrebko Blackface scandal', *BBC Music Magazine* (15 July 2022).
14 E. Harrison, 'Gal Gadot defends Cleopatra casting after "whitewashing" backlash', *Independent* (23 December 2020).

15 M. Paulson, '"Prince of Egypt" musical reading canceled after diversity complaints', *New York Times* (28 July 2016).

16 For examples from Poland of a populist government's forcible replacement of museum directors, see P. d'Alancaisez, 'How to lose a culture war', *The Critic* (5 March 2023).

17 See L. Smith, *Uses of Heritage* (Routledge 2006), p. 11.

18 For a code of conduct for dialogue, see B. Pruitt and P. Thomas, *Democratic Dialogue: A Handbook for Practitioners* (Organization of American States/United Nations Development Programme 2007), p. 33.

19 S. Benhabib, *The Claims of Culture: Equality and Diversity in the Global Era* (Princeton University Press 2002), p. 135; P. Bienkowski, 'Whose past? Archaeological knowledge, community knowledge, and the embracing of conflict', in G. Scarre and R. Coningham (eds.). *Appropriating the Past: Philosophical Perspectives on the Practice of Archaeology* (Cambridge University Press 2013), pp. 59–6.

Appendix A

Resources to help you

This selective list focuses on web-based resources on leadership in the cultural sector that provide practical advice and case studies, in both written and video formats.

aam-us.org

The resource library of the American Alliance of Museums, although focused primarily on museums and galleries, has useful content on leadership, governance, advocacy, funding and business models that is transferable to other cultural organisations. It includes resources specifically aimed at trustees, including tips on diversifying boards.

americansforthearts.org

Americans for the Arts is an advocacy organisation: its website has resources on leadership development, arts and business, funding, strategic partnerships, cultural equity, and offers webinars and e-learning.

changeleadersnetwork.com

A worldwide network of change leaders, including free articles and webinars on all aspects of leadership and organisational change.

cloreleadership.org

Clore Leadership runs development programmes for emerging leaders: its online library collates research projects completed by its fellows and alumni, on a wide range of topics in cultural leadership and governance.

culturalleadership.org.uk

Although the UK's Cultural Leadership Programme closed in 2011, its website archives lots of useful resources such as essays, case studies and videos about leadership.

culturalpartnership.eu

The Culture and Creativity website of the European Union is a useful resource on best practice and tools for the cultural and creative industries, also offering free web-based courses (in eight languages) for cultural leaders on a range of topics including developing strategy, advocacy, finance and fundraising.

ofbyforall.org

Includes a self-assessment tool to check how your organisation rates in being 'of, by and for' your community, and other toolkits and resources supporting leadership and change.

ourmuseum.org.uk

Over 200 multi-media resources on organisational change, leadership and community participation, with practical insights and case studies, aimed primarily at museums and galleries, but transferable to other cultural organisations.

ted.com/talks/simon_sinek_how_great_leaders_inspire_action

Simon Sinek on inspirational leadership and finding your 'Why?'—why your organisation exists and what it exists to do.

Appendix B
Useful publications

This brief list highlights publications which give at least some element of practical guidance about all the different aspects of cultural leadership. It is not an exhaustive bibliography of publications on cultural leadership, many of which focus on leadership theory and are aimed more at academics than practitioners. For references to a wider range of publications on specific topics, see the notes at the end of chapters.

The short annotations are intended to guide readers as to whether a particular publication might be useful for their purposes.

P. Bienkowski and H. McGowan, *Managing Change in Museums and Galleries: A Practical Guide* (Routledge 2021).

A similar format to the present book, aimed at practitioners, with short, cross-referenced chapters providing practical guidance on how to lead organisational change in museums and galleries, but transferable to all other cultural organisations.

T. Bovaird and E. Loeffler (eds), *Public Management and Governance* (third edition, Routledge 2016).

Edited collection of essays on all aspects of public management and governance. Each chapter includes learning objectives, questions for review and discussion, and reader and class exercises.

Governance Now: The hidden challenge of leadership (Cultural Leadership Programme 2009).

Reviews the issues, structures and characteristics of good governance for cultural organisations, offers practical recommendations and tools, and advice about what to do when things go wrong.

R. Hewison and J. Holden, *The Cultural Leadership Handbook: How to Run a Creative Organization* (Routledge 2011).

Essentially a curriculum handbook, presented through a series of challenges and exercises for students/leaders, quite theoretical in parts, for example, discussing the nature of power and cultural value at some length.

S. Kay and K. Venner (eds), *A Cultural Leadership Reader* (Cultural Leadership Programme/ Creative Choices 2010).

Edited collection of reflective and sometimes provocative essays about leaders and leadership in the cultural sector.

K.L. Mallia, *Leadership in the Creative Industries: Principles and Practice* (Wiley 2019).

Aimed primarily at those who manage 'creatives' in advertising agencies and architectural and design studios.

L. Varbanova, *Strategic Management in the Arts* (Routledge 2013).

Comprehensive overview of arts management structures and strategies, with practical recommendations and detailed case studies, and learning objectives for each chapter.

J. Ventura, *Law for Dummies* (second edition, Wiley 2005).

Useful reference for cultural leaders on common legal issues and terminology, but be aware that this book is based on US law.

Index

Pages in *italics* refer to figures, pages in **bold** refer to tables, and pages followed by "n" refer to notes.

For Product Safety Concerns and Information please contact our EU
representative GPSR@taylorandfrancis.com
Taylor & Francis Verlag GmbH, Kaufingerstraße 24, 80331 München, Germany

www.ingramcontent.com/pod-product-compliance
Ingram Content Group UK Ltd.
Pitfield, Milton Keynes, MK11 3LW, UK
UKHW050933280126
467416UK00025B/834
* 9 7 8 1 0 3 2 5 0 7 5 2 1 *